Where Peter Is

ALBA · HOUSE NEW · YORK

SOCIETY OF ST. PAUL, 2187 VICTORY BLVD., STATEN ISLAND, NEW YORK 10314

Where Peter Is
A Survey of Ecclesiology

Edward J. Gratsch

906

Library of Congress Cataloging in Publication
Gratsch, Edward J.
    Where Peter is.
    Includes bibliographical references.
    1. Church—History of doctrienes. I.Title.
BV598.G72   262'.02   74-34578
ISBN 0-8189-0302-3

Nihil obstat:
Daniel Pilarczk, S.T.D., Ph.D.

Imprimatur:
†Joseph L. Bernardin
Archbishop of Cincinnati
June 7, 1974

*Designed, printed and bound in the United States of
America by the Fathers and Brothers of the Society of St. Paul,
2187 Victory Boulevard, Staten Island, New York, 10314,
as part of their communications apostolate.*

3 4 5 6 7 8 9 (Current Printing: first digit).

Dedicated to

MOST REV. KARL J. ALTER, D.D., LL.D.
Archbishop of Cincinnati
1950-1969

ACKNOWLEDGMENT

The author wishes to thank the Rev. Gerald Van Ackeren, S.J. for permission to use the quotations taken from *The Church Teaches*.

CONTENTS

ABBREVIATIONS

AAS	*Acta Apostolicae Sedis,* Rome, 1909.
CSEL	*Corpus scriptorum ecclesiasticorum latinorum,* Vienna, 1866.
CT	*The Church Teaches,* St. Louis, 1957.
DACL	*Dictionnaire d'Archéologie chrétienne et de Liturgie,* Paris, 1924.
DG	J. Schwane, *Dogmengeschichte,* Münster, 1862.
DS	H. Denziger, A. Schönmetzer, *Enchiridion Symbolorum,* Barcelona, 1965.
DTC	*Dictionnaire de Théologie Catholique,* Paris, 1903.
EP	Encyclopedia of Philosophy, New York-London, 1967.
HC	J. Hefele, *Histoire des Conciles,* Paris, 1907.
HD	A. Harnack, *History of Dogma,* New York, 1961.
MGH	*Monumenta Germaniae Historica,* Hanover, 1826.
NCE	*The New Catholic Encyclopedia,* New York, 1967.
PG	*Patrologium Graecum,* Paris, 1857.
PL	*Patrologium Latinum,* Paris, 1844.
THD	R. Seeberg, *Textbook of the History of Doctrines,* Grand Rapids, 1952.

INTRODUCTION

The Church is a mystery. On the one hand, the Church is human and temporal. The Church is led by men and its message is expressed in human terms. Its rite of initiation, baptism, is similar to the common act of washing; and its principal act of worship, the Holy Eucharist, resembles a meal. The Church includes sinful men among its members, and in the Church there are misunderstandings and the misuse of heavenly things. To a considerable degree, the Church is subject to the vicissitudes of history, and it must contend with contradiction and persecution.

At the same time, the Church is divine and eternal. Those who lead the Church do so in virtue of a divine commission. The message which they teach is the message of God and it has the power to remit sins and beget eternal life. The invisible head of the Church, Jesus Christ, now sits at the right hand of His heavenly Father; and, because of their relationship to Him, the members of the Church have been incorporated into His kingdom.

The Church, therefore, is a reality composed of disparate elements: human and divine, earthly and heavenly, temporal and eternal. One finds it difficult to understand the union of these disparate elements in the Church. For this reason, the Church is a mystery, something revealed by God but incapable of being fully understood by men.

From the beginning, the faithful have reflected upon the mystery of the Church in order to achieve some understanding of it at least. Often the reflection of the faithful has been contingent upon the prevailing historical situation; and the result has been a new insight into the nature and function of the Church. For example, the primitive Christian community proclaimed Jesus as the Messiah whom the Jewish nation had long expected.

By and large, the Jews rejected the Christian proclamation. Controversy over this issue led the Christians to separate themselves from the Jewish community and to reflect upon their relationship to it. The Christian community came to the conclusion that it (and not the Jews) was the people of God, the heir of the promises made to Abraham. The Christians regarded themselves as the true Israel, the new Israel, to be distinguished from the Old Israel which had forfeited its privileged position. The historical situation had determined the focus of the Christian reflection upon the mystery of the Church. The result was a greater understanding of the Church on the part of Christians.

Another example. In the 16th century, Martin Luther (1483-1546) challenged the Catholic conception of the Church. The Church of Christ, Luther maintained, was essentially invisible since its members were those who had been justified by faith and were known to God alone. The Catholic response to the ecclesiological problems raised by Luther came from St. Robert Bellarmine (d. 1612). In opposition to the Lutheran view, Bellarmine emphasized the visibility of the Church. The Church, he said, was as visible as the kingdom of France or the republic of Venice. He developed an apologetics by which the Church of Christ could be recognized by means of certain visible notes or signs. The ecclesiology (that is, theological doctrine relating to the Church) elaborated by Bellarmine exerted a profound influence upon many generations of Catholic theologians. But the point is this: Bellarmine's reflection upon the Church was determined in large measure by the problems created by the Reformation. One result of his study was that the visibility of the Church was understood more clearly.

From the examples given in the preceding paragraphs the Catholic will not draw the erroneous conclusion that his Church has been shaped solely and entirely by the forces of history acting blindly. In this manner, the elements have carved the rocks and mountains haphazardly. No, the basic structure of the Church has been established by Christ. As the Church has encountered different historical situations, the true proportions of this structure have been revealed as a light illumines a painting. Or to use another image: history acts upon the Church as the milieu acts upon a man: it does not change him radically although it may change him significantly for better or worse.

The purpose of this book is to study ecclesiology in its historical setting. Such a study has particular advantages: it discloses the true significance of magisterial and theological statements about the Church by weighing them in their historical context; it reveals what God wills or permits in the case of the Church; it affords insights into the nature and function of the Church; it helps Catholics to distinguish between the divine and human elements of the Church; it affords them an abundance of facts and ideas for making judgments about the present; it reveals the potentialities and limitations of Church members; and it discloses the future which is contained in the past and present.

To assist in recalling the historical context of theological reflection upon the Church, a brief history of the period has been prefixed to each chapter. Often history speaks more tellingly about the Church than an abstract statement.

This book is concerned primarily with Catholic ecclesiology; nevertheless, for the purposes of comparison and contrast, non-Catholic views of the Church have been introduced. As a survey, the book is not intended to be a detailed examination of particular theologians and ideas; but it is intended to convey something of the sweep and development of Catholic ecclesiology.

Catholics will understand that the statements of Popes, bishops and theologians about the Church vary in significance. In general, the pronouncements of the Popes and the college of bishops (whether assembled in an ecumenical council or dispersed throughout the world) express the official position of the Catholic Church and expect the assent of Catholics. The statements of theologians possess such significance only to the extent that they reflect the teaching authority of the Church. Frequently, the statements of theologians concern matters on which the Church has taken no official stand.

May an increased understanding of the mystery of the Church inspire a deeper commitment to it.

I. THE NEW TESTAMENT

The world of the New Testament was the world of the eastern Roman Empire. By the force of its arms, Rome had extended its dominion over the lands surrounding the Mediterranean sea. Augustus (27 B.C.-A.D.14) established himself as the first emperor. With his accession the Roman world experienced a comparative peace after two hundred years of incessant warfare. Roads were built; trade increased; wealth accumulated; and a common language and culture prevailed. These were the benefits of Roman rule. Its attendant evils were rapacity, cruelty, luxury and the multiplication of slaves, among others.

In 63 B.C., Pompey, the Roman general and statesman, captured Jerusalem. The land where Christianity was born became part of the Roman Empire. Palestine was placed under the jurisdiction of Roman procurators, such as Pontius Pilate, and vassal kings, such as the Herods. While the Romans granted the Jews a measure of freedom, especially in religious matters, they imposed heavy taxes and deposed Jewish officials readily. The relationship between Roman and Jew was characterized by mutual contempt. Not infrequently the hatred of the Jew for the Roman erupted into outright rebellion. The rebellion of A.D. 66-70 resulted in the destruction of Jerusalem by a Roman army.

Although Rome was the political master of the Mediterranean world, the dominant culture was Hellenism which is the thought, art, literature, religion, customs, styles and language of ancient Greece. By his conquests, Alexander the Great (356-323 B.C.), the Greek king, had given the initial impetus to the spread of

Greek culture. The intrinsic power of the culture itself secured its dominant position.

The classical religion of Greece with its gods and goddesses, such as Zeus, Apollo and Aphrodite, was also widely adopted. Nevertheless, the Greek religion was not often maintained in its pure form, other gods and goddesses, native and foreign, being admitted readily. It is difficult to say to what degree the cult of religion was a matter of conviction. As far as the cult of the emperor was concerned, it seems to have been something similar to a pledge of allegiance.

Besides the Greek religion, there were other exotic cults brought back from the East by soldiers, civil officials and slaves. These cults included those of the Phrygian goddess, Cybele, and her lover, Attis; the Egyptian, Isis, goddess of immortality; the Persian, Mithra, a cult that appealed to soldiers especially; and the Eleusinian mysteries, celebrated in worship of Demeter and Persephone. The mystery religions, with their rites of initiation, esoteric doctrines, and promise of communion with the divinity, exercised a strange attraction. They were based on ancient fertility rites that were concerned with the annual decay and resurgence of nature.

In the midst of religious confusion, many members of the ruling classes of the Roman Empire turned to philosophy and especially to the Greek philosophy, Stoicism. The emperor, Marcus Aurelius (A.D. 121-180), was an exponent of Stoicism. For the Stoics, the paramount problem of philosophy was the problem of human destiny and human happiness. According to the Stoics, everything in the world of reality obeys and must obey inevitable law. Man, it is true, is endowed with reason and is thereby enabled to know the law he obeys. Nevertheless, he is obliged to obey it. The supreme canon of conduct is to live conformably to nature. The Stoics sought to eradicate all emotions for they can lead a man to oppose nature. This doctrine of apathy is one of the most characteristic Stoic doctrines.

According to the Stoics, the majority of men pass their lives in wickedness, slaves to custom, pleasure, and a multitude of desires. The wise man is indifferent to pain. He is independent of all ties of blood and kinship. He is a citizen of the world. If his peace of mind is threatened, he may take his own life.

There were other philosophical systems too, including the neo-Platonism of Philo of Alexandria (1st century, A.D.). He attempted to bring the revealed religion of the Old Testament into agreement with the philosophy of Plato. At the same time, the neo-Pythagoreans attached great importance to mysticism, ecstasy and prophecy.

The Jews were a distinct group within the Roman Empire. They were distinguished by their acceptance of the Law of Moses. The Romans granted the Jews considerable liberty in following the religious and social demands of the Mosaic Law. At the head of the Jewish community in Palestine was the high priest. He was assisted by the Sanhedrin, the supreme council and tribunal of the Jews in New Testament times. This council had religious, civil and criminal jurisdiction. Of course, Judaism was not confined to Palestine. Large colonies of Jews lived in other important cities such as Alexandria and Rome. These colonies were known as the diaspora. The Jews of the diaspora worshiped in synagogues in services not unlike the first part of the Catholic Mass. Animal sacrifices were legitimate only in the temple at Jerusalem. Because of their devotion to the Law of Moses, the Jews were characterized by their monotheistic belief in God and their freedom from the grosser vices of the pagans.

Within Palestinian Judaism there were a number of parties or groups. The scribes or lawyers were dedicated to the interpretation of the Law of Moses. They attempted to apply it to the myriad circumstances of daily life. The Pharisees were noted for their strict observance of the rites and ceremonies of the written Law of Moses and for their insistence upon the scribal traditions by which this Law was interpreted. They were especially hostile to the introduction of foreign ideas into Jewish life. The Sadducees accepted the Law of Moses, but (unlike the Pharisees) they did not accept the scribal interpretations of the Law. They rejected such doctrines as the resurrection, retribution in a future life and the existence of angels because they were not found in the written Law. The Zealots were a fanatical group bitterly opposed to the Roman domination of Palestine. In large measure, they were responsible for the rebellion that led to the destruction of Jerusalem by the Romans in A.D. 70. The Essenes were a monastic brotherhood of Jews in Palestine from the 2nd century B.C. to the 2nd century A.D. We have learned much more about them in recent decades as the result of certain discoveries at Khirbet Qumran. Distinct from all these groups were the common people.

The Church was born in this historical setting. Near the year A.D. 30 "Jesus came into Galilee, preaching the good news of the kingdom of God and saying, 'The time is fulfilled and the kingdom of God is at hand. Repent and believe in the good news'" (Mk 1:14-15). Just as any other rabbi or teacher was accustomed to do, Jesus gathered disciples around himself in order to instruct them in His teaching. In this gathering of teacher and disciples we must see an initial stage in the foundation of the Church, for the Church is a community of people committed to Christ and His message. Afterwards, Jesus incurred the hostility of the ruling powers; He was put to death; but He rose from the dead. Though scattered by His death, the disciples of Jesus reassembled after His resurrection. "They went forth and preached everywhere, while the Lord worked with them and confirmed the preaching by the signs that followed" (Mk 16:20). What they preached was written down later in the pages of the New Testament. These pages also reveal the mind of the first Christians about the Church.

THE PEOPLE OF GOD

The books of the Old Testament repeatedly speak of the Israelites as the people of God. Leviticus, for example, records God's promise to his people: "I will look with favor upon you and make you fruitful and numerous, as I carry out my covenant with you... I will set my dwelling among you and will not disdain you. Ever present in your midst, I will be your God and you will be my people" (Lv 26:9-12). The selection of the Israelites as the people of God was a matter of free choice and love on the part of God: "You are a people sacred to the Lord, your God; he has chosen you from all the nations of the earth to be a people peculiarly his own. It was not because you are the largest of nations that the Lord set his heart on you and chose you, for you are really the smallest of all nations. It was because the Lord loved you and because of his fidelity to the oath he had sworn to your fathers" (Dt 7:6-8). Fundamental to the idea of Israel's relationship to God was the fact that God had freely chosen the Israelites for their privileged position; He had made a covenant or agreement with them; as a consequence, they were the beneficiaries of His promises and the people of God.

The books of the New Testament are deeply impregnated with the thought that the Christian community has become the new or true Israel, the people of God. This thought is expressed in many ways. One very important way is the use of the Greek word, *ekklesia,* by the New Testament to designate the Christian community. (The New Testament, of course, was written originally in Greek.) The Greek word, *ekklesia,* is usually translated by the English word, church. When the early Church referred to itself by the term, *ekklesia,* it understood itself to be the people of God.

The significance of the term, *ekklesia,* for the early Church was dependent upon its usage in the Septuagint. In the Septuagint, which is a pre-Christian version of the Old Testament, which, moreover, was the Bible of the authors of the New Testament, the word, *ekklesia,* is used as a translation of the Hebrew word, *qahal.* The Old Testament, originally written for the most part in Hebrew, uses the Hebrew word, *qahal,* especially to signify the people of God assembled for worship or for a holy war (Nb 16:3; 20:4; Dt 23:24).

By designating itself as the *ekklesia* or Church, the early Church expressed its consciousness of being the legitimate successor of the people of God under the Mosaic covenant and the people of God in the final period. This consciousness contained a recognition on the one hand of the Christian Church's close connection with the Israel of the Old Testament and on the other hand of its sharp opposition to it. Because the "fleshly" Israel had rejected Jesus as its Messiah, it had deprived itself of its privileged position as the chosen people. The Church had succeeded it as the new people of God. The thought that the Christians are the true or new Israel, the "spiritual" Israel, was expressed by Paul with particular emphasis (Rm 2:28-29; Col 2:11-15; Ph 3:2-3). The carnal descendants of Abraham are not the true Jews or Israelites and heirs of the promises given to Abraham by God, but Christians are because as believers they alone are related to Abraham who believed God (Rm 4:1-25; 11; Gal 3-4).

Paul uses the word, *ekklesia,* most frequently in the New Testament. He often uses the word to signify the local community of Christians (1 Th 1:1; 2 Th 1:1; Gal 1:1-2; 1 Cor 1:1-2; 2 Cor 1:1). In this sense there is a plurality of Churches. However, Paul also uses *ekklesia* to signify the universal community of Christians (Gal 1:13; 1 Cor 10:32; 12:28; 15:9). The universal community of Christians manifests itself in the local community, an idea that Paul suggests when he speaks of the local Corinthian community as the bride of Christ, a designation that is applicable to the whole Church (2 Cor 11:2). Often too Paul speaks of the *ekklesia tou theou,* the Church of God (1 Th 2:14; 2 Th 1:4; 1 Cor 1:1-2; etc.) He does not speak of the Church of Christ (except in Rm 16:16) even though he thought of the Church as the body of Christ. Paul's use of the phrase, Church of God, is to be explained on the grounds that he—and the primitive Christian community before him—did not invent the phrase but borrowed it from Judaism and the Old Testament where the Israelites are styled the *qahal Jahweh,* the people or Church of God.

In the Septuagint the Hebrew word, *qahal,* is also translated by the Greek word, *synagoge* (Lv 16:17; Nm 10:7; etc.) This Greek word was not taken over by the primitive Christian community to designate itself; but it was reserved for the Jewish community.

Besides the term, *ekklesia* or Church, the New Testament also employs other words derived from the Old Testament to express the same idea. One of these words is the Greek word, *oi agioi,* which means "the saints" or "the holy ones". The Jewish-

Christian community at Jerusalem was the first to speak of itself in this way; but later the name was applied to all Christians (1 Cor 6:1-2; Rv 20:8). When Paul speaks of the collection for Jerusalem, he speaks simply of the collection being made for "the saints" (1 Cor 16:1; 2 Cor 8:4; etc.) Israel was called "holy" in the Old Testament because it had been chosen by God as His possession through the covenant of Mt. Sinai (Ex 19:5-6). When the early Church spoke of itself as "the saints" or "the holy ones," it expressed once more its conviction of being the people of God in the final age.

The title, "the chosen ones" or "the elect" is identical with the title, "the saints." The Christians as such are called "the chosen ones" or "the elect" (Rm 8:33; Col 3:12; 2 Tm 2:10; etc.) Sometimes they are referred to as "the called" (Rm 1:6; 1 Cor 1:24) or "the called to be saints" (Rm 1:7; 1 Cor 1:2). Similarly in the Old Testament the people of Israel are called "the chosen ones" (Ps 105:43; Si 46:1). Sometimes the early Church referred to itself simply as "a people" or "the people of God" (Ti 2:14; Heb 2:17; 13:12; 1 P 2:10). No longer are the Gentiles excluded from the people of God; rather, God has "visited the Gentiles to take from among them a people to bear His name" (Ac 15:14).

THE BODY OF CHRIST

One of the most important images employed by Paul to describe the Church is the body of Christ. Paul did not derive this conception of the Church from the Old Testament. It is possible that he borrowed it from other ancient (Hellenistic) sources. In antiquity it was common to compare a community to a living organism whose members shared a common life. In 1 Cor 12:12-31 and Rm 12:4-5, Paul compares the Church to a human body. Just as the members of a human body—the eye, ear, foot—have different functions which serve the whole body, so the members of the Church have different functions which serve the whole Church. However, Paul goes on to refine this idea still further: the Church is not just a body; it is the body of Christ; indeed, it is Christ. He writes: "For as the body is one and has many members, and all the members of the body, many as they are, form one body, so also it is with Christ [the Church]" (1 Cor 12:12).

In his major letters, Paul emphasizes the relationship of the members to each other and their unity in Christ: "We, the many, are one body in Christ, but severally members of one another," Paul writes (Rm 12:5). However, in his letters to the Colossians and the Ephesians, he emphasizes the relationship of the members to Christ their head: "Christ is the head of his body, the Church" (Col 1:18). "We are to practice the truth in love, and so grow up in all things in him who is the head, Christ. For from him the whole body (being closely joined and knit together through every joint of the system according to the functioning in due measure of each single part) derives its increase to the building up of itself in love" (Ep 4:15-16).

In the letter to the Ephesians Paul speaks of the Church as "the mystery of Christ" because in the Church God has fulfilled His intention to save all men, Jews and Gentiles (Ep 3:4-6). Moreover, the Church is a heavenly reality endowed with numinous powers because God has given Christ "as head over all the Church, which indeed is his body, the completion of him who fills all with all" (Ep 1:22-23), the same Christ through whom He has created all and reconciled all to Himself (Col 1:18-20). The saving activity of Christ is completed in the Church (Ep 2:13-16; 5:25-33; Col 1:20-22). The principle of the Church's life is the Spirit (Ep 4:4; 1 Cor 12:3-10.13).

OTHER IMAGES OF THE CHURCH

The New Testament speaks of the Church as the spouse of Christ. In one passage, Paul wrote to the Christians at Corinth: "I betrothed you to one spouse, that I might present you a chaste virgin to Christ" (2 Cor 11:2). This remark means that Paul, by his missionary activity among the Corinthians, had brought them to Christ as a father presents his daughter to her husband.

In another beautiful passage (Ep 5:21-23), Paul thinks of the Church as the bride of Christ when he calls upon husbands to love their wives as Christ loves the Church. According to Paul, Christ has sacrificed Himself for the Church and sanctified it through baptism. He continues to cherish the Church as His own body. The Church in turn is subject to Christ as a dutiful wife is subject to her husband.

For Paul, the Church is also a building or a temple. He wrote to the Corinthians: "You are God's building... As a wise builder, I laid the foundation, and another builds thereon. For other foundation no one can lay, but that which has been laid, which is Christ Jesus... Do you not know that you are the temple of God and that the Spirit of God dwells in you?" (1 Cor 3:9-16) The duty of the faithful is to "build up" the Church (Ep 4:12).

The Holy Spirit too builds up the Church in a variety of ways. The Spirit was responsible for certain extraordinary gifts enjoyed by the early Christians (1 Cor 12:4-11). The Spirit unites the members of the Church among themselves so that, many as they are, they form one body which is the Church (1 Cor 12:13). The Holy Spirit provides for order in the Church where He has placed the bishops to rule the Church of God (Ac 20:28). The Holy Spirit dwells with the Apostles forever (Jn 14:16-17). He does so in order to teach and remind them what Christ has said (Jn 14:26). John regards the presence and activity of the Holy Spirit in the Church as the fruit of Christ's work (Jn 7:38-39).

The New Testament also describes the Christian Church as a pilgrim in this world. As "saints" and "chosen ones" the Christians had been taken out of the world and separated from "those outside" (1 Th 4:12; 1 Cor 5:12; Col 4:5). As a result, the early Christians experienced a feeling of alienation from the world. Hence, they were "strangers" and "pilgrims" in this world (Heb 11:13; 1 P 2:11); and they were obliged "to be blameless and guileless, children of God without blemish in the midst of a depraved and perverse generation" (Ph 2:15). As the people of God upon the earth, they had here no lasting city but sought after a future one (Heb 13:14). Their citizenship was in heaven (Ph 3:20). Because the Gospel is foolishness to the world (1 Cor 1:13), the world hates Christians and this hatred is proof that they do not belong to the world (Jn 15:18-21). They are in the world (Jn 17:11) but not of it (Jn 17:14-16). They live in the certainty that this world is passing away (1 Cor 7:31).

THE CHURCH AND THE KINGDOM OF GOD

The central theme of Jesus' preaching was the kingdom of God or the kingdom of heaven. The kingdom of heaven signifies not so much a kingdom that exists or will exist in heaven; rather, it signifies the reign of God who is in heaven. It is a situation in which the will of God alone prevails. The fundamental conditions for admission to the kingdom of God are repentance and belief (Mk 1:15).

Frequently Jesus spoke of the kingdom of God as a reality of the future. In the "Our Father," for example, Jesus taught His disciples to pray for the coming of the kingdom (Mt 6:10). Paradoxically, Jesus also spoke of the kingdom as present. Thus we read in Mark's Gospel that Jesus proclaimed the presence of the kingdom (Mk 1:15). What is the explanation of this paradox? How can the kingdom be present and yet off in the future? One answer is this: the person and activity of Jesus indicate the actual presence of the kingdom. For the time being, though, the kingdom remains hidden to a large extent; and it is plagued by the presence of evil, especially death and temptation to sin. However, the kingdom of God will appear in all its perfection at a future moment—at the judgment of mankind when all evil will be removed (Mk 13:24-30).

What is the relationship between the Church and the kingdom of God? Although the Church is more than a religious community established by the mutual consent of Christians, it is not at all identical with the kingdom of God. The New Testament does not permit us to say that the Church is the kingdom of God on earth or the present form of the kingdom. Surely the forces of the kingdom are active within the Church; however, this activity means only that the kingdom and the Church are related. The Church is a community of salvation which exists for the sake of the kingdom. The Church will become the kingdom only after the final judgment and the separation of the saved from the damned.

As the community of those who await the kingdom in its perfect form, the Church is in a certain sense the preparatory stage of the kingdom. Nevertheless, adherence to the Church is no' guarantee of belonging to the kingdom. The Church is still exposed to temptation because it still lives in the present age. The relationship between the Church and the kingdom is clearly expressed in the prayer of the *Didache* (10:5): "Be mindful, O Lord, of your Church, to save her from all evil and to perfect her in your love; and bring her together from the four winds, the holy one, into your kingdom which you have prepared for her."

CULT

Baptism was the rite by which a convert was incorporated into the Church. The reception of baptism was regularly demanded of those who believed in Christ (Ac 2:38; 8:12; Rm 6:3; etc.) Jesus had spoken of the necessity of baptism (Jn 3:5) and commanded its administration (Mt 28-19). Those who were baptized committed themselves to Jesus as their heavenly Lord. By baptism a person "put on Christ" (Gal 3:27), obtained the remission of sins (Ac 2:38), and received the Holy Spirit (1 Cor 12: 13; etc.)

In the very earliest period of its existence, apart from baptism, the Church did not conduct any other cultic rite of its own because it had not yet separated itself from the Jewish community (Ac 2:46; 3:1; 5:42). Nevertheless, the tendency to initiate its own forms of worship was present when the community assembled in private homes for common meals although these did not have a cultic character at first. A distinct trace of a specifically Christian worship is the Aramaic prayer, *Maranatha* (1 Cor 16:22), which means "The Lord comes" or "Our Lord, come." When at the behest of Christ, the early Christians did come to celebrate a cultic meal of their own, the Eucharist, they did so in the spirit of this brief prayer. The Christians ate this meal with longing expectation of the return of their glorified Lord (1 Cor 11:26). Furthermore, at this meal the Christians identified Christ with the food (1 Cor 11:27) and they saw in it the memorial of His death (1 Cor 11:26).

OFFICES AND CHARISMS

Because the Church is a community living in the context of history, it needs a social structure. Accordingly, the Spirit (1 Cor 12:4-11) or (according to Ep 4:7-12) the glorified Lord has provided the Church with different offices and charisms. In 1 Cor 12:28, Paul speaks about this matter: "God indeed has placed some in the Church, first apostles, secondly prophets, thirdly teachers; after that miracles, then gifts of healing, services of help, power of administration, and the speaking of various tongues." The first three offices seem to be listed in the order of their importance. "Speaking of various tongues" seems to have been put in the last place because it was of slight importance for building up the Church (as Paul suggests in 1 Cor 14:4).

The most important office is that of apostle. The New Testament uses the word in a broad and restricted sense. In the restricted sense, it refers for the most part to one who has seen the risen Lord and has received from Him a commission to preach the Gospels. In the broad sense, apostle refers to one who was sent not by the Lord but by men.

After the apostles come the prophets. The function of the prophets is principally to reveal and disclose (Ac 11:28; Ac 21:10; 1 Th 3:4). Teachers, the third category mentioned by Paul, may have been persons who instructed others in the Christian faith.

Toward the end of his list, Paul mentions the gift of administration. Surely the apostles shared this gift; but it was shared by others too who exercised supervision over the local communities. Among the administrators and supervisors are the presbyters (Ac 11:30; 14:22; 21:18; Jm 5:14; 1 P 5:1-4) and those identical with them, the *episkopoi* or bishops (Ac 20:28; Tt 1:7; Ph 1:1; 1 Tm 3:2).

There can be no doubt that Paul was not particularly concerned with structural and legal matters. His attitude is to be explained on the one hand by his personality and on the other hand by his paternal relationship with the communities which he founded. Furthermore, Paul seems to have lived in the expectation of an imminent Parousia. He was not impressed with the necessity of establishing permanent structures. Hence, the Church presented in the principal Pauline letters (Gal, Ph, 1-2 Cor, Rm) and the captivity epistles (Phm, Col, Ep) has a "pneumatic" appearance.

When the pastoral epistles (1-2 Tm, Ti) were composed however, more permanent structures had become necessary because of the danger to the Christian communities through heresy. Hence, the pastoral letters reflect a fixed order within the communities which had assumed a more institutional character.

In Ph 1:1 and 1 Tm 3:8-13, there are references to deacons who exercised a ministerial function in the Church subordinate to that of the bishop-presbyters.

Induction into a Church office was often accompanied by an imposition of hands (Ac 6:6; 1 Tm 4:14; 5:22; 2 Tm 1:6). The laying on of hands to signify the conferral of an office was common in late Judaism and was reminiscent of the occasion when Moses chose Joshua as his successor, laying his hands upon him (Nb 27:18. 23; Dt 34:9).

JESUS, THE FOUNDER OF THE CHURCH

In what sense is Jesus the founder of the Church? In the past some maintained that the Church arose out of a voluntary association of believers and communities so that some time elapsed between the death and resurrection of Christ and the foundation of the Church. At the present time, however, there seems to be general agreement among Catholic and non-Catholic scholars upon a number of points: that the Church existed immediately after Easter, that it looked to God as its founder, that somehow it went back to the person and activity of Jesus, that Jesus Himself had expected the disciples, whom He had gathered around Himself during His earthly ministry, to be united again after His death. The common experience of personal contact with Jesus and His resurrection had to lead to such a reunion.

Some scholars, however, do not attribute to Jesus a greater role in the foundation of the Church. If the disciples of Jesus came to regard themselves as the new people of God—as an *ekklesia* or Church, this conviction must not be ascribed to the words and deeds of Jesus but to other causes. Jesus, they say, could not have considered the foundation of a Church because He regarded the appearance of the kingdom of God as imminent. Hence, the passage in Matthew's Gospel (16:17-19) in which Jesus speaks of building His Church upon Peter cannot be an authentic word of the Lord. This passage is surrounded by a host of other difficulties too. Only in this place (apart from Mt 18:18) does the word *ekklesia* appear in the Synoptic Gospels. Moreover, the idea of a Church which was to embrace all nations must have been foreign to the mind of Jesus because He was conscious of a personal mission to Israel only (Mt 15:24). He also directed the Twelve not to preach to the Gentiles (Mt 10:5-6). Hence, the initial hesitation of the primitive Church to go to the Gentiles (Ac 10). Finally, the historical character of the passage in Matthew's Gospel (16: 17-19) is questioned on the grounds that Peter's position in the primitive community did not actually correspond to the words of the promise. Did he not have to justify his going to the Gentiles before the community (Ac 11:1-18)?

Despite these objections, Jesus must be considered the founder of the Church in a very specific sense—not by a single act, but by a series of acts on His part. First of all, "Jesus came into Galilee, preaching the gospel of the kingdom of God and saying, 'The time is fulfilled, and the kingdom of God is at hand. Repent and believe in the gospel' " (Mk 1:14-15). The proclamation of the kingdom of God was Jesus' principal concern. The Church was established to continue the proclamation.

Second, just as the Jewish rabbis gathered disciples around themselves in order to instruct them in the Law, so Jesus gathered disciples around Himself in order to attach them to His person and to His mission of preaching the kingdom. From the circle of His disciples, Jesus selected twelve of them that they might be with Him and that He might send them forth to preach (Mk 3:14-19). Jesus chose the Twelve for a symbolic reason—to represent the people of God in the New Testament, just as the twelve sons of Jacob symbolically represented the people of God in the Old Testament. In the kingdom of God the Twelve will sit upon thrones judging the twelve tribes of Israel (Lk 22:30; Mt 19:28). By gathering disciples, by choosing the Twelve, by entrusting them with the mission of preaching, Jesus established in effect a religious society. By so doing, He took an important step in the establishment of the Church which is a group committed to Jesus and the proclamation of His message.

Third, Jesus chose Peter to be the foundation of His Church. He gave him the keys of the kingdom of heaven and the authority to bind and loose (Mt 16:18-19). He made him the shepherd of His flock (Jn 21:15-17). Hence, Jesus provided His Church with visible leadership. (This matter will be taken up in greater detail in the following section.)

Fourth, Jesus celebrated the Last Supper in anticipation of His death on Calvary. In this manner He founded a new covenant. We read in Mark: "While they were eating, Jesus took bread and blessing it, he broke and gave it to them, and said, 'Take; this is my body.' And taking a cup and giving thanks, he gave it to them, and they all drank of it; and he said to them, 'This is my blood of the new covenant which is being shed for many'" (Mk 14:22-23). When Jesus forged a new covenant by shedding His blood, He established the Church as the new people of God. He made available to all the remission of sins and life eternal.

Fifth, the risen Lord sent His apostles and disciples to announce the good news of the kingdom to all nations (Mt 28:19-20; Lk 24:44-49; Jn 20:21-23). The mission of those sent by Jesus—the Church—was now enlarged to include the Gentiles. The Church's mission to the Gentiles is consonant with Jesus' universal point of view. Jesus Himself and, at the outset, His disciples announced the kingdom of God only to the Jews. As sons of the old covenant, they enjoyed a privileged position. At the same time, though, Jesus explained that the Gentiles too would enter the kingdom of God (Mt 8:11; Lk 13:29). Further, Jesus acknowledged that He had been sent to give His life for the whole world (Mk 10:45; 14:24). Jesus anticipated the gathering of His elect from the four winds (Mk 13:27) and His judging all the nations of the earth (Mt 25-31-46). Moreover, Jesus accepted the prophetic expectation of the Old Testament which envisioned the admission of the Gentiles into the blessings of the Messianic period. Jesus' universal point of view was shaped by His conception of God as the Father of all mankind.

Finally, on Pentecost Jesus sent the Holy Spirit upon the Church. He did so in accordance with His promise: "I will ask the Father and he will give you another Advocate to dwell with you forever" (Jn 14:16). In the Old Testament God had promised His spirit to those who lived under the new covenant (Jl 2:28-32). On Pentecost this promise was fulfilled (Ac 2:14-21).

By a series of acts, therefore, Jesus founded the Church. A review of these acts enables us to achieve some understanding of the mystery of the Church. The Church is a community of persons committed to Jesus and the spread of His message. This community is the new people of God. It possesses the Holy Spirit and the visible leadership of Peter and the apostles.

Surely, then, Jesus expected a certain interval of time to elapse between His death and the appearance of the kingdom of God. Without such an expectation on His part, many of His actions would have been meaningless. The interval though is to be not merely a period of waiting, but a period of preparation of the people of God.

PETER

The New Testament attests to the leading role of the Twelve and the preeminent position of Simon Peter in the circle of the Twelve. He is named first on all the lists of the apostles (Mt 10:2; Mk 3:16; Lk 6:14; Ac 1:13). Christ changed his name from Simon to Peter (Mk 3:16; Lk 6:14; Mt 16:18; Jn 1:42). The name Peter means "rock." The change of name implies that Peter was to assume an exalted position in the Church (cf. Gn 17:5; 32:28; 35:9-10). Christ made him the foundation of the Church and handed over to him the keys of the kingdom of heaven with full authority to bind and loose (Mt 16:18-19). Christ enjoined Peter to strengthen his brethren (Lk 22:32). After His resurrection, the Lord "appeared to Peter and then to the Twelve" (1 Cor 15:5); and He made Peter the shepherd of His flock (Jn 21:15-17). Peter played a uniquely important role in the primitive Christian community as the first half of the Acts of the Apostles testifies. Because of Peter's position, Paul was anxious to make his acquaintance (Gal 1:18) and was quite concerned about the consequences of Peter's conduct in one instance (Gal 2:11-14).

The nature of Peter's primacy is disclosed especially in the passages, Mt 16:18-19 and Jn 21:15-17. In these passages Peter is said to be the foundation of the Church, the bearer of the keys and the shepherd of Christ's flock. To be the foundation of the Church, the rock upon which it is built, suggests a primacy of leadership and authority without which no social entity can exist. To be the bearer of the keys is to have supreme authority such as Christ has over death and hell (Rv 1:18) and Eliakim had over Jerusalem (Is 22:21-22). To be the shepherd of Christ's flock is to fill a position comparable to David's role in his kingdom (2 S 5:2) and the Messiah's role among His people (Ezk 34:23).

Furthermore, Peter being the rock upon which the Church has been built suggests that he will have successors in his capacity as the visible head of the Church. If the Church is to endure, the foundation must endure.

Of course, objections have been raised against the estimate of Peter's position sustained in the preceding paragraphs. Some believe that Mt 16:18-19 cannot be an authentic word of the Lord because only in this place (and Mt 18:17) does the word, *ekklesia* or church, appear in the Synoptic Gospels. A number of observations can be made in reply to this objection. First, if we were to reject as authentic those words of the Lord which appear only once in the Synoptic Gospels, we should have to reject a good many other passages too. Second, the idea of a church was not foreign to the mind of Jesus. At the Last Supper, for example, Jesus established a new covenant which includes the notion of the new people of God, the Church. Third, the passage in question (Mt 16:18-19) is in accord with the other passages of the New Testament relating to Peter; indeed, it furnishes an explanation for the prominent role of Peter. Hence, Mt 16:18-19 ought to be accepted as a *logion* revealing the mind of Christ about Peter and the Church.

Some have attacked the authenticity of Mt 16:18-19 on the grounds that Peter's position in the primitive Church did not actually correspond to the promise of the primacy contained in this passage. In reply: the New Testament gives a rich insight into the preeminent position of Peter in the primitive community. Recall the remarks at the beginning of this section on Peter. If Peter did not exercise his authority with all the assertiveness of some leaders, the fact may be ascribed partially to the familiar circumstances in which he moved. Moreover, it is possible that the primitive Christian community did not fully appreciate at the outset all the implications of Peter's position. In this matter as in others, we must recognize the possibility of clearer insights.

II. THE FATHERS

In general, the Fathers of the Church are the ancient writers who are witnesses to, and teachers of, the faith of the early Church. The patristic period extends from the close of the era of the New Testament up to the death of Gregory the Great (d. 604) or Isidore of Seville (d. 636) in the West and to the death of John Damascene (d. 749) in the East.

In ancient times, a teacher was considered to be the father of his pupil in a spiritual sense. Irenaeus (d. ca. 202), a Father of the Church, wrote: "One who is taught by another is said to be the son of his teacher and his teacher is said to be his father" (*Against Heresies* 4, 41, 2). At first Christians reserved the name, father, for bishops, the official teachers of the Church. Later, however, they gave the name to all ecclesiastical writers who taught the Christian faith in antiquity.

Today those individuals are considered to be Fathers of the Church who meet four requirements: orthodoxy, holiness of life, antiquity, and recognition by the Church as a Father. It must be noted that not all "Doctors" of the Church are Fathers of the Church; for some Doctors of the Church, such as Thomas Aquinas (d. 1274) and Robert Bellarmine (d. 1621), lived after the close of the patristic period. The Catholic Church recognizes four great Fathers in the West (Ambrose, Jerome, Augustine, and Gregory the Great) and four great Fathers in the East (Basil the Great, Gregory of Nazianzus, John Chrysostom, and Athanasius).

Within the ranks of the Fathers it is possible to distinguish various groups. The Apostolic Fathers lived at the close of the first century and during the first part of the second century. They had personal contact with the apostles or their immediate disciples. The Apostolic Fathers are Barnabas, Clement of Rome, Ignatius of Antioch, Polycarp of Smyrna, Hermas, Papias of Hieropolis, and the unknown authors of the *Epistle to Diognetus* and the Didache. The writings of these Fathers bear a resemblance to the epistles of the New Testament; and they are characterized by an expectation that the second coming of Christ is imminent, the same Christ whom the authors remember vividly.

The Greek Apologists of the second century wrote with two purposes in mind. First, they sought to answer the calumnies directed against Christianity by the pagans. Some pagans entertained fantastic ideas about Christianity which they regarded as a threat to the State and a mixture of superstition and fanaticism. Second, the Apologists attempted to show the absurdity of paganism and the sublimity of the Christian understanding of God. In their writings they present Christianity as the religion of truth, a religion far older than the Greek thinkers and religions because it has its roots in the Old Testament of the Bible. Among the Greek Apologists are Aristides of Athens and Justin Martyr.

The Alexandrians were members of the Christian catechetical school at Alexandria, Egypt. The school was one of the oldest centers of sacred science in the history of Christianity; and it existed for the purpose of instructing converts and preparing teachers. The Alexandrians were characterized by a preference for the philosophy of Plato and the allegorical interpretation of the Bible. The allegorical interpretation finds deeper meanings in the Bible than the literal sense of the words conveys. Among the most famous members of the school were Clement (150-ca. 215) and Origen (185-254).

Another famous Christian school existed at Antioch in Syria. In opposition to the school at Alexandria, the school of Antioch stressed the literal sense of the Bible, that is, the sense expressed by the words themselves. This school inclined to the philosophy of Aristotle and rationalism. The founder of the school was

Lucian of Samosata and its most famous student was John Chrysostom (345?-407).

The Cappadocian Fathers sprang from the province of Cappadocia in (what is today) Turkey. They are Basil the Great (330?-379?), Gregory of Nazianzus (330?-390?) and his brother, Gregory of Nyssa (331?-396?). They made notable contributions to the progress of theology and to monasticism.

Undoubtedly, the Fathers occupy an important place in the history of Greek and Roman literature; however, the Catholic Church reveres the Fathers for another reason. The First Vatican Council (1869-70) explained: "The Fathers have supreme authority whenever they all explain in one and the same way any passage in the Bible as pertaining to the teaching of faith and morals. For the holy Fathers, 'who came after the apostles, planted and watered, built, shepherded and nurtured the growing Church' " (CT no. 103). The reason the Church accepts the authority of the Fathers is that they testify to the belief of the universal Church which is infallible in matters of faith and morals.

Many Fathers wrote in Greek and specifically in Koine, the Greek language commonly spoken and written in eastern Mediterranean countries in the Hellenistic and Roman periods. From the third century of the Christian era, Latin became the language of the western Fathers. Some Fathers employed neither Greek nor Latin but the language of a particular country such as Syriac and Armenian.

THE WORLD OF THE FATHERS

The world of the Fathers preserved many important elements of the world of the New Testament. The Empire continued to dominate although Constantine transferred its capital from Rome to Constantinople (A.D. 330). To be sure, the classical religion of Greece and Rome with its gods and goddesses had lost its vitality; but the mystery religions of the East continued to thrive at least in the first centuries of the patristic era. The more intelligent looked to philosophy for the solution of deeper problems and especially to the philosophies of Plato and the Stoics. The

influence of Palestinian Judaism upon Christian thinkers, great as
it was in the apostolic age, was curtailed sharply by the disaster
of 70 A.D. Alexandrian Judaism, however, and particularly the
Alexandrian Jew, Philo (1st century, A.D.), with his allegorical
interpretation of Sacred Scripture and his doctrine of the Logos,
were important influences.

From Palestine the Church spread to Asia Minor, to Greece,
to Italy, to Egypt and Africa, to Gaul and Spain, to Germany and
to Britain. As the Church spread, it came into contact with other
religions and philosophies. One of these was Gnosticism. Gnosticism drew its inspiration from Jewish, pagan, oriental and Christian sources. Gnosticism maintained that matter was evil. It was
not the product of the God of light and goodness but the product
of an inferior deity or Demiurge. Emancipation of the spiritual
element in man from matter was achieved through the help of
celestial mediators and gnosis. Gnosis was the knowledge of
these things. A practical consequence of Gnosticism was that
some Gnostics indulged the flesh unreservedly as a thing of little
consequence while other Gnostics practiced a severe asceticism
seeking to repress the flesh as an evil thing.

When the Church made converts among the Gnostics, some
of them attempted to explain the mysteries of Christianity in a
Gnostic way. The opponents of Gnosticism and false Christian
Gnosticism were the bishops and especially Irenaeus, bishop of
Lyons in (what is today) southern France. In his work, *Against
Heresies,* Irenaeus pointed out that Gnosticism contradicted the
teaching handed down by the apostles to their successors, the
bishops. What that teaching was might be learned quite easily
from the Roman Church which was founded by the apostles
Peter and Paul and with which every Church should agree. The
words of Irenaeus are these:

> It is within the power of all, therefore, in every Church, who
> may wish to see the truth, to contemplate clearly the
> tradition which the apostles manifested throughout the
> whole world; and we are in a position to reckon up those
> who were by the apostles instituted bishops in the Churches,
> and [to demonstrate] the succession of these men to our
> own times; those who neither taught nor knew anything like

what these [heretics] rave about. For if the apostles had known hidden mysteries, which they were in the habit of imparting to 'the perfect' apart and privily from the rest, they would have delivered them especially to those to whom they were also committing the Churches themselves. For they were desirous that these men should be perfect and blameless in all things, whom they also were leaving behind as their successors, delivering up their own place of government to these men; which men, if they discharged their functions honestly, would be a great boon [to the Church], but if they should fall away, the direst calamity.

Since, however, it would be very tedious, in such a volume as this, to reckon up the successions of all the Churches, we do put to confusion all those who, in whatever manner, whether by an evil self-pleasing, by vainglory, or by blindness and perverse opinion, assemble in unauthorized meetings; [we do this, I say,] by indicating that tradition derived from the apostles, of the very great, the very ancient, and universally known Church founded and organized at Rome by the two most glorious apostles, Peter and Paul; as also [by pointing out] the faith preached to men, which comes down to our time by means of the successions of the bishops. For it is a matter of necessity that every Church should agree with this Church, on account of its preeminent authority, that is, the faithful everywhere, inasmuch as the apostolical tradition has been preserved continuously by those [faithful men] who exist everywhere.[1]

The Gnostic challenge and Irenaeus' response to it indicate that Christianity is a traditional religion, preserving and holding fast to that teaching which has been handed down by the apostles to their successors, the bishops.

Marcionism was a form of Gnosticism. Marcion (1st half of the 2nd century A.D.), the founder, was the son of a bishop. He affirmed the existence of two gods, a god of love who revealed himself in Jesus Christ and an angry god, Demiurge, who created the visible world which is evil. Jesus was crucified, though in appearance only, by the subjects of the Demiurge whose kingdom He came to destroy. Marcion believed that the apostle Paul was the best guide in religious matters; and he rejected the Old Testament which he thought was opposed to the teachings of Paul. To his peculiar doctrines Marcion added an austere system of morality, forbidding marriage, meat and wine. Marcionism won many adherents and still existed in many countries in the fifth century.

Another adversary of Christianity was Montanism. The founder, Montanus, declared himself to be the spokesman of the Holy Spirit in the second half of the 2nd century. He wished to bring Christianity to a more mature state in which the Holy Spirit would have complete freedom. Montanus foretold the coming of Jesus for the second time within his own lifetime. He enjoined an exceedingly strict code of morality upon his followers as a preparation for the Parousia. A prominent convert to the sect was Tertullian (160?-230?), one of the most brilliant minds of the age. Despite the prolonged delay of the Parousia, Montanism persisted for several centuries.

It is also necessary to speak of Manichaeism which retained fewer Christian elements than the religions mentioned above. Its teachings were a curious mixture of Buddhist, Zoroastrian, Gnostic and Christian ideas. The founder of the religion was Mani (A.D. 216-276), a Persian. Mani claimed to teach the fullness of religious truth which the prophets prior to him had communicated only fragmentarily. Mani spoke of the conflict between Light and Darkness both of which had given rise, by emanation, to good and bad beings respectively. Jesus is the product of Light while the devil is the product of Darkness. The human soul is a fragment of Light but it is tragically involved in the material order. Man's salvation lay in grasping these ideas and withdrawing from the contamination of the flesh. The religion of Mani was highly organized with "hearers," "elect," "priests," "bishops," and "apostles." For a time Augustine of Hippo (354-430) was an adherent of this religion; and it persisted until the 13th century when it was destroyed by the Albigensian crusade.

Prior to Constantine's edict of toleration in 313, the Church was subject to periods of fearful persecution. Often the best emperors who were strong, capable administrators and reformers were the worst tormentors of the Church. The Christian was persecuted because he refused to take part in the cult of the State and the emperor. His refusal made him appear to be an enemy of the State. Sometimes the persecution of the Church was desultory; sometimes it was well-organized. Among the best known and fiercest persecutors of the Church were the emperors Nero, Domitian, Trajan, Marcus Aurelius, Septimius Severus, Decius and Diocletian.

The Edict of Milan gave the Church the legal right to exist; and Constantine favored it increasingly with the passage of time. After the death of Constantine (337) laws were enacted against paganism; but the first really Christian emperor was Theodosius (379-95). He made Christianity the religion of the State. With the establishment of Christianity, the problem of Church and State entered a new phase. Caesaropapism made its appearance almost at once.

From the outset, the emperor took it upon himself to intervene in the affairs of the Church. Not only did the emperor sometimes regulate such practical matters as episcopal elections and clerical and monastic discipline, but he also interfered in doctrinal disputes. For example, the emperor Justinian (483-565) condemned by official decree the heresy of Origen in 543 and the so-called "Three Chapters" of some fifth century theologians; and on the eve of his death in 565 he even claimed the right to enforce a theory which was patently unorthodox. The successors of Constantine and Justinian remained faithful to the policy of their predecessors. The emperors came to regard themselves as the guardians of the faith—a claim which nullified the independence of the Church. The Church in the East became completely subject to the State. This situation is known in Church history as caesaropapism.

The patristic period is the period of the first ecumenical councils of the Church. The first ecumenical council of the Church met at Nicea in 325 in (what is today) Turkey. The council was summoned by the emperor Constantine to deal with the errors of Arius, a priest of Alexandria in Egypt. According to Arius, Jesus was not equal to the Father who was God but only the creature of the Father. The Council of Nicea declared that the Son is true God and of one substance with the Father. The great champion of orthodoxy at Nicea was Athanasius of Alexandria (293?-373).

The second ecumenical council, held at Constantinople in

381, affirmed the divinity of the Holy Spirit. Arius had taught that the Holy Spirit was the creature of the Son. This council also accorded the bishop of Constantinople a primacy of honor above all the bishops of the world, the Pope alone excepted. The honor was accorded because Constantinople was now the capital of the empire, the new Rome.

The third ecumenical council met at Ephesus in 431. This council defined the unity of person in Christ in contradiction to the opinion of Nestorius who recognized two persons in Christ. The council also taught that Mary is truly the Mother of God. (*theotokos*). Cyril of Alexandria was the leading figure at the council.

The fourth ecumenical council met at Chalcedon in 451. It had 630 members and was the largest council of antiquity. Against the Monophysites who recognized only one nature, the divine, in our Lord, the council asserted that there are two natures in the Lord, the divine and the human, without confusion or conversion, without division or separation, the distinction between the two natures being in no wise abolished by their union; on the contrary, the properties peculiar to each being retained, and both being united in a single person or hypostasis.

The fifth ecumenical council was held at Constantinople in 553. The council condemned the so-called "Three Chapters" which the emperor Justinian had condemned nine years earlier (544). The "Three Chapters" were certain writings which were tinged with Nestorianism.

Finally, the sixth ecumenical council, held at Constantinople in 680-681, defined the existence of two wills in Christ, the divine and the human, against the Monothelites who recognized only one will in Christ, at once divine and human.

The patristic period is also noted for the invention of monasticism. Even in the first centuries certain souls consecrated themselves to God through a vow of perfect chastity. During the persecutions some Christians fled to desert places where they led a solitary life in caves or huts even after the persecutions had ceased. St. Anthony (d. 356) was one of the most famous solitaries. St. Pachomius (d. 346) established monasteries in Egypt with a common way of life and a superior for those pupils who flocked to him. The monastic movement spread from Egypt to Palestine, Syria, Asia Minor and western Europe. St. Basil the Great (330-379?) drew up a rule which was notable because it provided for a novitiate and regulated against overly large monasteries. In Italy, St. Benedict (490-543) drew up a rule for monks which was widely adopted in the West. His rule imposed the vow of stability which obliged the monk to remain in the same house until death. For the most part the monks were laymen who occupied their time with manual labor and prayer. Of course, convents for women were common too.

After the middle of the fifth century a decline in theological speculation ensued. It seemed that the first four ecumenical councils had settled the problems connected with the central mysteries of Christianity, the Trinity and the Incarnation. The great Fathers in the East and West had died. The West was subjected to invasions by barbarians while the East was experiencing the initial onslaught of Islam.

IN GENERAL

The Fathers are the interpreters of the Scriptures. They are consumed with the idea that the entire Bible speaks of Jesus and the Church. To a large extent their ecclesiology is concerned with the interpretation of Biblical terms and expressions in which they perceive a reference to, or a likeness of, the Church. These terms and expressions include people (of God), body of Christ, temple, house, bride, flock, vineyard, Jerusalem-Sion, holy city, field, net, paradise, heaven, dove, moon ship, ark and coat without seam. For example, the Second Epistle of Clement (ca. A.D. 150) speaks of the Church in these terms:

> Wherefore brethren, if we do the will of God our Father, we shall be of the first Church, that is, spiritual, that has been created before the sun and moon; ... So then let us choose to be of the Church of life, that we may be saved. I do not, however, suppose that you are ignorant that the living Church is the body of Christ; for the Scripture saith, 'God made man, male and female.' The male is Christ, the

female is the Church. And the Books and the Apostles plainly declare that the Church is not of the present, but from the beginning. For she was spiritual, as our Jesus was, but was manifested in the last days that He might save us. Now the Church, being spiritual, was manifested in the flesh of Christ, thus signifying to us that, if any of us keep her in the flesh and do not corrupt her, he shall receive her again in the Holy Spirit: for this flesh is the copy of the spirit. No one then who corrupts the copy, shall partake of the original. This, then is what He meaneth, 'Keep the flesh, that ye may partake of the spirit.' But if we say that the flesh is the Church and the spirit Christ, then he that hath shamefully used the flesh hath shamefully used the Church. Such a one then shall not partake of the spirit, which is Christ (ch. 14).

In the passage just cited, the author speaks of the Church as the body of Christ and His bride. These are Pauline figures. In an earlier passage (ch. 2), the author thinks of the Church as our mother.

Another example. In various works, Hippolytus of Rome (d. 235) speaks of the Church as the bride and spouse of Christ, as the woman of the Apocalypse (12:1-6) who gives birth to the Logos, and as the new Eden. He also pictures the Church as a ship sailing towards the East and the heavenly paradise. Christ is its pilot:

But we who hope for the Son of God are persecuted and trodden down by those unbelievers. For the wings of the vessels are the churches; and the sea is the world, in which the Church is set, like a ship tossed in the deep, but not destroyed; for she has with her the skilled Pilot, Christ. And she bears in her midst also the trophy (which is erected) over death; for she carries with her the cross of the Lord. For her prow is the east, and her storm is the west, and her hold is the south, and her tillers are the two Testaments; and the ropes that stretch around her are the love of Christ, which binds the Church; and the net which she bears with her is the laver of regeneration which renews the believing, whence too are these glories. As the wind the Spirit from heaven is present, by whom those who believe are sealed: she also has anchors of iron accompanying her, viz., the holy commandments of Christ Himself, which are strong as iron.

She has also mariners on the right and on the left, assessors like the holy angels, by whom the Church is always governed and defended. The ladder in her leading up to the sailyard is an emblem of the passion of Christ, which brings the faithful to the ascent of heaven. And the top sails aloft upon the yard are the company of prophets, martyrs, and apostles, who have entered into their rest in the kingdom of Christ.[2]

The Fathers compare the Church to Biblical personages such as Eve, Rahab, Mary Magdalene and the virgin Mary. For example, Methodius (d. 311) sees a likeness between the Church and Eve:

> The apostle [Paul] directly referred to Christ the words which had been spoken of Adam. For thus will it be most certainly agreed that the Church is formed out of His bones and flesh; and it was for this cause that the Word, leaving His Father in heaven, came down to be 'joined to His wife;' and slept in the trance of His passion, and willingly suffered death for her, that He might present the Church to Himself glorious and blameless, having cleansed her by the laver (Eph 5:26-27), for the receiving of the spiritual and blessed seed, which is sown by Him who with whispers implants it in the depths of the mind; and is conceived and **formed by the Church, as by a woman, so as to give birth** and nourishment to virtue. For in this way, too, the command, 'Increase and multiply,' is duly fulfilled, the Church increasing daily in greatness and beauty and multitude, by the union and communion of the World.[3]

The Fathers apply these images to the Church, not in every detail of course, but to the degree they represent the reality of the Church. Moreover, these images convey less an ontology of the Church than a pattern of Christian conduct; that is, they do not tell us primarily what the Church is in itself, but rather how Christians are to conduct themselves in relation to God. The picture of the Church which emerges from the writings of the Fathers is that of a Church which fasts and prays, is under attack, does penance, is converted, struggles against Satan and achieves its greatest measure of fulfillment in the saints, martyrs, virgins, ascetics and monks.

The Fathers were influenced in varying degrees by Platonism. According to Plato (427?-347 B.C.), there are two worlds: the

unchanging world of forms or ideas which have objective existence and the sensible, changing world in which we live. The
forms are arranged in a hierarchy at the top of which is the
form of the Good. The Good is the cause of all the other forms.
The sensible world is modelled on the world of forms. The soul
lives between the two worlds. By contact with this world the
soul is led to remember the world of ideas which is contemplated
in a previous existence.

Several centuries later Plotinus (A.D. 205?-270), a Roman
(though Egyptian-born) philosopher, did much to promote neo-
Platonism. He conceived reality as a vast hierarchical structure.
The various strata of being emanated from the One much as con-
centric circles emanate from a point. The *Nous* or intellect
emanated immediately from the One; the world-soul, from the
Nous; individual souls, from the world-soul; matter, from the
individual souls. All reality, Plotinus maintained, experiences an
ardent longing for union with what is higher and ultimately
with the One itself.

One encounters platonic ideas (without, however, acceptance
of the total platonic system) in the writings of Cyprian, Hilary,
Augustine and Gregory the Great as well as in the writings of
the Greek Fathers. For example, certain Fathers thought in
terms of a hierarchy of being, the highest stage of being or truth
being ideal (in the platonic sense), spiritual, heavenly and eternal. Sensible realities reflect the order of heaven. Men encounter
the heavenly world in the Church, specially in its sacraments and
ministers. Also from a platonic point of view, some Fathers
thought that the mystery of the Church could be realized in
different ways. It is realized only superficially in the case of
"fleshly" Christians who share only in the visible side of the
Church. The mystery of the Church is realized truly, however,
in the case of "spiritual" Christians who participate in the
heavenly and true form of the Church's being and in the influence
of the Spirit. This platonic view of things corresponds thoroughly
to the ontology of the Bible which evaluates things according to
their harmony with the plan of God. Nevertheless, we must not
confuse the historical, eschatological thrust of the Bible with
the platonic doctrine of forms.

THE LATIN TRADITION OF AFRICA

The first great theologian in this tradition was Tertullian (160?-230?), a native of Carthage. He was a convert to Christianity and a lawyer. About 207 he openly went over to the Montanists. Tertullian thinks of the Church as a mother. Speaking to candidates for baptism, he wrote:

> Therefore, blessed ones, whom the grace of God awaits, when you ascend from that most sacred font of your new birth, and spread your hands for the first time in the house of your mother [the Church], together with your brethren, ask from the Father, ask from the Lord, that his own specialties of grace and distributions of gifts may be supplied you.[4]

Before he went over to Montanism, Tertullian thought of the Church as the guardian of the faith and the Scriptures. The Church alone was capable of teaching the doctrine of the apostles because of episcopal succession from them. In this view Tertullian resembled Irenaeus. After he went over to Montanism, Tertullian rejected the Church of the bishops and extolled the Church of the Spirit:

> For the very Church itself is, properly and principally, the Spirit Himself, in whom is the Trinity of the One Divinity— Father, Son, and Holy Spirit. (The Spirit) combines that Church which the Lord has made to consist in 'three.' And thus, from that time forward, every number of persons who may have combined together into this faith is accounted 'a Church,' from the Author and Consecrator (of the Church). And accordingly 'the Church,' it is true, will forgive sins: but (it will be) the Church of the Spirit, by means of a spiritual man; not the Church which consists of a number of bishops.[5]

The second African theologian in this tradition was Cyprian (d. 258), bishop of Carthage and martyr. He acknowledged Tertullian to be his teacher. The Church was at the center of Cyprian's thought. For him the Church was made up of two groups, the laity and the hierarchy. The Church is a harbor of salvation which offers men protection from the storms of the time.[6] It is a house of faith in which one may not doubt the promises of God.[7] The Church is a mother: from her womb we are born, by her milk we are nourished, by her spirit we are animated.[8] The Church is the body of Christ and Christians are members of this body.[9]

For Cyprian, people and bishops belong together. Through union with their bishop the people are joined to God, Christ and the Church. The bishop is the visible authority around which the congregation is centered. The unity of the whole Church rests in turn on that of the bishops. (Cyprian's conception of the bishop's place in the Church will be discussed at greater length in a section that follows.)

According to Cyprian, the possession and exercise of priestly powers depends upon communion with the bishop. If a cleric withdraws from communion with the bishop and, therefore, from the Church, he loses his priestly powers. (Similarly, if a bishop withdraws from communion with the other bishops of the Church, he loses his powers.) Cyprian was convinced that one loses all spiritual powers when he deserts the bishops and the Church. Hence, heretical ministers cannot validly baptize nor celebrate the Eucharist. Because the Holy Spirit dwells in the Church and not outside it, heretics who are outside the Church cannot confer the Spirit since they do not have it.[10]

Cyprian believed that sinners do not belong to the Church. They too do not have the Holy Spirit. They are spiritually dead.[11]

The Donatist controversy provided an additional spark for the development of ecclesiology. The Donatists—the name is derived from Donatus, one of their leaders—were a schismatic group in northern Africa. They asserted that the validity of the sacraments depended upon the goodness of the minister, that the true Church was composed of just members only, that the true Church was in fact the Donatist sect. The theological opponents of the schismatic group were the African bishops, Optatus of Mileve and Augustine of Hippo. In his book *On the Schism of the Donatists* written in 366 or 367, Optatus pointed out that the sacraments derive their validity from God and not from the human minister.[12] Optatus agreed with the Donatists that the Church is holy; but it is holy not because of the presence of persons who say they are holy (as the Donatists said), but because it possesses the means of sanctification.[13] Good and bad will be mingled in the Church until the day of judgment.[14] Finally, Optatus singled out two great marks of the Church, catholicity and unity. The Donatists could not be the true Church because they lacked catholicity inasmuch as they were confined to a small corner of Africa.[15] They also lacked unity because they were cut off from the chair of Peter in Rome. The unity of all the Churches was preserved by reason of their communion with Rome.[16]

Augustine (354-430), before his conversion to Christianity (387), was a teacher of rhetoric and a follower of Manichaeism. Subsequently, he was ordained bishop of Hippo in Africa in 395. He developed the ideas of Optatus about the Church, often in the context of the Donatist controversy. Augustine too was concerned with the identity of the true Church. Was it the Catholic Church or the heretical and schismatical groups which had broken with the Catholic Church? For Augustine, the world-wide extension of the Catholic Church in fulfillment of the promises of the Scriptures was evidence of its truth. God had brought this situation to pass.[17] All over the earth men and women had accepted the lofty moral demands of Christianity, a sign of its truth.[18] The Christian religion was to be found in the Catholic Church, a name given to it not only by its members but also by heretics and schismatics.[19]

The Catholic Church, according to Augustine, is characterized by charity and unity. Charity is manifested by concern for the unity of the Church: "You can prove to me that you have charity by preserving unity," Augustine said to the Church of Caesarea. "If we adore one Father, why do we not recognize one mother [the Church]?"[20] Unity means mutual affection grounded on the charity of Christ. When one separates himself from the Church by schism, as the Donatists did, he cannot retain the charity because he does not accept the unity of the body of Christ, the Church.[21]

It is the Holy Spirit who is responsible for the unity of the Church. "When the schismatics come to us. . ., they receive first of all the Church itself and in her [they receive] peace, unity and charity through her proper and invisible source, the Holy Spirit."[22] The Holy Spirit is the soul of the Church:

What the soul is to the body of man, that the Holy Spirit
is to the body of Christ which is the Church. The Holy
Spirit does that in the Church which the soul does in all the
members of the one body.[23]

In opposition to the Donatists, Augustine adopted Optatus'
view about the presence of sinners in the Church. In the Church
which is the Lord's net, the bad fishes swim together with the
good ones until the net is drawn to the shore at the end of time
and the angels separate the good from the bad.[24] Augustine used
another analogy to explain the presence of sinners in the Church.
Despite their common presence in the house of the Church, the
good belong to the substance of the house while the bad do not:

There are some in the house of God after such a fashion as
not to be themselves the very house of God, which is said
to be built upon a rock, which is called the one dove, which
is styled the beauteous bride without spot or wrinkle...
For this house is composed of those who are good and faithful, and of the holy servants of God dispersed throughout the
world, and bound together by the unity of the Spirit,
whether they know each other personally or not. But
we hold that others are said to be in the house after such a
sort, that they belong not to the substance of the house, nor
to the society of fruitful and peaceful justice, but only as
the chaff is said to be among the corn; for that they are in
the house we cannot deny, when the Apostle says: But in
a great house there are not only vessels of gold and silver,
but also of wood and earth; and some to honor, and some to
dishonor.[25]

The distinction made by Augustine between the good who
belong to the substance of the house and the bad who do not
was probably influenced by his platonic background. He distinguished easily between the ideal form of the Church and the
actual condition of it in this world.

In common with many other Fathers, Augustine thought of
the Church as a mother who begets us in the sacrament of
baptism and patiently educates us in Christian teaching and
morality. Augustine was thinking especially of the holy members
of the Church who are united to Christ in faith and love:

When young children are brought to baptism so that they
may receive spiritual grace, they are presented not so much

by those who actually carry them—although by them too if they are believers—as by the whole community of saints and believers. For one can rightly understand that they are brought to baptism by all who rejoice therein, whose holy and undivided love helps them to communion with the Holy Spirit. Mother Church—all the saints—does this because she has given birth to all and each one.[26]

The Church is the body of Christ:

There are many Christians but only one Christ. Christians together with their head who has ascended into heaven are one Christ. Not that He is many and we are many; but we who are many are one in Him. Therefore there is one man Christ with His head and body. What is His Body? It is the Church.[27]

Augustine's conception of the Church as the body of Christ was quite extensive:

The body of Christ is that Church which is spread throughout the world. It is not this Church or that one. It includes not only the living but also those who have gone before and those who will come after. For the Church which includes all the faithful because all the faithful are members of Christ has its head in heaven where He governs His body. Although the Church is separated from Him because it lacks the vision [of God], it is joined to Him in charity.[28]

Augustine's conception of the Church as the body of Christ goes back, of course, to Paul. For Augustine, Christ became the head of His body, the Church, through His incarnation and redemptive activity. He continues to act as the head of His body by the vivifying influence of His grace and charity. The latter effect the union of the members of the body with Christ. One who has lost charity and, therefore, the Holy Spirit, is no longer united to Christ; he has divided the body of Christ; he has separated himself from the source of life.

The Church is the bride of Christ:

When Adam was asleep, a rib was taken from him and Eve was created; so also while the Lord slept on the cross, His side was transfixed by a spear and the sacraments flowed forth whence the Church was born. For the Church, the Lord's bride, was created from His side as Eve was created from the side of Adam.[29]

Along with Optatus, Augustine recognized the validity of sacraments administered by heretics, schismatics and sinners.[30] The reason is that the sacraments derive their validity from Christ and not from the human minister: "It is Christ who baptizes if Peter baptizes; it is Christ who baptizes if Paul baptizes; it is Christ who baptizes if Judas baptizes."[31] But one obtains the forgiveness of sins only in the Church, for only the Church has the Holy Spirit who is the source of forgiveness. The Holy Spirit effects the forgiveness of sins in the Church even through an unworthy minister.[32]

In summary, Augustine was convinced that the union of the individual soul with God through faith, hope and charity was of paramount importance. But the merit of Augustine, the follower of Optatus in this respect, was to see the visible, institutional and sacramental elements of the Church in their true light—not as incidental but as important too. For him, a basic manifestation of charity was adherence to the one, visible Church. True, adherence to the Church did not necessarily make one a Christian; but the Spirit was active only in the Church. Only in the Church did the Spirit awaken faith, hope and charity.

NO SALVATION OUTSIDE THE CHURCH

The belief that there is no salvation outside the Church was graphically suggested when the Fathers compared the Church to the ark of Noah. Only those were saved who were taken into the ark (Gn 6:9-8:19). Origen (d. 253), a member of the Alexandrian school, was one of the first to formulate explicitly the principle: "Outside of this house, the Church, there is no salvation." The reason, Origen said, is that the doctrine and laws of Christ as well as the efficacy of His blood shed for our sins are to be found only in the Church.[33]

Cyprian, the contemporary of Origen, expressed the same idea:

> The spouse of Christ cannot be adulterous; she is uncorrupted and pure. She knows one home; she guards with chaste modesty the sanctity of one couch. She keeps us for God. She appoints sons whom she has born for the kingdom. Whoever is separated from the Church and is joined to an

adulteress, is separated from the promises of the Church; nor can he who forsakes the Church of Christ attain to the rewards of Christ. He is a stranger; he is profane; he is an enemy. He can no longer have God for his Father, who has not the Church for his mother. If anyone could escape who was outside the ark of Noah, then he also may escape who shall be outside the Church. The Lord warns, saying 'He who is not with me is against me, and he who gathereth not with me scattereth.' He who breaks the peace and concord of Christ, does so in opposition to Christ; he who gathereth elsewhere than in the Church, scatters the Church of Christ. The Lord says, 'I and the Father are one;' and again it is written of the Father, and of the Son, and of the Holy Spirit, 'And these three are one.' And does anyone believe that this unity which comes from the divine strength and coheres in celestial sacraments, can be divided in the Church, and can be separated by the parting asunder of opposing wills? He who does not hold this unity does not hold God's law, does not hold the faith of the Father and the Son, does not hold life and salvation.[34]

For Cyprian, therefore, no one could have God as his Father who did not have the Church as his mother; and no one could be saved outside the Church just as no one could be saved outside the ark of Noah in the days of the flood. Apparently, neither Origen nor Cyprian distinguished between guilt and innocence in those outside the Church.

Augustine refined the thought of Origen and Cyprian. With them he agreed there was no salvation outside the Church.[35] He maintained there could be no just reason for separating oneself from the Church.[36] In his opinion heretics had separated themselves from the Church for unworthy motives.[37] Nevertheless, Augustine was prepared to say that those who had been born as Donatists, who were living according to their lights, were not to be regarded as heretics:

> The Apostle Paul has said, 'A man that is a heretic after the first and second admonition reject, knowing that he that is such is subverted and sins, being condemned of himself' (Tt 3:10-11). But though the doctrine which men hold be false and subverse, if they do not maintain it with passionate obstinacy, especially when they have not devised it by the rashness of their own presumption, but have accepted it from parents who have been misguided and have

fallen into error, and if they are with anxiety seeking the truth, and are prepared to be set right when they have found it, such men are not to be counted as heretics.[38]

Augustine, therefore, was prepared to make an allowance for heretics in good faith and not condemn them out of hand; yet, his view did not take hold at once. A fellow African, Fulgentius (d. 533), took an unyielding position: "Not only all pagans but also all Jews, all heretics and schismatics who finish this life outside of the Catholic Church will go into eternal fire, prepared for the devil and his angels."[39] The opinion of Fulgentius will be stated again in the following centuries.

"MONARCHICAL" BISHOPS

During the patristic period, the so-called "monarchical" bishops established themselves. The New Testament speaks of various offices and charisms in the Church: apostles, prophets, teachers, evangelists, bishops, presbyters, deacons and so forth. Some of these offices were destined to remain; some were merged with others; some disappeared entirely. The leaders of the early Christian communities were known sometimes as bishops, sometimes as presbyters or elders. It was the function of bishops and presbyters to administer the Christian community under the supreme government of the apostle who founded it. Probably, one of the bishops was elected to succeed the apostle after his death; and the title, bishop, came to be applied to him alone. He functioned as a monarchical bishop, that is, as the sole supreme religious guide in the Christian community entrusted to his care. Churches appear under a single bishop before the end of the first century; and the institution prevailed throughout the Christian world.

The martyr, Ignatius of Antioch, who died under the emperor Trajan (98-117), is one of the earliest witnesses to the position of the bishop in the Church. In his letters, Ignatius indicates that a single bishop presides over the Christian communities he addresses. The bishop presides as God's representative.[40] The bishop is, above all, the responsible teacher of the faithful and to be in communion with him is to be safeguarded against error and heresy.[41] The bishop is the high priest of the liturgy and the dispenser of the mysteries of God. Ignatius writes:

> See that ye all follow the bishop, even as Jesus Christ does the Father, and the presbytery as ye would the apostles; and reverence the deacons, as being the institution of God. Let no man do anything connected with the Church without the bishop. Let that be deemed a proper Eucharist which is administered either by the bishop, or by one to whom he has entrusted it. Wherever the bishop shall appear, there let the multitude of the people also be; even as, wherever Jesus Christ is, there is the Catholic Church. [This is the first use of the term, Catholic Church, to designate the faithful collectively.] It is not lawful without the bishop either to baptize or to celebrate a love-feast; but whatever he shall approve of, that is also pleasing to God, so that everything that is done may be secure and valid.[42]

Cyprian (d. 258) of Carthage in Africa also explained the position of the bishop. For Cyprian, union with the Church is secured by adherence to the bishop for "the bishop is in the Church and the Church in the bishop and whoever is not with the bishop is not in the Church."[43] The solidarity of the universal Church is maintained by the bishops who form a kind of senate. The bishops are the successors of the apostles and the apostles were the bishops of old.[44] The Church is built upon the bishops. Thus Cyprian interprets Mt 16:18 of the whole episcopate:

> Our Lord, whose precepts and admonitions we ought to observe, describing the honor of the bishop and the order of His Church, speaks in the Gospel, and says to Peter: 'I say unto thee, that thou art Peter, and upon this rock will I build my Church; and the gates of hell shall not prevail against it. And I will give unto thee the keys of the kingdom of heaven; and whatsoever thou shalt bind on earth shall be bound in heaven; and whatsoever thou shalt loose on earth shall be loosed in heaven.' Thence, through the changes of times and successions, the ordering of bishops and the plan of the Church flows onwards; so that the Church is founded upon the bishops, and every act of the Church is controlled by these same rulers. Since this, then, is founded on the divine law, I marvel that some, with daring temerity, have chosen to write to me as if they wrote in the name of the Church; when the Church is established in the bishop and the clergy and all who are steadfast.[45]

The idea expressed by Cyprian that the bishops are the successors of the apostles had been articulated by other Fathers too. Irenaeus' remarks about the role of bishops as the successors of the apostles in transmitting apostolic doctrine have already been cited. Clement of Rome,[46] Clement of Alexandria,[47] Tertullian,[48] and Firmilian also spoke of the bishops as the successors of the apostles. For example, Firmilian wrote:

> But what is the greatness of his error, and what the depth of his blindness, who says that the remission of sins can be granted in the synagogues of heretics, and does not abide on the foundation of the one Church which was once based by Christ upon the rock, may be perceived from this, that the power of remitting sins was given to the apostles, and to the Churches which they, sent by Christ, established, and to the bishops who succeeded them by vicarious ordination.[49]

In what sense are bishops the successors of the apostles? The Fathers regard the bishops as preeminently the pastoral and doctrinal heirs of the apostles. Yet one did not assume the responsibility on his own initiative. He had to be sent "as Christ was sent forth by God, and the apostles by Christ" (Clement of Rome). He had to be "instituted" by those who were delivering up to him their own place of government (Irenaeus). Very probably the mission and institution were conferred and symbolized by the laying on of hands. In this way, the principle of an episcopal chain was established. How the principle was implemented in every instance is a matter of uncertainty because of the meagerness of historical data.

What was the role of presbyters after the emergence of the monarchical bishop? It seems the presbyters were a kind of advisory body which assisted the bishop in the proper execution of his duties. Presbyters were superior to deacons because they were regularly mentioned in the second place of the threefold ministry of bishops, presbyters and deacons. Ordinarily, it would seem, a presbyter presided at the Eucharist in place of the absent bishop. Deacons were the assistants of the bishop and presbyters and servants of the community: "The deacons should please all in every way they can; for they are not merely ministers of food and drink, but the servants of the Church of God."[50]

THE BISHOP OF ROME

While the bishops were recognized as the successors of the apostles, the Bishop of Rome claimed to be the successor of Peter, the prince of the apostles, and the visible head of the Church. With the passage of time, this claim was presented by the Bishop of Rome and accepted by others in more explicit terms. One of the earliest instances of the exercise of papal authority was the intervention of Clement I (90?-99?) in the affairs of the Christian community at Corinth, Greece. In this instance, Clement acted in authoritative manner to settle a dispute in the community. A little later, in his Letter to the Romans, Ignatius of Antioch (who had spoken so forcefully about the role of bishops) spoke of the Roman Church and its bishop in terms that imply a unique position of honor and authority. Reference has already been made to the remarks of Irenaeus (d. c. 202) in his struggle with the Gnostics. Every Church, he wrote, must agree with the Roman Church.

Subsequently, there were other signs of Rome's preeminence. As a matter of course, the Popes claimed and received a leading position at the councils of Ephesus (431) and Chalcedon (451). When the great Christological controversies broke out, both Nestorius and Cyril hastened to present their cases to Rome. Cyril declared he felt obliged to present a matter of such weight to the Pope in accordance with an ancient custom of the Churches.[51]

Other signs of Rome's preeminence appeared in the West. Ambrose of Milan (340-397) regarded communion with Rome as a guarantee of correct belief.[52] He believed that questions of faith and order should be referred to the Pope.[53] Ambrose stated the famous dictum, "Where Peter is, there is the Church."[54] For Augustine (354-430) Peter was the apostle upon whom the primacy was bestowed.[55] The Roman Church, the seat of Peter, retained the primacy (*principatus*) of Peter.[56]

From the 3rd to the 5th centuries, the Popes themselves—men like Damasus (366-384), Siricius (384-399) and Innocent (402-417)—vigorously asserted the prerogatives of the papacy in quite explicit fashion. They appealed to Mt 16:18-19 ("Thou art Peter and upon this rock I will build my Church") as evidence that the Church was built upon Peter, the rock, who lived on in his successors, the Popes. The Popes claimed Peter's position as visible head of the Church which is the body of Christ. In this capacity they claimed a primacy of doctrinal authority and jurisdiction. The words of Philip, the papal legate to the Council of Ephesus (431), illustrate the nature of the papal claim:

> No one doubts, in fact, it is obvious to all ages that the holy and most blessed Peter, head and prince of the apostles, the pillar of the faith, and the foundation of the Catholic Church, received the keys of the kingdom from our Lord Jesus Christ, the savior and redeemer of the human race. Nor does anyone doubt that the power of forgiving and retaining sins was also given to this same Peter who, in his successors, lives and exercises judgment even to this time and forever.[57]

With Pope Leo the Great (440-461), the theology of the papacy reached a certain plateau of development. According to Leo, that which Christ established in Peter is permanent. Peter is the foundation of the Church, the bearer of the keys, the one who binds and looses. His power and authority survive *in sede sua*. The dignity of Peter is not lacking in an unworthy successor.[58] Christ charged all the apostles with preaching the gospel; but He placed the principal charge on the most blessed Peter from whom He wanted gifts to flow into the entire body as it were from the head.[59] Although there are many priests and pastors among the people of God, Peter rules them all. He is ruled by Christ. The same structure willed by Christ for the apostolic period is a permanent part of His Church.[60] Bishops and archbishops have been set up in each ecclesiastical province. Through them the care of the universal Church is to converge in the one see of Peter, and nothing is ever to be at odds with his leadership.[61]

The papal claim did not go unchallenged entirely. In the 2nd century, the Christians of Asia ignored the Popes when the Popes tried to set the date of Easter for them. Moreover, the position of Cyprian was somewhat ambiguous. Cyprian recognized only one Church, that built on Peter.[62] The Roman

Church was for Cyprian "the chief Church whence priestly unity takes its source."[63] Nonetheless, in his capacity as president of the African synod of 256, Cyprian refused to recognize the Bishop of Rome as his juridical superior. No bishop, he said, may be judged by another.[64] Furthermore, the silence of certain eastern Fathers must be mentioned. These Fathers spoke of Peter in exalted terms. John Chrysostom (345?-407), for example, described him as "the coryphaeus of the choir, the spokesman of the apostles, the head of the band, the ruler of the whole world, the foundation of the Church, the ardent lover of Christ."[65] Yet, when these Fathers spoke of Peter, frequently they made no reference to the transmission of his position and authority to the Roman Pontiff. Finally, the Fathers did not always understand the rock upon which the Church was built as the person of Peter; sometimes, they understood the rock to be the faith of Peter in the messiahship of Christ or His divinity, or else the Savior Himself, the object of Peter's faith.

What is to be said about the claim of the Bishop of Rome to be the successor of Peter and the visible head of the Church? Unquestionably this claim was stated by the Popes and accepted by others in less explicit terms at the beginning and more explicitly as time passed. Undoubtedly too historical factors contributed to this development, factors such as the connection of Peter, the prince of the apostles, with Rome, and the prestige of Rome as the ancient capital of the empire. Does the claim of the Bishop of Rome have a basis in the actions and words of Christ? The Catholic response to this question may be formulated in this way: Christ intended His Church to remain until the end of time. He placed Peter at the head of His Church and provided for successors to Peter in view of the permanence of the Church and the continuing need for a visible source of unity. The connection of Peter with Rome and the claim of the Bishop of Rome to be his successor as the visible head of the Church—a claim urged with unrivaled cogency—validates the papal claim as the realization of the will of Christ. Hence, the Church is built upon Peter, the rock, and his successors, the Popes, so that "where Peter is, there is the Church" (Ambrose).

CHURCH AND STATE

The Fathers also probed the relationship between the Church and the State. Even before Christianity became the official religion of the Roman empire in the 4th century, Polycarp (d. 156) enjoined prayers for civil authorities.[66] One of the Greek Apologists of the 2nd century, Melito of Sardis, advocated cooperation between the Church and the State; and he attributed the prosperity of the Roman empire to the appearance of Christianity.[67] Origen is the first to describe the Church as the city of God here on earth,[68] existing side by side with the secular State. The laws of Christians are "in harmony with the established constitution in all countries".[69] Eventually, though, the State will be superseded by the Church.[70]

When Christianity became the official religion of the Roman empire, the Church no longer had to contend with persecution; but it did have to suffer the interference of the emperor in its affairs. Ambrose of Milan (340-397) vigorously resisted this interference. According to Ambrose, bishops judge emperors and emperors do not judge bishops in matters of faith.[71] He noted that "the emperor is within the Church, not above it."[72] Furthermore, Ambrose insisted that the function of a Christian emperor was to defend the true religion and not to further superstition.[73] Probably Ambrose inspired some of the measures which the emperor Theodosius took against paganism.

Augustine expressed similar ideas. At first, he had opposed the use of force by the secular arm as a solution to the Donatist controversy. The danger of hypocritical conversions from Donatism to the Catholic faith was too great. He had hoped that the Donatists would come to see the light through argument and persuasion. Two things, however, caused him to change his mind. The excesses of the Donatists made the use of force necessary. Moreover, the civil laws against the Donatists actually effected conversions among them so that they rejected Donatism and accepted the Catholic faith. In many cases, the conversions were quite sincere. Augustine saw that force did not make hypocrites only. He explained the situation in this way: the physician is hateful to the madman in a frenzy because he ties the madman down. But once the madman has been restored to sanity by the restrictive measures of the physician, he is grateful.[74] Augustine's ideas about the use of force to deal with heretics were influential throughout the Middle Ages and even later.

In *The City of God* Augustine described the relationship between the city of God and the city of this world. The occasion for the composition of this work was the capture of Rome by the Goths in 410. Augustine wished to show that the city of God alone was eternal. He presented the history of mankind as an historical process which unfolds according to the plan of God. The decisive moments are the incarnation and the last judgment when the saved will be separated from the damned. The city of God is the community of the servants of God while the city of this world is the community of all the enemies of God. The earthly State is ordained by God to be a principle of peace in a sinful world. Governments with coercive powers have to exist to prevent men from robbery, rape and murder. In effect, the State is rooted in human sinfulness. The Church on earth is not yet the city of God. It includes both the good and the bad. It is the scene of the confusion of the two cities. The Church is a pilgrim on this earth and it will be fully integrated into the city of God only after the resurrection.

At the end of the 5th century, Pope Gelasius I (429-496) formulated the doctrine of the two powers which govern the world. The doctrine was expressed in a letter, *Famuli vestrae pietatis*, written by the Pope to the Byzantine emperor, Anastasius I, in 494. The occasion of the letter was the difficulties which had arisen when the Byzantine emperors interfered in doctrinal matters. A prime example was the emperor Zeno who drew up and imposed a creed called the Henoticon (484) in the midst of the Monophysite controversy. Pope Gelasius wrote:

> There are two powers which rule the world, the sacred authority of the Popes and the royal power of kings. The burden of priests is the heavier one because they must render an account for the kings of men. For you know, most clement son, that although you are supreme in human affairs you must submit to those who have charge of spiritual things and seek from them the means of your salvation.[75]

In the controversies between Pope and emperor during the
Middle Ages this statement was employed over and over again
both to assert papal superiority and to defend royal autonomy.
The interpretation of Gelasius' statement remains a matter of
dispute.

The patristic development of the Church-State theme came
to a conclusion with Isidore (ca. 560-639), archbishop of Seville,
Spain. His great contribution is to be found in the theories of
authority, the criterion for good government and the social
mission of the clergy. His views may be summed up as follows:
authority comes from God.[76] It is to be used to establish justice
among His people. The authority of the king exists for this purpose.[77] Earthly princes must give an accounting to God for the
Church which they receive from Christ to be cared for.[78] The
king determines the form of justice more by deeds than by words.
It is just for a prince to obey his own laws.[79] Isidore rebukes
those prelates who fail to defend the rights of their people
against those who oppress them. The priest must be concerned
for his flock.[80] The views of Isidore on the nature of the State and
its relationship to the Church were influential in the medieval
period.

THE END OF THE PATRISTIC ERA:

GREGORY, ISIDORE, BEDE

In some respects, Pope Gregory I (the Great) is a pivotal
figure recapitulating the ecclesiology of the patristic era and
giving direction to the future. For Gregory, the holy, Catholic
Church is Christ living among us. The Church is the garment of
Christ,[81] the moon which derives its light from the Light of the
world in order to shine in the darkness of this life, a large building whose stones are the believers.[82] The Church is the city of the
Lord,[83] the kingdom of God upon earth which reigns by reason
of its heavenly conversation.[84] The Church is one body with many
members who are distinct by reason of responsibility but joined
by charity.[85] The Church is a large city comprising, as it were,
many cities throughout the world in which the faithful live in
harmony. This harmony was foreshadowed when Jesus multiplied

the loaves for the many distinct groups of the large crowd.[86] Never can the Church cease to shine in the night of this life with the splendor of sanctity.[87]

The Church embraces all the elect from Abel to the last elect who will be born before the end of time.[88] The Church has a two-fold life, a temporal and an eternal one, the former upon earth, the latter in heaven. On earth there is labor; in heaven, reward. On earth the faithful offer the sacrifice of repentance; in heaven, the sacrifice of praise.[89] Peter was the first among the apostles while Paul, Andrew and John were members of the Church under one head.[90] When the Church speaks, the faithful listen, not to judge, but to follow.[91] The Church is holy; it shines in the night of this life with the virtues of the saints as the heaven shines with the stars.[92] The Lord allows both good and bad persons to exist side by side in the Church that evil persons may be changed by the example of the good, that good persons may be purged by the assaults of the evil.[93] The Church has a promise with which it can look forward to the future with confidence; yet, it has much to suffer from false friends, heretics and those who abuse the word of God.[94] The Church is the ark outside of which there is no salvation. It will come to rest in heaven as the ark of Noah came to rest on the mountain top.[95] Pope Gregory honored the first four ecumenical councils as he honored the four gospels.[96]

In his work, *Etymologiae*, Isidore of Seville (d. 639) offered definitions of certain words which give a clue to his understanding of the Church. Isidore understood the Greek word for Church, *ekklesia*, to mean a convocation. The Church is called a convocation because it summons all men to itself. The Church is called catholic or universal because it is dispersed throughout the world and is not confined to a particular corner of the world as the sects of heretics are.[97] The Church is called Zion—meaning "to observe," "to look at," according to Isidore—because it has its eyes upon heavenly things from the distance of this life.[98] The Church is called Jerusalem or "vision of peace" in view of the peace which it will possess and now sees from afar off.[99] By means of the Holy Eucharist the Holy Spirit transforms the faithful into members of Christ.[100] Councils are means for assuring the unity and well-being of the Church.[101] (One recalls the string of

councils held at Toledo, Spain, from 397 to 694 by which ecclesiastical life in that country was so effectively regulated.)

Bede (673-735), the English scholar, historian and theologian,
is important because he, along with Gregory the Great and
Isidore, is a link between the Fathers and the medieval theo-
logians. In the tradition of the Fathers, Bede noted a similarity
between the Church and biblical persons and objects such as
Noah's ark, the Mount of Olives, the widow assisted by
Elias, St. Peter, and the spouse and his beloved of the Song of
Songs. After the manner of Augustine, Bede thought of the
Church as the whole congregation of the elect—the faithful of the
old and new covenants, the saints and angels of heaven.[102]

Bede passionately defended the unity, universality, authority
and discipline of the "present" Church, that is, the visible
Church on earth founded by Christ.[103] Christ committed the
Church to men: "Christ constructs for Himself, teaches, governs,
and will dedicate to eternal life one Catholic Church by means
of various human persons."[104] One enters the Church through
baptism;[105] nevertheless, not all the baptized are members of
the elect:[106] there are bad Catholics.[107] Moreover, Bede recognized
the validity of baptism outside the Church.[108]

Bede was intensely conscious of the universality of the
Church. He gloried in the fact that the Church of the English
nation was one of the Churches dispersed throughout the world
which formed the Catholic Church.[109] Bede accepted the scale of
offices in the Church as easily as he accepted the scale of offices
in the State and monastery. Christ established the apostles with
the powers of teaching, judging and consecrating.[110] The first
order of bishops had been established in the apostles.[111] The
second order of priests was inaugurated when Christ appointed
seventy-two disciples.[112] The distinctive function of priests is
to be a minister of the Lord's body and blood, to offer sacrifice;[113]
but the priestly function most stressed by Bede was preaching.[114]

Peter had been the leader of the whole Church.[115] Rome was
the see of Peter.[116] The Church cannot teach falsehood. It imparts
truth through the decrees of the apostles and their successors,[117]
through the Sacred Scripture and the writings of the Fathers.[118]

Christ left the Church in body by His ascension; yet, He remains with it all days even to the consummation of the world.[119]

The patristic period came to a close in the 7th and 8th centuries. The western Fathers especially had made a major contribution to the development of ecclesiology, a contribution which the eastern Fathers could not match. For two centuries, however, theological speculation had been declining. External factors had made intellectual activity quite difficult. The decline was to continue.

NOTES TO CHAPTER II

1. *Against Heresies* 3, 3, 1-2. This and other quotations from the Fathers are taken from the series, The Ante-Nicene Fathers, published by T. & T. Clarke of Edinburgh, which is still the only English translation of the early Fathers which is more or less complete and easily accessible in libraries.
2. *On Christ and Antichrist* 59.
3. *On Virginity,* 3, 8.
4. *On Baptism* 20.
5. *On Modesty* 21.
6. Letter 1, 14.
7. *On the Mortality* 6.
8. *On the Unity of the Church* 5.
9. *On the Lapsed* 6.
10. Letter 73, 4.
11. *On the Unity of the Church* 9.
12. *On the Schism of the Donatists* 5, 4; 5, 7.
13. *Ibid.* 2, 1; 2, 9-10.
14. *Ibid.* 7, 2.
15. *Ibid.* 2, 1; 2, 11.
16. *Ibid.* 2, 2; 2, 9.
17. *On True Religion* 4, 6.
18. *Ibid.* 3, 5.
19. *Ibid.* 7, 12.
20. Sermon to the Church of Caesarea 5.
21. Letter 61.
22. *Against Cresconius* 2, 13, 16.
23. Sermon 267, 4.
24. *Against the Letters of Petilian* 3, 3, 4.
25. *On Baptism* 7, 51, 99.
26. Letter 98, 5.
27. *On the Psalms* 127, 3.
28. *Ibid.* 56, 1.
29. *Ibid.* 126, 7.

30. *On Baptism* 3, 10, 13; 5, 20. 28.
31. *Tract on John* 6, 7.
32. Sermon 71, 20, 33; 71, 23, 37. *Enchiridion* 65, 17.
33. Homily on Joshua 3, 5.
34. *On the Unity of the Church* 6.
35. *On Baptism* 4, 17, 25.
36. *Against the Letters of Petilian* 2, 11, 25.
37. Sermon 4, 30, 33.
38. Letter 43, 1.
39. *On Faith, to Peter* 38.
40. Letter to the Magnesians 6.
41. Letter to the Trallians 6-7.
42. Letter to the Smyrneans 8.
43. Letter 66, 8.
44. Letter 3, 3.
45. Letter 33, 1.
46. First Letter 42, 44.
47. *Who is the Rich Man that shall be saved?* 42.
48. *On Prescription Against Heretics* 32.
49. Letter to Cyprian.
50. Ignatius of Antioch, Letter to the Trallians 2.
51. Letter 11, 1; 11, 7.
52. Letter 42, 5; 11, 4. *De excess. Sat.* 1, 47.
53. Letter 56, 7. Letter 13, 7.
54. *Enarr. in ps.* 40, 30.
55. *On Baptism* 2, 1, 2.
56. Letter 43, 7.
57. *CT* no. 146.
58. Sermon 3, 2-4. *PL* 54, 145-147.
59. Letter 10, 1.
60. Sermon 4, 2-3. *PL* 54, 149-151.
61. Letter 14.
62. *On the Unity of the Church* 4-5.
63. Letter 59, 14.
64. *CSEL* 3, 1, 436.
65. *Hom. in illud "Hoc scitote".*
66. Letter to the Philippians 12.
67. Cf. Eusebius, *Ecclesiastical History* 4, 26.
68. *In Jer. hom.* 9, 2; *In Jos. hom.* 8, 7.
69. *Against Celsus* 4, 22.
70. *Ibid.* 8, 72.
71. Letter 21, 4.
72. Sermon against Auxentius 37.
73. Letter 17.
74. Letters 185 and 93.

75. DS 347.
76. *Lib. Sent.* 3, 48, 10. *PL* 83.
77. *Ibid.* 2, 49, 3.
78. *Ibid.* 3, 51, 6.
79. *Ibid.* 3, 49, 2; 3, 51, 1.
80. *Ibid.* 3, 45 and 57.
81. *Mor.* 20, no. 58.
82. *In Ezech.* 2, 1, no. 10.
83. *Mor.* 25, no. 21.
84. *Ibid.* 33, no. 34.
85. *Ibid.* 19, nos. 43-44.
86. *Ibid.* 16, no. 68.
87. *Ibid.* 32, no. 25.
88. *In evang.* 1, 19, no. 1.
89. *In Ezech.* 2, 1, no. 5.
90. Letter 5, 18.
91. *Mor.* 20, no. 2.
92. *Ibid.* 32, no. 25.
93. *Ibid.* 31, no. 28.
94. *Ibid.* 23, nos. 3-7.
95. Letter 11, 46.
96. Letter 1, 25.
97. *Etymol.* 8, no. 1. *PL* 82.
98. *Ibid.* no. 5.
99. *Ibid.* no. 6.
100. *Ibid.* 6, nos. 38, 41-42.
101. *Ibid.* 6, nos. 2-3.
102. *In Cant.* 2. *In E & N* 2. *PL* 91.
103. *De Mul. F. PL* 91, 1041.
104. *In Luc.* 2. *PL* 92, 412.
105. *In Luc.* 3. *PL* 92, 469.
106. *Hom.* 1, 11. *PL* 94, 62.
107. *In Apoc.* 2. *PL* 93, 162.
108. *Hex.* 2. *PL* 91, 101.
109. *In Marc.* 2. *PL* 92, 193.
110. *Expo. Act.* 4:33; *Hom.* 2, 9. *PL* 94.
111. *De Tabern.* 3. *PL* 91, 477.
112. *Ibid.*
113. *Retr. Act.* 6:6.
114. *Hom.* 1, 5. *PL* 94, 37.
115. *Hom.* 2, 23. *PL* 94, 259.
116. *HE* 5, 7.
117. *De Temp. PL* 91, 780.
118. *In E & N.* 3. *PL* 91, 919.
119. *In Marc.* 4. *PL* 92, 266.

III. THE CAROLINGIAN ERA AND THE GREGORIAN REFORM

By the end of the 5th century the whole of western Europe was ruled by barbarian kings. In 496, the king of the Franks, Clovis, was baptized by the Catholic bishop, Remy. His baptism marked the initial step in the conversion of the Franks. In the following century the Suevi and the Visigoths in the Spanish peninsula were won over from Arianism to Catholicism. In 596, Pope Gregory the Great sent a mission to convert the English. Boniface, an English monk who was martyred in 754, became the apostle of Germany. Christianity found its way into Denmark, Sweden and Norway. In 966, a Christian queen persuaded her husband, a Polish duke, to embrace Christianity; and a number of his subjects were baptized with him. A generation later, the whole country was Christian. During the same century, the Hungarians accepted Christianity and their king, Stephan (997-1038), did much to solidify the religion among them. During the same period, the Russians were converted by missionaries from the East. Other tribes too were baptized. Bishops and monks became the spiritual and moral educators of their people. In a real sense, they were the fathers of European civilization.

One hundred years after the death of Muhammad (632), the Moslems had conquered Arabia, Syria, Palestine, northern Africa, Spain and southern France. Their advance into northern and western Europe was halted by Charles Martel at the battle of Poitiers in 732; but for centuries thereafter they continued to be a serious threat to Europe.

Charles Martel was a member of the Frankish dynasty which had ruled France for several generations and was destined to rule France, Germany and Italy until the 10th century. This dynasty gave its name to the period, namely, the Carolingian. Charles Martel was succeeded as the real ruler of France by his son, Pepin. Pepin, in turn, was succeeded by his son, Charles or Charlemagne. In 800, Charles took the title of emperor. This restoration of the western empire, marked by the solemn coronation of Charlemagne by Pope Leo III in St. Peter's, reinforced the alliance established fifty years earlier between Pepin and the papacy; and it widened the breach between the West and the Byzantine East. Now the Frankish monarch was invested with a quasi-sacerdotal character which made it all the easier for him to encroach upon ecclesiastical affairs as Charlemagne actually did. Indeed he called himself *caput ecclesiae*, "the head of the Church."

Upon the conversion of the princes and kingdoms of Europe there followed a real symbiosis between the temporal and the spiritual. State Churches were created and participation in Church councils was delimited by the boundaries of the State. Typical of the situation was the string of councils held at Toledo in the kingdom of the West Goths in Spain. Bishops acted in the capacity of counsellors to the king. They achieved this position equally because of their position in the Church and because of the immense landed possessions which had come into their hands. Prelates gradually became civil princes. The greater the political importance of the higher ecclesiastical posts became, the more secular princes strove to win control over them. Princes gained the right to nominate candidates for the bishopric. They exercised this right sometimes to the advantage, ultimately to the disadvantage, of the Church. Nomination was signified by investing the candidate with the bishop's ring and staff.

Under the weak successors of Charlemagne, his empire disintegrated. Political chaos and chronic civil war ensued. The Moslems renewed their attacks on France and Italy. Savage tribes from Scandinavia attacked northern Europe, England and

Ireland. Learning disappeared. The papacy became the pawn of noble Roman families. The bishops proved unworthy. These were truly the Dark Ages.

In the 9th century came the first open break between the eastern and western Churches. For a long time there had been an estrangement between the two halves of the Church. The estrangement was aggravated when Charlemagne established a western Roman empire with the see of the Pope within its boundaries. The appointment of Photius as Patriarch of Constantinople (858) was the occasion of the first open break. The appointment of Photius was accompanied by certain irregularities which brought him into conflict with Rome. Nicholas I excommunicated him (863). Later Pope Adrian II excommunicated him again (869). During his conflict with Rome, Photius helped to lay the foundation of the schism between the eastern and western Churches by emphasizing the differences between the two of them. Ultimately, Photius was deposed by the emperor Leo VI (886); and comparatively friendly relations were reestablished by the Popes and Patriarchs. Under the Patriarch, Michael Cerularius, however, matters changed. He assailed various practices of the Latins; and, in turn, the Latins assailed the Greeks on various points. Legates of the Pope excommunicated the Patriarch in 1054; and the Patriarch for his part convened a council which anathematized the legates. Other eastern Churches soon followed Constantinople into schism. As a result of the break, the fate of the Catholic Church was tied up with the West.

Meanwhile, a movement for reform was gaining strength in the West. The Benedictine monastery at Cluny in France was founded in 910. The monks committed themselves to the strict observance of the rule and made the liturgy the center of monastic life. Eventually Cluny affiliated hundreds of monasteries with itself and infused its spirit into them. The reform movement continued under Pope Leo IX (1049-1054) who traveled throughout France and Italy holding councils and deposing unworthy bishops and clerics. Leo's efforts were seconded by Cardinal Humbert, the counsellor of the Pope and one of the papal legates who had excommunicated Michael Cerularius. In his treatise, *Adversus Simoniacos* (ca. 1057-58), he pointed out the necessity of changing the system under which the Church worked. He believed that the nomination of bishops by secular princes was highly improper. The reform continued under Nicholas II (1058-61) under whom the Lateran Council of 1059 made the law for the election of Popes. According to this law, the right of election belongs to the cardinals (and not, for example, to the emperor or to a faction of the nobility).

The reform reached its high point under Gregory VII (1073-1085). Gregory struggled relentlessly against the evil of simony and he forbade lay investiture, that is, the appointment of persons to ecclesiastical offices by laymen. When the emperor, Henry IV, violated this prohibition, Gregory excommunicated him and absolved his subjects from the oath of allegiance to him. In his fight to free the Church from the interference of the secular power, Gregory and his supporters elaborated an ecclesiology that was based upon divine law, canon law and feudal law.

Gregory did not live to see the end of the struggle for the freedom of the Church. Forty years after his death, however, a wise compromise was effected by the Concordat of Worms (1122). The compromise recognized the distinction between the exercise of religious ministry and the administration of temporal possessions and prerogatives. The emperor promised Pope Calixtus II (1119-24) to desist in the future from all investiture of bishops and abbots with the ring and staff and granted canonical freedom of election. In return, the Pope granted the emperor the right to confer temporal endowments symbolized by the sceptre. The emperor also had the right to demand the oath of loyalty. Hence, the Church gained a victory with the most serious consequences. On the one hand, the Church regained its position as an independent and spiritual community; on the other, the State set out on the road to secularization.

THE GROWTH OF THE PAPAL IDEA

The Carolingian theologians of the 8th and 9th centuries saw a dynamic relationship between the body of Christ born of the Virgin Mary, the sacramental body of Christ in the Holy Eucharist, and the body of Christ which is the Church.[1] The mystery of

Christ is accomplished in the Church through the Holy Eucharist. The Holy Eucharist transforms the faithful into living members of Christ's body, the Church. The Church is a visible communion of faith and sacraments and an invisible communion of life in Christ through the Holy Eucharist. The Eucharistic sacrifice is offered by the whole Church: that which is accomplished *proprie* by the ministry of priests is effected *generaliter* by the faith and devotion of the faithful.[2] Christ, of course, is the principal minister.[3]

The period under consideration is particularly notable, however, for the growth of the papal idea. Since the 3rd century, the Popes had vigorously asserted the prerogatives of the papacy in quite explicit terms. They had appealed to Mt 16:18-19 ("Your name is Peter, a rock, and on this rock I will build my Church") as evidence that the Church was built upon Peter who lived on in his successors, the Popes. As the successors of Peter, the Popes claimed universal jurisdiction over the Church. The Carolingian era and the era of the Gregorian reform marked the practical implementation of this idea in the life of the Church. No one in the West really opposed the claims of the papacy, but there was considerable discussion about the nature and extent of papal authority and the manner of its application. Questions about this matter were raised especially in the Gallic and Germanic countries. What was the relationship between papal authority and episcopal authority? Did the Pope have the power to depose kings in Christendom? The papal claims were not heeded widely on a practical level until the accession of Pope Leo IX (1049-54) to the reformed papacy.

The western Church of the 8th and 9th centuries was vividly conscious of the kingship of Christ. Christ is both priest and king after the manner of the biblical figure, Melchizedek (Gn 14:18). He is the absolute master of creation. The Church is inseparable from Christ: it is His body, His spouse, the new Eve, the mother of the faithful. The Church is ruled by bishops and princes[4] who share the priestly and royal dignity of Christ respectively. The prince has an important role *in* the Church: he pursues not only the temporal and earthly interest of his people, but also their eternal salvation, even by the use of the sword if necessary.

This conception of things is illustrated by the views of Alcuin (735-804), the teacher and friend of Charlemagne for almost a quarter of a century. Adopting the terminology of Gelasius, Alcuin spoke of two powers, the spiritual and the secular. The spiritual was the higher power because it was concerned with the souls of all men including the representatives of the secular power. "The duty of priests is to preach the word of God. It is the duty of princes to obey them humbly and fulfill the word of God diligently... Let princes be the defenders of the Church."[5] Hence, Alcuin praised Charlemagne because he did his duty: he subdued and converted pagan nations, he was diligent in spreading the word of God, he was watchful lest erroneous doctrines mar the purity of the faith.[6]

Alcuin recognized the Pope as the supreme shepherd of the flock of Christ in his capacity as the successor of Peter.[7] Yet, Alcuin restricted the role of the Pope considerably. In a letter to Pope Leo, undoubtedly written by Alcuin, Charlemagne stated that is was the task of the emperor to defend the Church and strengthen it while it was the task of the Pope, like a new Moses, to pray for the arms of Charlemagne that the Christian people might be victorious over their enemies.[8] Charlemagne and Alcuin regarded the emperor as the ruler of Christendom to which the Pope and the clergy gave spiritual care and nourishment.

While the Popes such as Nicholas I (858-867) and John VIII (872-882) continued to interpret Mt 16:19 as a reference to papal primacy, others, following Cyprian, Bede and Isidore, thought that the power of the keys had been given to Peter for all the apostles and their successors, the bishops and priests.[9] There was some tension between papal and episcopal authority. For example, Hincmar (806-882), archbishop of Reims, acknowledged papal primacy in forthright terms;[10] but at the same time he asserted the right of bishops to regulate actively the life of the local Churches without papal intervention. In 876, he and nearly all the Frankish bishops refused to accept an archbishop appointed by the Pope. He explained it was the ancient custom of the Church, sanctioned by many Popes and councils, to reserve the election of an archbishop to the bishops of a province.[11]

The mid-9th century marked the appearance of the Pseudo-

Isidorian decretals,[12] so-called to describe their alleged author and bogus origins. In general, a decretal is a papal letter giving an authoritative decision on a point of canon law. The first authentic decretals date from the late 4th century. Innocent I (401-417) issued decretals dealing with such matters as clerical continence, the sacraments, conjugal fidelity and the canon of Scripture. The Popes repeatedly demanded obedience to their decretal letters. Their attitude is summarized by the 19th distinction of Gratian's Decretum.[13] The individual decretals were a means by which the Popes influenced the doctrinal, moral and administrative policies of the Church.

At an early date, collections of papal decretals were made. Dionysius Exiguus made a collection of them in the early 6th century. Another collection was the Dionysio-Hadriana made in the Carolingian empire. The Pseudo-Isidorian collection of the 9th century contained both genuine and false decretals, although they were generally held to be genuine throughout the Middle Ages. The Pseudo-Isidorian decretals were drawn up to curtail the power of the metropolitans and to enhance papal authority and clerical privileges. These decretals reserved the more important decisions affecting ecclesiastical life to the See of Rome; and in this way they furthered the cause of the Roman primacy. Many of the decretals found their way eventually into Gratian's Decretum (ca. 1140-41). Gratian's collection, which contained both genuine and false decretals, became the standard text in the schools of law as well as an essential tool of the courts.

During this period the Popes bound the metropolitans (archbishops) to themselves by the conferral of the pallium. The pallium is a white woolen band with pendants in front and back worn over the chasuble by the Pope and archbishops. The origin of the pallium is uncertain; but the bishops of the eastern Church and the Pope began to wear it in the 4th century as a symbol of their episcopal authority. From the 6th to the 9th century, the Popes conferred the pallium upon their episcopal vicars and metropolitans in distant lands such as Gaul, Spain and Great Britain. The conferral of the pallium served to enhance the prestige of the papal representative among his episcopal brethren and to bind him more closely to the Pope.

The Council of Soissons (744) under the presidency of Boniface obliged all metropolitans to request the pallium from the Pope in order to signify their union with, and submission to, the vicar of Christ. Not all the metropolitans heeded the injunction because they feared some restrictions upon their independence. Charlemagne, however, encouraged the metropolitans of his realm to request the pallium from the Pope. Eventually, Rome made the bestowal of the pallium a *sine qua non* for the exercise of jurisdiction by the metropolitan. Nicholas I (858-867) and John VIII (872-882) enjoined metropolitans from any official act until the reception of the pallium. This prohibition was ultimately incorporated into the Code of Canon Law.[14]

The so-called Gregorian Reform began under Pope Leo IX (1049-54). Two churchmen who pushed the reform were Peter Damian and Cardinal Humbert. Peter Damian (1007-72) was cardinal-bishop of Ostia and the friend of Hildebrand, the future Gregory VII. He wrote the *Liber Gomorrhianus* (1049) against the vices of the clergy and the *Liber Gratissimus* (1052) against simony, the buying and selling of ecclesiastical office. In this matter he accepted the teaching of Augustine, recognizing the validity of simonical ordinations as long as the faith of the Church was preserved. Elsewhere Peter articulated several ideas vigorously defended by Pope Gregory and his supporters. The Roman Church is the mother of other Churches at whose breast her children have sucked the milk of apostolic faith.[15] The Pope alone is the universal bishop of all the Churches.[16] The Roman Church is an effective instrument of reform in virtue of its petrine authority and apostolic truth.[17] Peter Damian called for cooperation and mutual support from the Church and the temporal authority. The king was to use his authority to further the objectives of the Church.[18]

Cardinal Humbert's book, *Adversus Simoniacos* (*Against Simoniacs*), appeared a few years later (ca. 1057-58). In the book he spoke about the widespread evil of simony and the Churches plundered by simoniacal shepherds. He declared the consecration of a bishop who had bought his office to be invalid; and he denied the validity of ordinations conferred by him. Humbert condemned the interference of the secular power in episcopal elections. According to the rules of canonical discipline, he said, bishops are to be elected by the clergy and the people with the approbation of the metropolitan and the consent of the prince. But the situation had changed radically:

> The first are last and the last are first. It is the secular power which is the first to elect and confirm: afterwards come, willingly or unwillingly, the consent of the clergy and the people and finally the judgment of the metropolitan. Those who are promoted in this way are not to be regarded as bishops. . . By what right do laymen confer ecclesiastical sacraments and the grace of the episcopacy? By what right do they invest with the staff and the ring which are bound up with the consecration of a bishop?[19]

More than any other, the Roman Church had suffered from the lay interference denounced by Cardinal Humbert. The German king and the Roman aristocracy had very frequently taken the election of the Pope entirely out of the hands of those who should have had a powerful voice in the matter. The law promulgated by the Lateran Council (1059) under Nicholas II placed the election of the Pope solely in the hands of the cardinals, a decision of great consequence. The ideas expressed by Cardinal Humbert in his *Adversus Simoniacos* were largely responsible for the passage of the law.

The struggle for the freedom of the Church was continued by Gregory VII (1073-85) with an appeal to the direct foundation of papal authority by Christ. The *Dictatus Papae*,[20] a document emanating from the circle of Gregory and his supporters, did not hesitate to draw practical conclusions from the primacy of the Pope. According to the *Dictatus Papae*, the Roman Church was founded by the Lord. The Pope is the master of the Church. He can legislate for the whole Church and reserve the most important decisions to himself. The Roman Church has never erred and it will never err. The Pope can depose bishops or transfer them; and his legate has the right to preside over councils of bishops. The Pope cannot be judged by anyone. The Pope has the authority to depose kings and to free their subjects from the oath of allegiance to them.

Gregory claimed no temporal authority over this world; but he emphasized the subjection of temporal authority to his supreme priestly authority. This claim was supported by an appeal to biblical passages such as Jr 1:10: "This day I set you over nations and over kingdoms" and 1 Cor 2:15: "The spiritual man judges all things." The principle of papal primacy has been affirmed many times before; but Gregory was the first to draw from the principle such practical conclusions.

THE GREEK SCHISM

Prior to the Photian schism of the ninth century, the Greek conception of the Church had been derived from the Greek Fathers. According to them, the Church is a spiritual society established by God. It is the body of Christ, that is, the body of those who have been divinized by the humanity of Christ who took unto Himself that which He wished to save.[21] Baptism and the Holy Eucharist effect our incorporation in Christ. In baptism one receives the faith of the Church while the Holy Eucharist unites those who have been regenerated in baptism. The earthly Church is a reflection of the heavenly Church; indeed, it is one with the heavenly Church in praising the Father. The Church is indefectible because of Christ's promise to Peter (Mt 16:18). It is infallible for Paul described it as "the pillar and mainstay of the truth" (1 Tm 3:15). The Church is one, holy, catholic and apostolic. It is the fold in which the sheep of Christ are safe from the wolves. It is the bride of Christ and the mother of the faithful. It is the gate to eternal life.

The Byzantine emperor was considered to be the representative of God on earth and a sacred person. He presided over a baptized people and was responsible for the Church which was, as it were, the spiritual side of the empire. The unity of the empire was inextricably bound up with the unity of the Church. Hence, the coronation of Charlemagne as emperor by Pope Leo III was viewed by the Greeks as a blow to the unity of the Church. It was the practice of the Byzantine emperor to name patriarchs and bishops, to summon councils, to legislate for the Church and to implement its canons. Instances of his intervention in dogmatic disputes have already been mentioned. On these latter occasions imperial intervention was often met by resistance on the part of the Popes and Greek ecclesiastics. As a matter of fact, there were two currents within the Byzantine Church—one defending the Church's independence of the state, the other accepting the dependence of the Church upon the State.

In dogmatic conflicts with the emperor, Greek ecclesiastics frequently looked to the Pope for support. They spoke of Rome as the apostolic see, the foundation of orthodox doctrine (Sophronius of Jerusalem) with the power to bind and loose derived from the incarnate Word (Maximus the Confessor). The Pope, they said, proclaimed the faith of Peter. Rome was a norm of faith, the center of unity (Theodore the Studite). It owed its superior dignity to the apostles Peter and Paul (Nicephorus of Constantinople). The precise significance of these phrases, however, is not always clear.

The idea—possibly stemming from the emperor Justinian (527-565)—that the Church was ruled by a pentarchy was widespread in the East. Theodore the Studite (759-826) explained the idea in one of his letters:

> I am not speaking of worldly affairs. These are the concern of the emperor and the secular tribunal. I am concerned with divine and heavenly matters. These are the province of those to whom God the Word said: 'Whatsoever you bind on earth will be bound in heaven and whatsoever you loose on earth will be loosed in heaven.' Who are they to whom this command was given? They are the apostles and their successors. Who are their successors? First, the bishop of Rome; second, the bishop of Constantinople; and, after them, the bishops of Alexandria, Antioch and Jerusalem. This is the pentarchy of the Church. These bishops define the dogmas of the Church. The emperor and the secular power have the duty to help them and to approve what they decide.[22]

The synod in Trullo at Constantinople (692), which is sometimes called the "Quinisext" synod because its canons were passed as a complement to the fifth (553) and sixth (680-681) general councils, canonized certain Byzantine practices, a number of which were in opposition to Roman practices. The council repudiated clerical celibacy; it reaffirmed the position of Constantinople as the second see in Christendom despite the previous opposition of Pope Leo I; it prescribed excommunication for fasting on Saturdays of Lent and forbade the use of blood and suffocated animals. The synod renewed the condemnation of Pope Honorius I who had been condemned earlier by the sixth general council as a defender of monothelitism. The synod *in Trullo* is characterized by an intolerance of differing customs, especially those of the western Church. The synod had the effect of encouraging the growing antagonism between East and West. It is recognized as an ecumenical council in the East but not in the West.

In 863, Nicholas I, the bishop of Rome, excommunicated Photius, the bishop of Constantinople, because of irregularities in the election of the latter to his see. In the course of the controversy Nicholas issued his famous letter (865) reminding the Greeks of the primatial rights of the Roman Church. Christ Himself, Nicholas wrote, had granted supreme authority to the Roman Church in the person of the apostle Peter. The Roman Church was responsible for all the other Churches. No one might judge the see of Rome and no one might appeal from its judgement to another tribunal.[23]

Subsequently, Photius sent a letter to the bishops of the East in which he bitterly denounced the Latins. He made these charges: the Latins sent missionaries to Bulgaria which was Greek missionary territory; they observed Saturday as a fast day; they looked down upon married priests; they reconfirmed those who had been confirmed by a priest; and they said the Holy Spirit proceeded from the Father *and* the Son. Photius summoned the bishops to a council to condemn these errors and all who fostered them.[24] The Photian council met in 867 and condemned Nicholas; but the significance of the condemnation is uncertain. Was the condemnation directed against the papacy as such or merely against the person of Nicholas who had acted wrongly in the council's judgement?

The eighth ecumenical council, assembled at Constantinople (869-870), sustained the condemnation of Photius by Nicholas in vigorous terms. The council also reaffirmed the rights of the Pope and other patriarchs:

No secular authority may dishonor or attempt to remove a

patriarch; rather, patriarchs must be held in honor and reverence, especially the Pope of the elder Rome, then the
patriarch of Constantinople, then the patriarchs of Alexandria, Antioch and Jerusalem. No one is to direct libelous
writings against the Pope of the elder Rome, as Photius did
recently and Dioscorus did earlier... If a secular authority
should attempt to remove the Pope who occupies the
apostolic chair or another patriarch, let him be anathema.
Furthermore, if a general council is concerned with some
matter involving the Roman Church, the matter is to be
treated with becoming reverence, and no judgment is to be
given in defiance of the supreme pontiffs of the elder
Rome.[25]

After the conclusion of this council, Rome and Constantinople lived in union for two centuries, although contact between
the two sees diminished.

In the 11th century, Michael Cerularius, the patriarch of
Constantinople, reopened old wounds. He caused a letter to be
sent in 1053 to a Latin bishop in which he attacked the Latins for
using unleavened bread to celebrate the Eucharist, for fasting
on Saturdays, for eating meat from which the blood had not
been drained properly, and for suppressing the *Alleluia* in
Lent.[26] Cerularius' letter came into the hands of the Pope, Leo
IX. Cardinal Humbert replied to the letter in the name of the
Pope. Humbert defended the use of unleavened bread by pointing to Jesus' use of it at the Last Supper; among other things,
he bitterly recalled all the eastern heresies in which, he said, Constantinople had played a role; and he restated the Roman claim to
the primacy of Peter.[27]

After a complicated series of events, Cardinal Humbert and
two other papal legates excommunicated Michael while they were
on a papal mission to Constantinople. In a dramatic gesture, the
legates laid the bull of excommunication upon the altar of St.
Sophia on July 16, 1054. The bull reaffirms the primacy of the
Roman Church. The legates say they have no quarrel with the
emperor, the clergy and the people. Their quarrel is with
Michael and his supporters who have gone the way of ancient
heretics: the Simonists, the Arians, the Donatists, the Manicheans

and others. Moreover, Michael has refused to repent; he has not received the papal legates; he has closed Latin churches; he has anathematized the Holy See by persecuting its sons; and he is guilty of other crimes. In accordance with their instructions from the Pope, the legates excommunicated Michael because he is intransigent.[28]

Michael's reply was to convoke a synod which in turn excommunicated the legates. The excommunication was directed against the legates as individuals and not as representatives of the Pope. The legates, the synod said, had not been sent by the Pope; rather, they had come to Constantinople in their own name with the connivance of a certain Argyros, the enemy of Michael.[29]

For the benefit of the eastern patriarchs Michael also composed a letter—a kind of manifesto—in which he explained his side of the affair in greater detail. He noted that a rupture between East and West had existed since the 6th century and the days of Pope Vigilius. He renewed the old charges: the Latins use unleavened bread and fast on the Sabbath; they add the *Filioque* to the creed; they forbid priests to marry; they baptize with immersion only; they do not "adore" relics; and these things are not all. He did not see how those who admitted such "illicit, forbidden and shameful" things could be recognized as orthodox. He would have no part with them. The true religion of Jesus Christ was preserved by the Greeks.[30]

The breach created in 1054 has persisted. It was healed for brief moments—at the Second Council of Lyons (1274) and at the Council of Florence (1439)—under the stress of political necessity; but the union did not endure. Different traditions, national pride, mutual distrust, scandals in the West, and Greek scorn for Latin ignorance and barbarity prevented the reunion of Rome and Constantinople from being permanent. In recent years there has been a rapprochement. On December 7, 1965, Pope Paul VI and Athenagoras I, Patriarch of Constantinople, issued a joint statement in which they expressed publicly their regret for the events of 1054 and their wish to remove the sentences of excommunication *de la mémoire et du milieu de l'Église.*[31]

Curiously enough, the medieval debate between Rome and Constantinople never explicitly raised the question about the nature of the Church and the primacy of Rome. Later, however, after the sack of Constantinople by the Crusaders in 1204 and the installation of a Latin patriarch in the city, Eastern Orthodox[32] theologians such as Nilus Cabasilas (14th century) began to dispute the claim of the bishop of Rome to be the successor of Peter in an exclusive sense.[33] These theologians looked upon all bishops—not just the bishop of Rome—as the successor of Peter. All the bishops are the successors of Peter in his capacity as the foundation of the Church because they, like Peter, are teachers of the faith *ex officio*. If the bishop of Rome enjoyed a primacy of honor among other bishops, the reason was his position as the bishop of the ancient capital of the Roman empire.

For the Orthodox, the bishop is the leader of his Church. He presides over the Eucharistic assembly. He is the official teacher of his flock. (There is some disagreement among the Orthodox whether the bishop holds his commission directly from Christ or indirectly through the people.) When the bishops meet together (in an ecumenical council, for example) and manifest a consensus, they give infallible expression to the truth of Christ. The fullness of the truth of Christ from which other Churches have fallen away is preserved in the Orthodox Church. The unity of the local Orthodox Churches in the profession of the true faith, maintained by the abiding presence of the Spirit (Jn 16:13), assures the visible and indefectible unity of the Church of Christ. The Orthodox are true to their position, therefore, when they summon other Christians who have left the unity of the Church to return to the faith of the Fathers and Apostles.

NOTES TO CHAPTER III

1. Pasch. Radbertus, *De corp. et sang. Dom.* 7, 1. *PL* 120, 1284.
2. Florus of Lyons, *De actione missarum* 52. *PL* 119, 47- D-48 A.
3. *Ibid.* 43. *PL* 119, 44. Hincmar of Reims, *De cavendis vitiis* 10. *PL* 125, 924 D.
4. Synod of Paris (829), cc. 2-3. *MGH Concilia* 2, 610; *Capitularia* 2, 29.
5. Letter 11. *PL* 100, 159.
6. Letter 17. *PL* 100, 169.
7. Letter 18. *PL* 100, 170. Letter 24. *PL* 100, 178.
8. *MGH Epistolae* 4, 137.

9. Haymo, *Homil. de tempore* 81. *PL* 118, 493 D.

10. *Libellus expost.* (871), 26. *PL* 126, 609 A.

11. *De jure metropolitanorum. PL* 130.

12. *PL* 130.

13. *PL* 187, 103-112.

14. C. 276. *DACL* 13, 1, 931-940; *NCE* 10, 929-930.

15. *Opusc. 5um. PL* 145, 92 C.

16. *Opusc. 23um. PL* 145, 474 C.

17. *Opusc. 5um. PL* 145, 89-90.

18. Letter 6 (*lib.* 3). *PL* 144, 294 C. Letters 2-3 (*lib.* 7). *PL* 144, 437-442.

19. *Adversus Simoniacos* 3, 6. *PL* 143, 1148-49.

20. *PL* 148, 407-408.

21. Anastasius of Antioch, *De nostris rectis dogmat. verit., Oratio 3a. PG* 89, 1340.

22. *PG* 99, 1417.

23. DS 638-642.

24. *PG* 102, 722-742.

25. C. 21 DS 661-664.

26. *PG* 120, 835-844.

27. *PL* 143, 744-769.

28. *PL* 143, 1002-1003; *PG* 120, 741-744.

29. *PG* 120, 736-748.

30. *PG* 120, 781-796.

31. *AAS* 58 (1966) 20-21.

32. The term, Eastern Orthodox, is employed in modern times to designate eastern Churches of the Byzantine rite that do not recognize the primacy of the Pope, Churches which form a loose federation according a primacy of honor to the Patriarch of Constantinople and adhering to the decisions of the first seven ecumenical councils.

33. *PG* 149, 704.

IV. THE GOLDEN AGE OF SCHOLASTICISM

THE AGE

The 12th and 13th centuries were a period of powerful activity. This is the period of the Crusades, the first one in 1099 and the last one in 1270. The main object of the Crusades, of course, was the liberation of the Christian holy places in Palestine from the hands of the Muslims. Organized by the Popes and directed by their legates, the Crusades created a popular support and enthusiasm for the papacy hitherto unknown. The Crusades failed to achieve their main objective; but they widened the intellectual horizon of Europe by bringing it into closer contact with Grecian and Arabic civilization. The Crusades contributed significantly to the development of commerce, art, literature and architecture.

This was an age of freedom and enterprise. There was an increasing recognition of the worth of the individual; yet a communal spirit was quite evident. The citizens of a medieval town took a common oath to maintain peace among themselves and defend the rights of each member against attack. The townsmen formed themselves into associations, confraternities and guilds. The result was political, social and industrial advancement. The communal spirit also manifested itself in the formation of new religious communities. These new religious communities included the Premonstratensians (founded by St. Norbert in 1120), the Cistercians (founded by St. Stephen Harding in 1134), the Dominicans (founded by St. Dominic in 1215) and the Franciscans (founded by St. Francis about the same time). The Dominicans and Franciscans (unlike monks and hermits) were free to

travel wherever their mission required. They served the Church
as preachers, teachers, missionaries, writers and reformers.

The age is characterized by devotion to the humanity of
Christ. This devotion was manifested by new signs of reverence
for the body and blood of Christ in the Holy Eucharist—communication under the species of bread alone for fear of profaning
the species of wine, the elevation of the Host after the consecration of the Mass, kneeling during Mass, and the institution of the
feast of Corpus Christi (1264). There was a new devotion to the
passion of Christ and His five wounds. The crucifix made its appearance and the way of the cross. Mary, the holy mother of
God, was honored in a new way. The Hail Mary, the *Salve
Regina*, the rosary and the feast of the Immaculate Conception
were introduced. Pilgrimages and fasting were popular; and each
locality and occupation had its patron saint. Gothic art and
architecture, paintings and statues attempted to present the
supernatural to the senses. Hospitals, orphanages, homes for the
aged and penitents were built; and associations, lay and religious,
were established to support and serve them.

Among the most important sects of the 12th and 13th centuries were the Albigenses (or Cathari) and Waldenses. The
Albigenses sustained the errors of the ancient Manichaeans who
acknowledged two absolute principles, the one good and the
other bad. In particular, the Albigenses regarded the God of
Catholics as an evil power and the Church itself as an evil
creation; hence, they rejected the bishops of the Church and its
sacraments; they believed in the migration of souls; they regarded
civil government as unlawful; and they abstained from marriage
and meat. The Albigenses administered the *Consolamentum,* a
sacrament given by the imposition of hands. The possibility of
receiving this sacrament, which was necessary for salvation,
induced many Albigenses to give full vent to their passions.

The Waldenses, founded by Waldes, a native of Lyons, dedicated themselves to poverty, chastity and obedience. One branch,
the French, remained, externally at least, within the Church.
The Italian branch, believing the validity of the sacraments depended upon the holiness of the minister, rejected the sacraments
of the Church and conducted their own services. In the 16th

century the Waldenses became part of the Protestant movement.

In 1208 a crusade was declared against the Albigenses. In 1215 the Fourth Lateran Council decreed the confiscation of goods and banishment of all heretics; in 1231 Pope Gregory IX established the Inquisition to deal with them, Innocent IV sanctioning the use of torture as a means of extracting the truth (1252).

The doctrinal reaction of the Church to the Albigenses and Waldenses was expected by the Fourth Lateran Council. Against the Albigenses the council defined that "the universal Church of the faithful is one; outside it no one at all is saved."[3] The same council condemned those (the Waldenses) who undertook to preach without a canonical appointment from the Holy See or the local Catholic bishop.[2] The most important theological work of the period written expressly against the Albigenses and Waldenses was the *Adversus catharos et valdenses libri quinque* of Moneta of Cremona (d. ca. 1250). In the fifth book of this work, Moncta defended the apostolic origin of the Roman Church, the truth of its teaching, its uniqueness and indefectibility, the uninterrupted succession of its bishops, its authority to legislate, and its right to temporal possessions in order to further its mission.

Shortly after the beginning of the 12th century, the Concordat of Worms became effective (1122). The emperor renounced his right to appoint the bishops of the Church. Pope and emperor were at peace. The peace was broken by the German emperor, Frederick Barbarossa (1152-90) who drove the Pope from Rome. Finally though Frederick's armies were defeated by an Italian army (1176). The 13th century opened with the reign of Pope Innocent III (1198-1216). Innocent exercised a political sovereignty over Europe greater than any of his predecessors or successors. A few decades later, the grandson of Barbarossa, Frederick II (1215-50), sought to become master of the Church: but ultimately he achieved no greater success than his grandfather.

The 12th and 13th centuries were the golden age of scholasticism. The term scholasticism designates first of all the educational tradition of the medieval schools, the curriculum of the seven liberal arts. The term designates, secondly and more com-

monly, the systems of speculative thought which employed
reason to explain the mysteries of faith. These systems sought
to demonstrate the harmony between natural and supernatural
truth. Anselm (1033-1109) is called the father of scholasticism
in this sense. The scholastics made wide use of dialectic, that is,
the juxtaposition of opposed and contrary ideas, in order to grasp
the meaning of Christian dogmas.

There were two main currents within scholasticism. One was
the mystical, intuitional current which was inspired by Augustine.
Followed by the Franciscans especially, it reached its culmination
in the teaching of Bonaventure (1221-74). The other current employed the philosophy of Aristotle in the exposition of the Christian faith. This current culminated in the teaching of Albert the
Great (d. 1280) and Thomas Aquinas (1225-74). The age of
scholasticism, apart from its contribution to philosophy and
theology, contributed to the development of modern science by its
recovery of the Hellenistic scientific tradition and by its confidence in the power of reason and the rationality of the universe
without which science would be impossible.

BERNARD OF CLAIRVAUX

Bernard (1091-1153), abbot of the monastery of Clairvaux,
was the greatest religious figure of the century. He revealed his
mind about the Church in his sermons on the Song of Songs.
Bernard applied the Song to the mystical union of the Word
with the individual soul which is simply an expression of the
union of the incarnate Word with His Church. "We are all called
to a spiritual marriage," Bernard wrote, "in which Christ is the
spouse... At one and the same time we are all one bride and
individual souls are, as it were, individual brides."[3] The Church
is holy and its sanctity must shine in its members.[4] By Church,
though, Bernard meant in this case not the individual soul, but
the unanimity of a great number of them.[5] Sinners have a place
in the Church: they can receive the sacraments; they profess
the faith of the Church; and they associate visibly with the
faithful.[6] Bernard was convinced that the Church had to trod

historically the same path of humiliation in order to share the exaltation of its head.[7]

Bernard ardently desired the integration of nations and individuals into the life and order of the Church; hence, he called for missionary activity. Writing to Pope Eugene III, he said: "How in good conscience can we fail to offer Christ to those who do not have Him... Who believes by chance? How shall they believe unless someone preaches? Was not Peter sent to Cornelius and Philip to the eunuch? Was not Augustine sent to the English by St. Gregory?" Bernard held out little hope of success in evangelizing the Jews, for the time of their conversion had not yet come. He hoped for the return of the Greeks: they are and are not with Catholics, being joined in faith but separated in peace. Schismatics and heretics were to be set right lest they perish and prevented from destroying others.[8]

Bernard spoke of the papal office in the highest terms describing the Pope as the defender of the faith, the teacher of nations, the leader of Christendom, the father of kings, the vicar of Christ and the anointed of the Lord.[9] The bishops too are pastors of the flocks assigned to them by divine institution; but the whole flock of Christ has been entrusted to the successor of Peter, the shepherd even of the other pastors.[10] Bernard counseled the Pope to abstain from worldly trappings which make him appear to be the successor of Constantine, not the successor of Peter.[11] The papacy ought not to become a worldly tribunal in which the laws of Justinian rather than those of Christ are operative.[12] Bernard set himself against the abuse of appeals and exemptions which impaired the authority of bishops and disrupted traditional order.

Bernard sustained the theory of the two swords at the disposal of the Church. One sword was spiritual and involved the imposition of spiritual sanctions such as excommunication; the other was material and implied physical force. Writing to Pope Eugene, Bernard explained the theory in this way:

> Do the work of an evangelist and you have done the work of a shepherd. You will say that I admonish you to shepherd dragons and scorpions, the rebellious citizens of Rome. For

this reason, I say, go to meet them with the word and not with the sword. Why should you use the sword again when you have once been told to put it back into the scabbard. If anyone says the sword is not yours, he does not pay enough attention to the word of the Lord who said, 'Put up your sword' (Jn 18:11). The sword is yours therefore, although it is not wielded by you but at your wish. Otherwise, if the sword did not belong to you in any way, when the apostles said, 'Here are two swords,' the Lord would not have replied, 'Enough' (Lk 22:38) but rather 'Too many.' The Church, therefore, has a spiritual sword and a material sword; the latter is to be wielded for the Church; the former, by the Church. The spiritual sword is to be wielded by the hand of the priest; the material sword, by the hand of the soldier, but at the wish of the priest and the command of the emperor.[13]

Bernard called for cooperation between the Church and the emperor to insure peace and further the salvation of souls. In a letter to Conrad, king of the Romans, Bernard requested him to come to the aid of the Pope in dealing with the Romans. Kings and priests, Bernard wrote, "should be of one mind since they are of one religion. Let them help and defend each other and bear each other's burdens."[14] Hence, the emperor had a twofold responsibility: as king, he had to insure the peace and welfare of his people; as defender of the Church, he had to insure its liberty and safety.

THE DECRETUM OF GRATIAN AND THE DEVELOPMENT OF CANON LAW

The development of canon law influenced the history of the medieval Church as much as the theological and philosophical movement. An important factor in this development was the *Decretum*[15] of Gratian which is a collection of almost 4000 legal canons or chapters. Very little is known about Gratian's life except that he was a Camaldolese monk of the monastery of Sts. Felix and Nabor at Bologna, Italy. Gratian issued his collection ca. 1140-41. In making his compilation he drew upon earlier collections of conciliar canons and papal decretals, supplementing them with material issued subsequently. But Gratian was no mere compiler. He took a position on questions of the law, supporting his position by appropriate arguments. When he was confronted by contradictory canons, he attempted to resolve the contradiction or indicate the more authoritative law. His work was a private attempt to adapt earlier canonical legislation to the existing needs of the Church. He is known as the founder of the science of ecclesiastical jurisprudence.

The success of Gratian's *Decretum* was enormous. It became the standard text in the schools of law as well as an essential tool of the courts. Its success was due to the rich amount of material it provided, the arrangement of this material, and the teaching it set forth. What is even more significant is that the *Decretum* provided a juridical basis for the centralization of authority and jurisdiction in the hands of the Popes. The decretals and canons cited by the *Decretum* pronounced the primacy of the Roman Church to be a matter of divine institution. The Roman Church is the head of all the other Churches. The Pope is the supreme legislator. It is the prerogative of the Roman see to convene councils. Its faith is untainted. The Pope judges all others, but no one judges the Pope unless he has erred in faith.

The papacy had been the instrument of reforms; bishops continued to turn to it for the solution of problems confronting them; dissensions between civil authorities were referred to it for arbitration; questions about contracts, marriages, patrimonies, and privileges of clerics were presented. The new system of canon law embodied in the *Decretum* was invaluable in this situation. The most effective Popes of this period—Alexander III (1159-81), Innocent III (1198-1216), Gregory IX (1227-41), Innocent IV (1243-54) and Alexander VI (1254-61)—were all ardent canonists.

CHURCH AND EUCHARIST

Augustine had stressed the relationship between the Holy Eucharist, the physical body of Christ, and the community of the faithful. It was the common and emphatic teaching of the period under consideration that the Eucharist is the sacrament of ecclesiastical unity, that its object is to incorporate us in Christ and with one another. One of the first to touch upon this point was Alger of Liege (d. 1131) in his work, *De sacramento corporis et sanguinis dominici.*[16] Peter the Lombard (d. ca. 1160) expressed the formulation that was adopted by all the scholastics after him: "This sacrament [the Holy Eucharist] has a twofold reality: one contained and signified, the other signified but not contained. The reality which is contained and signified [by the sacramental species] is the body of Christ born of the Virgin and the blood which He shed for us. The reality which is signified but not contained is the unity of the Church."[17] Often the reality of the sacramental body of Christ was deduced from the reality of the Church. The Church could not be a real entity if the sacramental body of Christ were not real. Often enough, the Eucharist was said to be the image of the body of Christ. Such a conception was not a denial of the reality of the body of Christ in the Eucharist but a reference to its relationship to the ecclesial body of Christ.

After Berengarius of Tours (1000-88) had denied transubstantiation and the real presence, the scholastics began to speak of the sacramental body of Christ as the *corpus verum,* the true body. Previously the Eucharist had been called the *mystical* body of Christ or the equivalent. From the middle of the 12th century the scholastics began to speak about the *Church* as the mystical body of Christ in order to distinguish it from the Eucharistic body, the *true* body. The words of Master Simon (ca. 1160) illustrate the terminology employed: "In the sacrament of the altar there are two things: the true body of Christ, and that which is signified by it, His mystical body which is the Church."[18] When applied to the Church, the expression, mystical body of Christ, was intended to signify the mysterious and ineffable union of Christ with His Church.

THE BODY OF CHRIST

The dominant theological conception of the Church in the 12th and 13th centuries was that the Church is the body of Christ. There were two reasons that prompted theologians to reflect upon the Church as the body of Christ. One reason was the greater attention paid to the humanity of Christ. The scholastics were agreed that Christ as man is the head of the Church. The connection between the Church and Christ its head was studied to a greater degree. Theologians studied this connection in treatises called *De Christo capite* (*On Christ the Head*) or *De gratia capitis* (*On the Grace of the Head*). A second reason for the prominence of this theme was the great influence of Augustine upon the scholastics. For Augustine, the Church was the community or assembly of the faithful.[19] The faithful were those who were united to Christ by faith and participation in the sacraments which He instituted. In virtue of their union with Christ, the faithful were members of His body and were vivified by His Spirit.[20]

The scholastics accepted these ideas and developed them. Hugh of St. Victor, William of Auxerre, Albert the Great, Thomas Aquinas and others also spoke of the Church as the *Collectio* or *congregatio fidelium* (the assembly or congregation of the faithful) who are united to Christ by faith and baptism. The members of the Church are the body of Christ and are vivified by His Spirit. Hugh of St. Victor (d. 1141), for example, wrote: "Holy Church is the body of Christ; united in faith the Church is sanctified and vivified by the one Spirit. The faithful are members of this body. They are one body because of one spirit and one faith."[21]

The *Sententiarum libri quattuor* (*Four Books of Sentences*) of Peter the Lombard (d. ca. 1160), composed between 1150 and 1152, provided a springboard for subsequent theologizing about the body of Christ by the scholastics. Peter stated that Christ's human nature possesses wisdom and grace because among other reasons, it has been made the principle of sanctification for all Christians.[22] In his biblical commentaries Peter explained why Christ is the *head* of the body: because He possesses the fulness of grace, because He rules the minds of men, because grace flows from Him as from a fountain.[23] Similar ideas are found in the *Libri quinque Sententiarum*[24] of Peter of Poitiers (d. 1205), a distinguished disciple of Peter the Lombard, and in the *Summa aurea*[25] of William of Auxerre (d. 1231).

Other scholastics too, following the inspiration of Paul and

Augustine and building upon the work of their immediate predecessors, spoke of Christ as the *head* of the mystical body, the
Church. They gave various reasons for the suitability of this
designation. In general, they saw a likeness between the head of
the human body and Christ, the head of the Church. Alexander
of Hales (d. 1245) explained the likeness in this way: just as
sensation and movement flow from the head through the nerves to
the different members of the human body, so faith and love flow
from Christ to the members of the Church.[26] Albert the Great
enumerated three functions of the head which he then applied
to Christ. The head, he wrote, is a source of sensation and movement for the other members of the body; the soul functions as the
form of the body by means of the head; and the head has the
same nature as the other members of the body.[27] Bonaventure
wrote in a similar vein: "In spiritual matters something is called
the head because of its likeness to some property of a material
head." Then he enumerated some properties of a material head.
He drew this conclusion: "All these properties are to be found in
Christ with respect to the just. Therefore, Scripture says quite
reasonably that Christ is the head of the Church."[28] Aquinas
viewed the matter in substantially the same way:

> The whole Church is said to be one mystical body by reason
> of its similarity to the natural body of a man which has
> different functions in virtue of its different members...
> Christ is said to be the head of the Church because of a
> similarity to a human head. In the human head we can
> consider three things, namely, order, perfection and power
> —order, because the head is the first part of a man if we be-
> gin with what is higher; perfection, because all the exterior
> and interior senses are to be found in the head while only
> the sense of touch is to be found in the other members;
> power, because the power, movement and government of
> the other members are derived from the head...
>
> These three things belong spiritually to Christ. First, by
> reason of His nearness to God, His grace is the highest and
> the first, although not in a temporal sense, for all have
> received grace on account of His grace... Second, He is
> perfect with respect to the fullness of grace... Third, He
> has the power to bestow grace on all the members of the
> Church....[29]

The scholastics made a distinction among the members of the Church. Both the just and sinners are members of the Church, but in different ways. According to Alexander of Hales (d. 1245), for example, sinners do not share in the unity of the mystical body of the Church. He distinguished between the unity of the Church and the unity of the mystical body of the Church. Both the just and sinners share in the unity of the Church. In this case, the bond of unity is faith alone. Alexander illustrated this point of view by citing the parable of the wheat and the tares in Matthew's gospel (13:24-30). The Church is the field in which wheat (the just) and weeds (sinners) are to be found. Only the just, however, share in the unity of the mystical body of the Church. In this case, the bond of unity is faith and charity.[30] Hence, all the members of the body of the Church are also members of the Church; but not all the members of the Church are also members of the body of the Church.

The scholastics placed the beginning of the Church in the Old Testament. Again Alexander of Hales is representative of them. According to Alexander, the Church began with Abel for a number of reasons: Abel was the first to manifest faith in the coming Redeemer by the visible sacrifice he offered; he displayed the holiness of the Church; he was the first martyr to sanctify the Church by his blood; finally, he was recognized as just by the Lord Himself (Mt 23:35). From the very beginning, though, the Church was the mystical body of Christ. It is Christ, the head of the mystical body, who unites all the members of the body through faith and love whether they have lived before or after His birth.

Just as the Church reaches back to Abel, so it will continue to the end of the world. Alexander drew this conclusion from two premises: the permanent union between Christ and His bride, the Church, and the mission of the Church to make full the number of the elect. If this mission were fulfilled before the end of the world, the days remaining would serve no useful purpose, an hypothesis opposed to divine providence. Furthermore, Paul wrote that the just who are still living at the coming of Christ will be glorified with those who have fallen asleep through Jesus (1 Th 4:14-15). Even though faith will diminish

(Lk 18:8) and charity will grow cold (Mt 24:12), not all will be affected. Jesus promised (Mt 28:20) to be with the apostles to the end.[31]

The scholastics compared the Church not only to the human body but also to a marriage and to the formation of Eve from the side of Adam. They employed the image of a consummated marriage to illustrate the union between the human nature of Christ and the person of the Word on the one hand and the union between Christ and the Church on the other. They (Hugh of St. Victor, Peter Lombard, Alexander of Hales, Albert the Great, Thomas Aquinas, Bonaventure and others) also saw a parallel between the formation of Eve from the side of Adam and the foundation of the Church from the side of Christ as He hung upon the cross.

THOMAS AQUINAS

For Aquinas (1225-1274), the Church was the body of Christ; the soul which quickened the body was the Holy Spirit. When Aquinas studied the Church as the body of Christ, he placed himself within the dominant ecclesiological current of the 13th century. In his *Summa theologica* Aquinas considered the connection between Christ and the Church. Christ, he wrote, is said to be the head of the Church because His function in the Church is similar to the function of a head with respect to the body.[32] All men in heaven and on earth share in the influence of the head in different degrees:

> First and foremost Christ is the head of all those who are actually united to Him in glory. Second, He is the head of those who are actually united to Him in charity. Third, He is the head of those who are united to Him in faith. Fourth, He is the head of them who are united to Him potentially, a potentiality which has not yet been actualized but will be actualized according to divine predestination. Fifth, Christ is the head of those who are united to Him with a potentiality which will never be actualized as in the case of those who are living in the world but are not predestined. Those who die in sin totally cease to be members of Christ because they are not even potentially united to Christ.[33]

In this way, Thomas viewed Christ as the head of redeemed humanity somewhat as Adam was the head of fallen humanity. As Adam was the source of sin, so Christ was the source of grace. Christ as man possessed the fullness of grace.[34] From Christ as from a fountain overflowing upon the Church, all the effects of grace come to men in varying degrees. Christ as man is the conjoined living instrument of the divinity for the conferral of grace. In this matter, Christ in His humanity exercises a true instrumental causality.

Another passage which reveals (partially at least) Aquinas' conception of the Church is his commentary upon the article of the creed which speaks of the one, holy, catholic and apostolic Church:

> Just as in a man there is one body and one soul, yet a diversity of members, so the Catholic Church is one body with a diversity of members. The soul which quickens the body is the Holy Spirit. Therefore, after we have faith in the Holy Spirit, we are commanded to have faith in the holy, catholic church, as the creed indicates.

> The Church is an assembly. The holy Church is the assembly of the faithful. Each Christian is a member of the Church. . . This holy Church has four properties: it is one, holy, catholic (or universal), and strong or firm. . .

> The unity of the Church is the result of three things. First, the unity of faith. All Christians who belong to the body of the Church believe the same thing as Scripture says: 'Let all say the same thing, and let there be no divisions among you' (1 Cor 1:10); 'One Lord, one faith, one baptism' (Ep 4:5). Second, the unity of hope. All Christians are rooted in the one hope of attaining eternal life as the Apostle says: 'One body and one Spirit, even as you are called in one hope of your calling' (Ep 4:4). Third, the unity of love. All are united in the love of God and to one another in mutual love as John says: 'The glory that thou hast given me, I have given to them, that they may be one even as we are one' (Jn 17:22). If it be true, this love is manifested when the members are concerned for one another and feel for one another. . .

> The faithful are sanctified, first, because they have been washed by the blood of Christ; second, because they are anointed with the grace of the Holy Spirit. . ; third, because the Trinity dwells within them. . .

The Church is catholic or universal, first, by reason of her geographical extension throughout the whole world. . ; second, by reason of her inclusion of all classes of men. . ; third, by reason of her universal duration. . . The Church began at the time of Abel and will endure until the end of the world. . ; after which she shall continue in heaven. . .

The Church is strong or firm. A house is said to be strong or firm, first, if it has good foundations. The principal foundation of the Church is Christ as Paul says: 'For other foundation no one can lay, but that which has been laid, which is Christ Jesus' (1 Cor 3:11). The secondary foundation is the apostles and their doctrine. . . That is why the Church is called apostolic. . . Second, the strength of a house appears when it cannot be destroyed even if it is shaken. The Church however can never be destroyed: either by persecution. . ; or by error. . ; or by the temptations of the demons. . . Hence it is that the Church of Peter alone has always been firm in the faith. . .[35]

In this passage, Thomas speaks of the Holy Spirit as the soul of the Church because the Spirit is the principle of the Church's life. The designation of the Holy Spirit as the principle of the Church's life was justified by Thomas on the basis of appropriation. The first cause of the life of grace in man is God. Man's sharing in God's life is an effect *ad extra* common to all three persons of the Trinity. Man's created sharing in God's life is a work of love on God's part; hence, it is attributed or "appropriated" to the Holy Spirit who is personal Love.

In his explanation of the creed (given above) Aquinas spoke of the Church as a body with a diversity of members. He was thinking of the Church as an organized body, as a society whose members perform different functions in view of a common good. In another passage Aquinas gave the reasons for the different states and functions within the Church: first, the fullness of grace possessed by Christ, the head of the Church, is shared by His members in a variety of ways just as creatures share in the perfection of God in a variety of ways. Second, good order within the Church demands that certain members be responsible for certain tasks. Paul wrote: Christ gave some men as apostles, others as prophets, evangelists, pastors and teachers for the building up of the Church (Ep 4:11-12). Third, a diversity of ministries contributes to the dignity and beauty of the Church. Such a diversity does not impair the unity of the Church which is preserved by the unity of faith, love and service. Moreover cooperative action on the part of the members of the Church insures peace within the Church.[36]

Sometimes, therefore, as in the preceding paragraph, Aquinas thought of the Church as a body because of its social unity, the members of the Church functioning in different ways for the benefit of the whole Church. Sometimes, however, as in the third part of his *Summa theologica* (cited at the very beginning of this section), Aquinas thought of the Church as a body because its members shared a common life in the biological sense of the term.

Aquinas' commentary on the text of the creed also makes quite clear that he regarded the Church as one complex reality, that is, as a community of faith, hope, and charity whose soul is the Holy Spirit, a community established by Christ, propagated by the apostles, spread abroad in the world, united under the visible leadership of the Pope, a community which goes back to Abel. As the body and soul are one person, as the soul manifests itself through the body, so there is only one Church whose interior life manifests itself in a visible society.

As a visible society, the Church is the sacrament of salvation; that is; the Church is the visible sign and cause whereby men are incorporated into Christ. The preaching and sacramental ministry of the institutional Church beget members of Christ and build up the body of Christ. Faith and the sacraments of faith have the effect of communicating the merits of Christ's passion to the individual Christian. The Church is not merely the body of Christ, but the effective instrument of its growth and development.

The sacrament of ecclesiastical unity is the Holy Eucharist. The Eucharist is the sign and cause of the union between Christ and the faithful. Because the faithful are one with Christ through the Eucharist, the effect of the Eucharist is to unite the faithful among themselves.[37] The bread and wine used in the sacrament signify this effect: just as the bread and wine are made of many grains and grapes, so the Church is composed of many members.[38] The whole ministry of the Church is devoted to the celebration of the Eucharist or to functions which prepare the faithful for the celebration of the Eucharist or follow therefrom.

A complete summary of Aquinas' ecclesiology would also have to consider his teaching about the priesthood (4 *C.G.* 74-76; *S. Th.* 3, 22; etc.), jurisdiction (*S. Th.* 3, 59; 1-2, 108, 1-2; 2-2, 39, 3; etc.), the papacy (to be considered in the next section), the episcopacy (4 *Sent.* 7, 3, 1; 4 *C.G.* 76; etc..), the magisterium (*S. Th* 2-2, 1, 9-10; etc.), the relations between Church and State (*De regimine princ.* 1, 14; etc. and (what came to be known as) the marks of the Church (*Expos. in Symb.* 9; etc.)

PAPAL PRIMACY AND INFALLIBILITY

Alexander of Hales (d. 1245), the first great theologian of the 13th century, touched upon the place of the Pope in the Church when he spoke of the power of the keys (Mt 16:19) in connection with the sacrament of penance. The power of the keys is concentrated in the hands of the Pope in order to secure the unity of the Church upon earth.[39]

Bonaventure (1217-74), the student of Alexander of Hales at Paris and later general of the Franciscan order, is one of the principal architects of the monarchical conception of the papacy. His vision of the Church is dominated by his Christology. Enlightened by the Word made flesh, man is recreated in the likeness of God and prepared for attaining the wisdom of contemplating the Holy Trinity. This preparation is accomplished on earth within the Church by its sacraments and ministers through whom Christ continues to act from heaven. The Pope is the vicar of Christ, the supreme father of all fathers, the chief hierarch of all the faithful, the source and norm of all ecclesiastical authority.[40] The Roman see has the fulness of that authority which Christ conferred upon His Church. Others share that authority in different degrees just as the saints share the glory of their Savior in different degrees.[41] Those who exercise jurisdiction within the Church derive their jurisdiction from the Pope.[42] "If the Pope were alone in the Church and all else had been destroyed, he could restore all."[43] The patriarchs of Constantinople,

Alexandria, Jerusalem and Antioch have authority over a limited area; but the authority of the bishop of Rome is universal.[44]

One of the sources upon which Bonaventure (and along with him Hugh of St. Victor, Peter the Lombard, Alexander of Hales, Albert the Great, Thomas Aquinas and others) drew was the writings of Dionysius the Pseudo-Areopagite.[45] He passed himself off, and was accepted by the scholastics, as the convert of Paul (Ac 17:34). It was believed that Paul, who had communicated his revelations to his disciple in Athens, spoke through these writings. Probably though the Pseudo-Areopagite lived and wrote at the beginning of the 6th century. His teaching is characterized by his hierarchical conception of being. The universe is organized hierarchically, every intelligent being having its proper place and function. Every being is divinized by a twofold action—by personal effort toward purification and conversion and by the influence of the higher strata of beings transmitting the divine light to the lower strata.

This hierarchical conception of reality furnished the Franciscan theologians above all—Bonaventure included—with an apt model for a monarchical papacy. Christ was the principal hierarch. The Pope was His vicar. The papacy was the source of whatever power and jurisdiction the lower ecclesiastical orders possessed. The influence of Christ reached the humblest members of the Church through the mediation of the clerical orders. The action of the higher upon the lower, however, was intended to bring all intelligent beings back to God, just as the circle returns into itself.

Albert the Great spoke about the power of the keys. The function of the keys, as Alexander of Hales had said, is to secure the unity of the Church. The power of the keys has been committed fully to one individual, the Pope, who shares this power with others according to their pastoral responsibility.[46] The Pope is the bishop of all men; he has the fullness of episcopal authority; and he is the vicar of Christ on earth.[47] Albert recognized the infallibility of the Pope in the matter of indulgences. The Popes, Albert argued, preach indulgences and have others preach them. (The preaching of indulgences had become more frequent after Urban II had granted a plenary indulgence to all who pledged

themselves to fight the Turks during the first crusade in 1099.)
Albert drew this conclusion about the Pope's granting indulgences: "The universal ruler of the Church must not be thought
to deceive anyone especially in those matters which the whole
Church receives and approves."[48]

Thomas Aquinas wrote no systematic treatise about the position of the Pope in the Church; but he discussed it in many places
within his works. According to Aquinas, there must be one head
of the whole Church for the sake of unity. If the Church is to be
one in faith, there must be one who can settle disputes about the
faith. If the Church is to be governed in the best way, it must
have a monarchical constitution since peace and unity are
achieved more easily by a single ruler than by many of them. If
the Church on earth is to be a type of the Church in heaven,
there must be a single ruler on earth just as there is a single ruler
in heaven. Christ made Peter the visible head of His Church on
earth. Because the Church is to continue until the end of time,
Christ provided for successors to Peter. These are the Roman
Pontiffs.[49]

In virtue of his authority, comprehensive as it is, the Pope
cannot alter or suppress ecclesial elements derived from Christ.
For example, the Pope cannot originate or suppress articles of
faith; he cannot institute new sacraments or suppress those which
already exist. All these things have been derived from Christ and
are beyond the scope of papal authority.[50]

The authority of the Pope is universal and immediate. It is
universal because it extends to all the faithful and bishops. The
authority of the bishop is restricted to a particular locality and
group of the faithful. Even so, papal authority is not generically
different from episcopal authority. Peter shared the apostolate and
apostolic authority with the other apostles.[51] The authority of the
Pope is immediate in two senses: it is derived immediately from
God and not from the Christian community; and it can reach
every member of the Church immediately. The fact that both
Pope and bishop can exercise authority over the same individuals
does not foster disunity because the Pope is superior to the
bishop.[52]

Toward the close of the 13th century, the Second Council of

Lyons (1274), the 14th ecumenical council, defined the common faith:

> The Holy Roman Church has supreme and full primacy and jurisdiction over the universal catholic Church. This was received from the Lord Himself in the person of Peter, the prince of the apostles, whose successor in the fullness of power is the Roman Pontiff. Just as the Roman Church is bound before all others to defend the truth of the faith, so it must render judgment about questions of faith. Any aggrieved person can appeal to it in ecclesiastical matters and have recourse to its judgment. All Churches are subject to it and their prelates obey and reverence it. The Roman Church has the fullness of authority but grants other Churches a share of its responsibility. The Roman Church has honored many Churches, especially those of the patriarchs, with special privileges; but at the same time it has maintained its own rights both in general councils and in other instances.[53]

The Pope's fullness of power of which the council spoke was subject to a variety of interpretations. Contemporary canonists tended to understand this fullness as extending even to temporal affairs in which the Pope could intervene for the good of the Church—by deposing a contumacious emperor, for example. Others, as Aquinas,[54] understood the papal fullness of power to be without practical temporal implications. No one attributed to the Pope the power to dispense from the divine or natural law or to modify the constitution of the Church as established by Christ.

The Second Council of Lyons had been a council of reunion with the Greeks. The Greek envoys had accepted the prescribed profession of faith which included a recognition of papal primacy. The union did not last, however, because the Greek emperor had supported it only from political motives and the Greek clergy and people would not agree to it. The Greeks continued to insist that the bishop of Rome was not the bishop of the entire world but only the bishop of a particular Church; therefore, he was not the head of the Church as the Latins understood the term. The Greeks were prepared to accept only those decisions reached *collegialiter* and to rely upon a unity achieved by the Spirit rather than by administrative procedures.

While medieval canonists and theologians generally did not

formulate the doctrine of papal infallibility in the explicit terms of Vatican I, they did take strides in this direction. It was universally agreed that the Church as a whole, the *congregatio fidelium*, could not err in matters of faith. The inerrancy of the Church was recognized as operative in a general council over which the Pope, the head of the Church, necessarily presided. There was a tendency, however, to make the inerrancy of the Church dependent upon the inerrancy of the Pope; but there was also a general feeling that the Pope could err and fall into heresy ceasing to be, as a consequence, head and member of the Church.

The canonists of the 12th and 13th centuries vigorously asserted papal primacy over the Church; thus, they laid the basis for later theories of papal infallibility which tied it to papal supremacy. Nevertheless, the canonists held that the Pope, the head of the Church, could err; but they were confident that divine providence would always prevent the Church as a whole from being led astray.

Bonaventure too did not explicitly speak of papal infallibility but he did teach that the Pope was the source and norm of all ecclesiastical authority. This teaching could certainly have led to the conclusion that, since the universal Church was unerring, its head was unerring.

For Aquinas, it is the responsibility of the Pope to determine what matters are of faith. By adhering to the decision of the Pope in matters of faith, the members of the Church maintain their unity.[55] A person is guilty of heresy if he rejects a doctrine taught by ecclesiastical authority, an authority which resides principally in the Supreme Pontiff.[56] The Church can never be destroyed by persecutions or error or the temptations of the demons. The Church of Peter alone has always been firm in the faith.[57]

The Franciscan theologian, Duns Scotus (d. 1308), again and again expressed a complete and unreserved confidence in the public teachings of the universal Church. For him, the Church was the one certain guide to all the truths of Christian revelation; and the Church spoke through the Pope and councils.[58]

NOTES TO CHAPTER IV

1. DS 802.
2. DS 809.
3. *PL* 183, 158.
4. *De consid.* 1, 8. *PL* 182, 737-738.
5. *Cant.* 61, 2. *PL* 183, 1071.
6. *Cant.* 25, 2. *PL* 183, 899.
7. Sermon 68, 2. *PL* 183, 682.
8. *De consider.* 3, 1, 3-4. *PL* 182, 759-760.
9. *Ibid.* 4, 7. *PL* 182, 788.
10. *Ibid.* 2, 8. *PL* 182, 751.
11. *Ibid.* 4, 3, 6. *PL* 182, 776.
12. *Ibid.* 1, 4. *PL* 182, 732.
13. *Ibid.* 4, 3, 7. *PL* 182, 776.
14. Letter 244, 1. *PL* 182, 441.
15. A Latin text can be found in Migne *PL* 187.
16. *PL* 180, 745-750.
17. *PL* 192, 857.
18. *Tract. de Sacram.* H. Weisweiler, *Maître Simon et son groupe,* (Louvain, 1937) 27 and 34.
19. *Quaest. evang.* 2, 40. PL 35, 1355.
20. *Tract. Jo. Evang.* 26, 13; 27, 6. PL 35, 1612. 1618.
21. *De Sac.* 2, 2, 2. *PL* 176, 416.
22. 3, 13, 1-5. *PL* 192, 781-783.
23. *PL* 191, 1629; 192, 178-179 and 263-264.
24. 4, 20.
25. 3, 1, 4.
26. *S. Th.* 3, 12, 2, 1.
27. 3 *Sent.* 13, 2.
28. 3 *Sent.* 13, 2, 1.
29. *S. Th.* 3, 8, 1.
30. *S. Th.* 3, 12, 2, 3.
31. *S. Th.* 4, 2, 4.
32. *S. Th.* 3, 8, 1.
33. *S. Th.* 3, 8, 3.
34. *S. Th.* 3, 7, 9.
35. *Explanation of the Apostles Creed* 9.
36. *S. Th.* 2-2, 183, 2.
37. *S. Th.* 3, 73, 4.
38. *S. Th.* 3, 74, 1.
39. *S. Th.* 4, 20, 6, 3.
40. *Breviloquim* 6, 12.
41. *Quare Fratres Minores praedicent* at the beginning.

42. *De perf. evang.* 4, 3, *corp.*
43. *Ibid. ad* 15.
44. *In Hexaem.* 22.
45. *PG* 3.
46. *De sacrificio Missae* 3, 6, 9.
47. *S. Th.* 2, 24, 141.
48. 4 *Sent.* 20, 17.
49. *C.G.* 4, 76. Aquinas did not regard these reasons as apodictic in every case; often he suggested reasons to explain the suitability of the divine plan.
50. 4 *Sent.* 17, 3, 1, 5.
51. *Ibid.* 24, 3, 2, *ad* 3.
52. *Ibid.* 17, 3, 3, 5, *ad* 3.
53. DS 861.
54. *S. Th.* 3, 59, 4, *ad* 1 and 2.
55. *S. Th.* 2-2, 1, 10.
56. *Ibid.* 2-2, 11, 2, *ad* 3.
57. *Explanation of the Apostles Creed* 9.
58. In his book, *Origins of Papal Infallibility* (Leiden, 1972), B. Tierney points to the Franciscan, Pietro Olivi (d. 1289) as the first theologian to formulate explicitly the doctrine of papal infallibility.

V. THE 14th & 15th CENTURIES

THE DECLINE

The 14th and 15th centuries were a period of decline for the Church in western Europe. The supranational unity of Christendom was weakened by the formation of new national monarchies. Toward the middle of the 14th century, the Black Death carried away millions of people in less than two years. In many ways the plague broke the spirit of the survivors. The Hundred Years War between France and England ravaged France especially. The prestige of the papacy was enormously diminished by its political quarrels and the worldly lives of the Popes. Concubinage was widespread among the clergy. Rival claimants to the chair of Peter at Rome during the course of the Great Schism divided the loyalty of Catholics. Conciliarism maintained the superiority of a general council over the Pope. Ecclesiastical bureaucracy and its financial demands became intolerable. Theology declined because it lacked a fuller and more exact knowledge of history. Exaggerated emphasis upon one's personal, inner life led to a deterioration of ecclesiastical consciousness.

The political power of the papacy declined from the pontificate of Boniface VIII (1294-1303) and his political quarrels with Philip IV of France. The Pope issued the famous bull *Unam sanctam* (1302) in the course of these quarrels. The so-called Babylonian exile of the papacy, when the Popes resided at Avignon, France, and not in Rome, began in 1305 with the election of a Frenchman, Clement V (1305-14), as Pope. The Popes were absent from Rome about seventy years until 1376 when Gregory XI (1370-78) returned at the urging of Catherine

of Siena. The Popes remained at Avignon during this period because of the political turmoil in the city of Rome. The Great
Western Schism followed upon the return of the Popes to Rome.
Urban VI (1378-89), an Italian, succeeded Gregory XI. The
French cardinals, displeased with Urban, elected Clement VII
(1378-94), formerly Cardinal Robert of Geneva. The schism
continued for forty years or so, two and sometimes three individuals claiming the chair of Peter at the same time. The schism
was healed at the Council of Constance (1414-18) which elected
Martin V (1417-31) as Pope. This council declared in explicit
terms that general councils were superior to Popes.

The Council of Basle assembled under the successor of Martin
V, Eugene IV (1431-47). Eugene transferred the council to
Ferrara (1438) and then to Florence (1439). At Florence, a
reunion was achieved between Rome and the Greeks, Armenians,
Jacobites, Mesopotamians, Nestorians and Maronites. The union
was disrupted (1453) when the Greeks realized they would receive no help from the West against the Turks. The Turks captured Constantinople in 1453. The patriarchs of Alexandria,
Antioch and Jerusalem had withdrawn their consent to the union
ten years earlier. The Popes who presided over the Church for
the last half of the 15th century were engrossed in temporal
interests, warning Christendom against the menace of the Turks,
securing their dominion over the Papal States, furthering the
worldly fortunes of their own families, and promoting the arts.
The Fifth Lateran Council met between 1512 and 1517 with
meager results.

Voices calling for reform were not silent. John Wycliffe
(1320?-84), an Englishman, condemned the wealth of the
Church. He went on to reject monasticism, the papacy, auricular
confession, celibacy and prayers for the dead. He wished to reform Christianity on the basis of the Scriptures alone. John Hus,
a university professor and preacher in Prague, was burned at the
stake (1415) for views similar to those of Wycliffe. Within the
Church, Bernardine of Siena (d. 1444) and John Capistran
(d. 1456) pressed for the reform of the religious orders. New
religious societies came into existence: the Brethren of the Common Life (1386), the Minims founded by Francis of Paula

(1474), the Olivetans, Jesuats, Alexian Brothers, Jeronymites and Bridgittines. There was great enthusiasm for the writings of the mystics: Meister Eckhart (d. 1327), John Tauler, a persuasive preacher (d. 1361), Henry Suso (d. 1366), Jan van Ruysbroek (d. 1381), John Gerson, professor and chancellor of the University of Paris (d. 1429), and Thomas à Kempis (d. 1417), author of the *Imitation of Christ,* possibly the most widely read Christian book after the Bible. Numerous churches and charitable foundations attested to the piety of many laymen.

The Renaissance *par excellence* began with two Italians, Petrarch (d. 1374), the poet, and Boccaccio (d. 1375), the author. It flourished especially in Italy and Germany; and it continued into the 17th century. The movement was marked by its enthusiasm for Greek and Latin literature, by its preoccupation with purely human values and with the individual and personal, and by the flowering of the arts and the beginnings of modern science. The Renaissance was not necessarily incompatible with Christianity; but its most ardent devotees were often infected with pagan ideas. Among the most famous artists, architects and engineers of the period were Giotto (d. 1336), Fra Angelico (d. 1455), Leonardo da Vinci (d. 1519), Raphael (d. 1520), Michelangelo (d. 1564) and Titian (d. 1576).

During the 14th and 15th centuries and earlier the Jews suffered considerably at the hands of the people. Wild charges, widely accepted in some instances, were made against them. Sometimes they were forced to accept baptism. Their lot was especially difficult in Spain where the Inquisition was re-activated in 1480. In 1492 Ferdinand and Isabella expelled all Jews from Spain. Another melancholy aspect of the period was the persecution of women thought to be witches, the highest authorities of the Church sometimes lending their support.

THE 14TH CENTURY
CHURCH AND STATE

In the midst of his difficulties with Philip IV of France, Pope Boniface VIII issued the bull, *Unam sanctam* (1302), probably the most famous of all the medieval documents on Church and

State that has come down to us. In the bull, the Pope made these
points: there is only one, holy, catholic and apostolic Church;
outside this Church there is no salvation; this Church has been
committed to Peter and his successors, the Popes; in this Church
there are two swords: the spiritual sword wielded by the Church
and the temporal sword wielded by the kings at the wish of the
Church; spiritual power is superior to earthly power, establishes
it and judges it. In its only dogmatic definition the bull concludes:
"We declare, say, define and pronounce that it is absolutely
necessary for the salvation of every creature to be subject to the
Roman Pontiff."[1]

In this document Boniface was concerned with Church unity
and the subordination of temporal authority to spiritual authority.
Boniface claimed spiritual authority over the whole Church of
Christ to which all men are called as to the ark of salvation. He
asserted the supremacy of the Pope in the temporal sphere to the
extent that "the spiritual power can both establish the earthly
power and judge it, if it proves to be no good."[2] The precise
meaning and implications of this statement are uncertain. Some
interpret the statement to mean that the power of kings was
delegated to them by the papacy.

The bull, *Unam sanctam,* reflects the thought of Giles of
Rome. Giles wrote *De ecclesiastica potestate*[3] toward the end of
1301. According to Giles, spiritual authority is necessarily superior
to the temporal authority of kings; indeed, the latter authority
is derived from the former. It follows that all temporal goods
are subject to the Pope, the highest spiritual authority in his
capacity as the vicar of Christ. Nevertheless, prudence dictates
that the Pope ordinarily concern himself only with spiritual
matters, leaving mundane affairs to temporal rulers.

James of Viterbo, a supporter of Boniface VIII, wrote his
De regimine christiano in 1301-2. It was dedicated to the Pope.
In the first part, James speaks of the Church as a kingdom which
is orthodox, one, holy, catholic and apostolic. In the second part
he speaks of the dominion of Christ, the king of the Church, and
of His vicar, the Pope. Christ has communicated His divine
authority to bishops and princes. Bishops are spiritual kings while
princes are temporal kings. The latter are subject to the former.

Bishops have the right and duty to reprimand and even depose tyrannical princes. The plenitude of sacerdotal and royal power resides in the bishop of bishops, the Pope.[4]

Occasionally, James of Viterbo's *De regimine christiano* is described as the first formal treatise on the Church. Actually it is only a treatise about papal and royal power and not a complete dogmatic study of the Church.

Agostino Trionfo (d. 1328) wrote his *Summa de potestate ecclesiastica* seemingly at the behest of Pope John XXII (1316-34), one of the immediate successors of Boniface VIII. Trionfo reaffirms the position of Giles of Rome and James of Viterbo. The Pope is supreme in spiritual and temporal matters. The primary concern of the Pope is the spiritual order where doctrinal and social authority are concentrated in his hands. The jurisdiction of bishops is derived immediately from him. The spiritual authority of the Pope has consequences in the temporal order which is related to the spiritual order. The unity of the Christian world demands a single head. This head is the Pope who has the power of the keys from Christ. Since the emperor or king is the vassal of Christ, he is the vassal of the Pope, the vicar of Christ. The Pope may demand an account of his reign from the prince, impose penalties on him and even depose him.[5] Alvaro Pelaio sounded a similar note in his *De planctu ecclesiae* written between 1320 and 1330.

The French Dominican, John of Paris, took a different stance in his *Tractatus de potestate regia et papali* (1302-3).[6] For John, the Church needed a single head to settle questions of faith. By the will of Christ, this head was the Pope. Yet the highest authority for defining matters of faith was a general council representing the whole Church. The Pope was the source neither of episcopal authority nor of royal authority. While he was the head and principal member of the Church, the Pope's authority was not greater than that of all the members together. The Church could depose him for heresy, notorious wrongdoing and even for incompetence. The papal office was of divine origin; but the Church which had appointed an individual to that office had the authority to remove him. John's views foreshadowed the conciliarism of the next century.

Though the bishop of Rome retained his religious supremacy in this period, the storms of the time did not pass without some of his prerogatives being called into question or rejected. France was unwilling to admit any papal claim of political supremacy. Germany denied to the Pope the right of ratification in the election of the emperor. The disputes between the Pope and French king had other consequences too. Marsilio of Padua (1280?-1342), rector of the university of Paris in 1313, denied the divine institution of the papacy in *The Defender of Peace* (1324).[7] The goal of the State, he explained, is the welfare of its citizens. The State achieves this goal by assigning its citizens to different functions and supervising the performance of these functions. The priesthood must make its contribution to the goal of the State. It does so by exercising a ministry of teaching and worship. This ministry is from God. It is the right of the State, however, to assign priests to a specific pastorate and hierarchical rank. This assignment is from man. The civil legislator must designate priests to particular posts, fill the offices of bishop and Pope, and summon general councils. The papal claim to the plenitude of authority disrupts the orderly functioning of the State.

William of Ockham (*ca.* 1285-1349), an English Franciscan, also debated the extent of papal authority. Involved in a controversy with Pope John XXII about the nature of apostolic poverty, Ockham placed himself under the protection of the emperor Louis of Bavaria who had denied to the Pope the right of ratifying the election of the emperor. Ockham expounded his views about papal and imperial authority especially in three works: *Dialogus* (written between 1334 and 1338), *Octo quaestiones super potestate ac dignitate papali* (1340), and *Tractatus de imperatorum et pontificum potestate* (1347). According to Ockham, the authority of the apostle Peter, as defined by Christ, was limited to spiritual matters, that is, to teaching God's word, conducting divine worship, and supervising those things necessary for eternal salvation. In no way does the authority of the Pope extend to temporal matters. These matters pertain to the competence of the emperor in accordance with the injunction of Christ: Render to Caesar what is Caesar's. Imperial authority is from God and not the Pope. The election of the emperor needs no confirmation by the Pope. Hence, Ockham did not question the position of the Pope as the head of the Church and the vicar of Christ; but he did deny the right of the Pope to intervene in temporal affairs.[8]

Another Englishman, John Wycliffe (1320?-1384), went further. In his work, *De ecclesia* (1378) he spoke of the Church triumphant, the Church in purgatory, and the Church militant. The Church militant is the *universitas praedestinatorum*, the community of the predestined. Only the elect are members of the Church. (Wycliffe based this teaching upon Paul's doctrine of predestination.) Since predestination is a matter known only to God, no one can be certain that he belongs to the Church. It follows that the Church is essentially invisible. There is a continual struggle between the predestined and those who are not. The head of the former group is Christ; the head of the latter group is the Antichrist.

Wycliffe drew the consequences of this theory for the papacy. It is possible that the Pope is not a member of the Church because he is not predestined. In this case he does not have authority over the Church militant. Every papal decree must be judged by its conformity to the law of God enshrined in the Bible. Hence, every Christian must know the Bible. Wycliffe also maintained that papal and episcopal excommunication can do no harm to him whom God does not excommunicate.

After the Great Schism, Wycliffe passed from attacks on individual Popes to attacks on the papacy itself. A Pope, he said, could not claim authority over the Church on the pretext that Peter died at Rome. The antiquity of the see proved nothing about the wisdom and sanctity of the occupant. As the papacy functioned, it was full of poison. He seemed to say that the Church would be better off if it recognized only Christ as its head and rejected the papacy entirely.[9]

THE 15TH CENTURY
CONCILIARISM

Far worse than the quarrels between the spiritual and temporal powers in the 14th century was the commotion aroused in the bosom of the Church upon the outbreak of the Great Schism (1378-1417). The needs of the time secured wide acceptance for the false theory of conciliarism, that is, the doctrine asserting that a general council constitutes the supreme authority in the Church, the Pope being inferior to such a council. The seeds of this theory had been sown earlier. Commonly the Church had been defined as the congregation or assembly of the faithful sustained by the Spirit under the headship of Christ. The general council was viewed as an expression of the corporate nature of the universal Church. Representative of the whole Church, the general council was superior to any parts of the Church including the Pope. Moreover, there was a general conviction that a Pope could fall into heresy. To deal with such a possibility, canonists held that the Pope was bound by the canons of councils in matters touching upon the faith and the general state of the Church. Hugh of Pisa (d. 1210), the most prominent canonist of his day and the teacher of the future Innocent III, held that the Church acting through a council could depose an heretical and notoriously sinful Pope.

Conciliarism sprang from other ideas too. Some viewed a general council as a means of restricting the growing centralization of authority in the hands of the papal curia. Others considered the authority of the Church to rest with the people, the Pope being its minister. A council, acting on behalf of the whole Christian people, might recall the authority of the minister and depose him. Still others believed that the only solution to the existence of rival claimants to the papacy was to convoke a general council which should decide among them. True, they said, a legitimate council had to be convoked by the Pope; but in the abnormal circumstances of the Great Schism, convocation without the Pope was justified through the use of *epikeia*.

Conciliarism is encountered in a developed form in the *Epistola concordiae* (1380) of Conrad of Gelnhausen, the first major work of conciliar scholarship to appear after the inception of the Great Schism. Conrad distinguished between the universal Church and the Roman Church (the Pope and the cardinals). The universal Church could not err while the Roman Church could err; therefore, the former was superior to the latter. Conrad called for a general council of the whole Church to put an end to the Schism. If the rival claimants to the see of Peter were unwilling to convoke such a council, the cardinals should do so. Once the Schism had been healed, Pope and council should act together.[10]

A few months later, Henry of Langenstein, a theologian of the University of Paris, took a similar position in his *Epistola concilii pacis* (1381). He saw no alternative to a general council as a solution to the Great Schism. By the Lateran Council of 1059, he wrote, the Church had delegated the cardinals to elect the Pope. Nevertheless, primary responsibility for electing the Pope rests with the bishops, a responsibility which they must exercise when the cardinals choose an unworthy candidate. The Church has the right to depose an unworthy Pope and elect a new one.[11]

The Council of Pisa (1409) furthered the conciliar idea. A number of cardinals, bishops and theologians met at Pisa and pronounced the deposition of the two rival Popes, Benedict XIII and Gregory XII. The council described the Popes as schismatics, heretics and scandals. It released all Christians from obedience to either of them and declared their acts to be null. For its part the council elected Alexander V as Pope.[12]

One of those who participated in the Council of Pisa and played a prominent role at the Council of Constance (1414-1418) was Peter D'Ailly (1350-1420), cardinal of Cambrai, chancellor of the University of Paris, and an ardent advocate of the conciliar theory. In his treatise, *Recommendatio sacrae Scripturae,* he expressed doubts that Christ had founded His Church upon such a weak individual as Peter. It was more likely that Christ Himself or Sacred Scripture was the foundation of the Church. His work, *De ecclesiae auctoritate*, was an extended expression of his views. The Pope, he wrote, is inferior to a general council which has the right to depose him not only for heresy but also for other crimes. The reason is that the whole Church represented by a general council is greater than any of its parts. The papacy is only a part of the Church just as the head is only a part of the body. Only the universal Church is infallible. The Popes are not infallible; in fact, they have erred commencing with Peter who denied Christ and was corrected by Paul. Lk 22:32 was a promise made to the universal Church and not to Peter and the Popes.[13]

Gerson (1363-1429) was the disciple of D'Ailly, his successor as chancellor of the University of Paris, and a leading figure at the Council of Constance. He too espoused the conciliar theory which he defended by several arguments. One argument was this: Christ established the papacy for the sake of peace and unity within the Church. When, however, the papacy becomes a source of conflict and disruption—Gerson was thinking of the situation created by the Great Schism—then a general council which represents the universal Church has the authority to do what is necessary to end the intolerable situation. A second argument Gerson employed was this: if the Pope is able to sever his relationship with the Church by resigning his office, as Pope Celestine had done, then the Church too, represented by a general council, is able to sever its relationship with the Pope when he abuses his office. A third argument: according to Mt 18: 17, one who does not hear the Church is to be considered as a heathen and a publican. From the use of the word, Church, in this passage, it follows that Christ made the universal Church the highest authority of all. Therefore, even the Pope is subject to a general council which represents the Church. Indeed, the laws made by the Pope must be accepted by the Church before they take effect.[14]

The decree, *Sacrosancta*, issued by the Council of Constance (1414-18) in 1415, is a classical formulation of the conciliar theory:

> This holy synod of Constance, assembled in a lawful manner in the Holy Spirit and being a general council representing the Catholic Church, has authority immediately from Christ and everyone, no matter what his rank or dignity even if he be a Pope, is bound to obey it in matters pertaining to the faith, the extirpation of the present schism and the reformation of the Church in its head and members.[15]

It must be noted that the decree just cited never received papal approbation although Pope Martin V approved the acts of the council in a general way. In another decree, *Frequens*

(1417), the council called for general councils on a regular basis to ensure the good government of the Church.

For the first part of his life, Nicholas of Cusa (1401-64)— cardinal, mathematician and philosopher—supported the conciliar theory. In his book, *De concordantia catholica* (1433-34), he defended the superiority of a general council to the Pope because a general council represents all the faithful. The Pope has only an administrative primacy. A council can depose the Pope if he errs in matters of faith. In his book, *On the Supremacy of General Councils* (1440), he expressed no doubt that the Pope is the "rector" of the universal Church and the ship of Peter; therefore, the validity of fundamental laws depends on him since it is impossible to legislate for a corporation without its head. Nevertheless, the authority of enacting canons depends not on the Pope alone but on common agreement. The Pope can claim no primacy in this respect because all the apostles were equal to Peter.

Nicholas changed his views in 1442 when he abandoned the conciliar theory. He seemed to go to the opposite extreme by asserting that all authority in the Church is derived from the Holy See just as all being is derived from God.[16]

The Council of Florence (1438-45), the 17th ecumenical council, *opposed* the conciliar theory by asserting vigorously the primacy of the Roman Pontiff. The council effected a shortlived union with the Eastern Churches, the Greeks subscribing to this profession of faith:

> We define that the holy apostolic See and the Roman Pontiff have the primacy over the whole world, and that the same Roman Pontiff is the successor of St. Peter, the Prince of the Apostles, and the true vicar of Christ, the head of the whole Church, the father and teacher of all Christians; and that to him, in the person of St. Peter, was given by our Lord Jesus Christ the full power of feeding, ruling and governing the whole Church; as is also contained in the proceedings of the ecumenical councils and in the sacred canons.[17]

In a decree directed to the Jacobites, the council took this position about the necessity of the Church for salvation:

> The holy Roman Church believes, professes, and preaches that no one remaining outside the Catholic Church, not just

pagans, but also Jews or heretics or schismatics, can become partakers of eternal life; but will go to the everlasting fire which was prepared for the devil and his angels (Mt 25: 41), unless before the end of life they are joined to the Church. For union with the body of the Church is of such importance that the sacraments of the Church are helpful to salvation only for those remaining in it; and fasts, alms-giving, other works of piety, and the exercise of Christian warfare bear eternal rewards for them alone. And no one can be saved, no matter how much alms he has given, even if he sheds his blood for the name of Christ, unless he remains in the bosom and the unity of the Catholic Church.[18]

One of those who took part in the discussions with the Greeks at the Council of Florence was John of Torquemada (1384-1468), not to be confused with his nephew, Thomas of Tor-quemada, the inquisitor. John of Torquemada wrote a *Summa de Ecclesia* (1450), the first work dealing *ex professo* with the Church in an integral way. The *Summa* is divided into four books devoted to the Universal Church, the Primacy of the Pope, Gen-eral Councils, and Heretics and Schismatics. In the second book, John attributes the primacy of the Pope to Christ. Christ bestowed the fullness of authority immediately upon Peter whose successor is the Pope. Therefore the Pope is the head of the Church in virtue of a commission stemming from Christ and not from the Church. No power on earth, not even a general council, can in-fringe upon the Pope's position. Even though the Pope is only a part of the Church, he is superior to a general council which represents the whole Church because he is the vicar of Christ, the invisible head of the Church.

According to John of Torquemada, the authority of the Pope does not extend to the revelation of new truths, for the Pope, like Peter, is the minister of Christ. Christ conferred the power of or-ders for the administration of the sacraments immediately upon the apostles (and the bishops, their successors). Christ conferred the power of jurisdiction for the government of the Church im-mediately upon Peter (and the Pope, his successor) and through Peter mediately upon the apostles (and the bishops). John de-fended papal infallibility by appealing to Mt 16:18 and Lk 22:32. The primacy of the Pope necessarily includes infallibility which is also necessary for the unity of the Church. The Pope exercises the charism of infallibility when he speaks *de sede sua.*[19]

A contemporary of Torquemada, Antoninus (1389-1459), archbishop of Florence, also recognized papal infallibility. Infallibility, he noted in his *Summa theologica,* is granted to the teaching office of the Pope through the assistance of the Holy Spirit. In judicial matters, however, the Pope is not infallibile because his decisions rest upon human witnesses who can err.[20] Antoninus qualified his position still further: "Although the Pope as an individual can err..., when he employs a council and seeks the help of the universal Church, he cannot err in accordance with the word of God to Peter: 'I have prayed for you that your faith may not fail.' Nor can it happen that the universal Church should accept as true what is erroneous."[21] The mind of Antoninus about the relationship between papal and conciliar infallibility was a subject of dispute at Vatican I.

The bull, *Exsecrabilis* (1460), of Pius II is particularly noteworthy. It is an explicit and solemn condemnation of the conciliar theory. Before his ordination to the priesthood, Pius II (Aeneas Silvio de' Piccolomini) had vigorously supported the conciliar theory. Subsequently, he changed his mind and supported the idea of papal supremacy. Three years after he issued the bull, *Exsecrabilis,* Pius wrote to the university of Cologne: "Reject Aeneas and support Pius." The important words of the bull are these:

> A detestable abuse—one unheard of in ancient times—has come to pass in our times. It is this: some individuals, imbued with the spirit of rebellion and not with a desire for a more balanced judgment, presume to appeal to a future general council over the head of the Roman Pontiff, the vicar of Jesus Christ, to whom Christ said in the person of St. Peter: 'Feed my sheep' and 'Whatever you bind on earth will be bound in heaven...' Wishing therefore to remove this pestilent venom from Christ's Church..., we condemn such appeals and reprobate them as erroneous and detestable.[22]

The German theologian, Gabriel Biel (1425-1495), of the university of Tübingen, was one of the last to sustain the conciliar theory. While Christ is the primary foundation of the Church,

Peter was a secondary foundation resting upon Christ. The Church does not have two heads, for the Pope is only the vicar of Christ. As a *viator,* the Pope cannot only sin but also err. Nevertheless, the primacy of the Pope means that he has the fullness of power whence stems directly or indirectly the spiritual power of bishops and priests. The Pope has the prerogative of confirming conciliar decisions. Simultaneously, Biel held that a council is the highest tribunal on earth where the faith is concerned. It has authority even over the Pope. What then is the relationship between papal and conciliar authority? For Biel the question was somewhat academic. At the end of the 15th century conciliarism was no longer a particularly live issue. Biel did not regard the Pope and a general council as rivals; both represented the authority of the Church; and in his opinion it was normal for both to cooperate; nonetheless, in case of a conflict, the council stands above the Pope in Biel's judgment.[23]

Cardinal Thomas de Vio (1468-1534), commonly known as Cajetan, was a staunch defender of papal supremacy. He wrote two works explicitly dealing with the papal-conciliar relationship: *De comparatione auctoritatis Papae et Concilii* (1511) and *Apologia de comparata auctoritate Papae et Concilii* (1512). Both works were reprinted under the direction of V. Pollet (Rome, 1936) and the references are taken from this edition. For Cajetan, a council represents the Church which is a body with a head. The head of the council, the Pope, represents Christ, the head of the Church, and the body of the council represents the body of the Church. Cajetan rejected the application of the principle that the whole is greater than any of its parts to the papal-conciliar relationship: although the Pope is a part of the universal Church *quoad personam et merita,* nevertheless the total power of the Church resides in the Pope as the vicar of Christ, and all others merely participate in this power.[24] Christ established the Church as a monarchy by making Peter the one head of the whole body of the Church. From this one head all ministers of the Church ordinarily derive the power of jurisdiction and orders.[25] Evidently, Cajetan applied to Peter and his successors, the Popes, the scholastic teaching about the relationship of Christ the head, to His body, the Church.

Cajetan was prepared to admit that the Pope could err in faith as a private individual; but he defended papal infallibility as a corollary of papal supremacy in an infallible Church. He argued thus: the Church as a whole cannot err in faith in virtue of the promise of Christ to abide with His Church until the end (Mt 28:20). Therefore, the Pope must be infallible when he defines matters of faith. Since the members of the Church are bound to accept the definitions of the Pope, the whole Church would be led into error if the Pope could err in these matters.[26]

Cajetan granted to a council the right to provide for the election of a new Pope when the Pope had been deposed for heresy or when the Pope had been doubtfully elected.[27] Cajetan was one of the early forerunners of Vatican I.

Finally, the Fifth Lateran Council (1512-17), the 18th ecumenical council, solemnly defined the relationship of the Pope to a general council. The occasion was the rejection of the so-called Pragmatic Sanction of Bourges by the Lateran Council. The Sanction was a document adopted by the French clergy at Bourges in 1438. The document was imbued with the spirit of conciliarism. In rejecting the Sanction, the Lateran Council adopted the bull, *Pastor aeternus,* of Leo X which said in part:

> We believe we cannot and must not be held back or desist in good conscience from revoking such an evil Sanction and the contents thereof. We must not be influenced by the fact that the Sanction itself and the contents which emanated from the Council of Basle were received and accepted by the assembly at Bourges at the urging of the council, for all these things happened at Basle after Eugene IV had transferred the council [to Ferrara in 1437]; hence, they had no validity. This is so because it is clear from Sacred Scripture, the Fathers, the Roman Pontiffs, the sacred canons, and councils that only the Roman Pontiff, having authority over all councils, has full authority and power to convoke, transfer and conclude councils.[28]

THE CARDINALS

As early as the 8th century, certain members of the Roman clergy who took part in liturgical functions of the great basilicas were called cardinals. Eventually the cardinals became a standing body of the Pope's most intimate counsellors. In 1059 Pope Nicholas II reserved the election of the Pope to the cardinals. Shortly thereafter one hears of "consistories" in which the Pope and cardinals met *collegialiter* to conduct important church business. Often enough the cardinals affixed their signature to papal decrees. In this way the cardinals exercised much greater power than they have today. This situation prompted a number of questions in the minds of contemporary theologians and canon lawyers: to what degree did the cardinals share the authority of the Pope? Was the college of cardinals the head of the Church when the Holy See was vacant? Was the college of cardinals able to act in opposition to the Pope? Did the college have the right to summon a general council?

A variety of answers were given to these questions from the 11th to the 14th century. Some, of course, regarded the cardinals simply as advisers and agents of the Pope incapable of acting independently of him. Ockham, for example, described the cardinals as a purely human institution, the college of bishops being superior to the college of cardinals. Those who accepted and justified what some called the "divine right" of cardinals to assist the Pope in the government of the Church appealed to the fact that they had elected him, that he needed their counsel, that the cardinals inherited the role of the apostolic college gathered around Peter prior to its dispersion. Generally these supporters of the cardinals regarded the college of cardinals as superior to the college of bishops.[29]

During the centuries under consideration the college of cardinals exercised the responsibility of the college of bishops, namely, the *sollicitudo omnium ecclesiarum* or concern for all Churches. The Second Vatican Council reaffirmed the responsibility of the bishop not only to his own Church but to other Churches as well.

NOTES TO CHAPTER V

1. *CT* no. 154.
2. *Ibid.*
3. Ed. R. Scholz (Weimar, 1929).
4. Cf. H. Arquillière, *DTC* 8: 1, 307-8.
5. Cf. J. Rivière, *DTC* 15: 2, 1855-60.
6. Ed. J. Leclercq (Paris, 1942). Cf. B. Tierney, *Foundation of the Conciliar Theory* (Cambridge, 1942), 157-178.
7. Tr. A. Gewirth (New York, 1956).
8. Cf. E. Amann, *DTC* 11:1, 864-876; E. Moody, *EP* 8, 306-317; Y. Congar, *L'Eglise* (Paris, 1970) 290-295; B. Tierney, *Origins of Papal Infallibility* (Leiden, 1972) 205-237.
9. Cf. L. Cristiani *DTC* 15:2, 3594-3600; A. Harnack *HD* 6 & 7, 141-149; Congar, *op. cit.,* 299-302.
10. Cf. G. Mollat, *NCE* 4, 188; B. Tierney, *Foundations of the Conciliar Theory* (Cambridge, 1955) *passim;* G. Alberigo, *Cardinalato e Collegialitá* (Firenze, 1969) 178-181; W. Ullmann, *The Origins of the Great Schism* (London, 1948) 176-181.
11. Cf. G. Alberigo, *o.c.* 180-181; W. Ullmann, *o.c.* 181-182; E. Jacob, *Essays in the Conciliar Epoch* (Notre Dame, 1963) *passim.*
12. Cf. Hefele-Leclercg, *HC* 7, 46-48, for the decree of deposition.
13. Cf. L. Salembier *DTC* 1:1, 647-650; J. Schwane *DGS* 3, 557-559; E. Jacob, *o.c.* 14-15.
14. Cf. L. Salembier, *DTC* 6:1, 1318-22; J. Schwane, *DGS* 3, 559-561; E. Jacob, *o.c.* 11-14.
15. DS 1151, introd.
16. Cf. F. Copleston, *A History of Philosophy* (Westminster, 1953) 3, 231-234; E. Jacob, *o.c.* 16-18; J. Schwane, *DGS* 3, 565-566.
17. *CT* 164.
18. *CT* 165.
19. Cf. J. Schwane, *DGS* 3, 567-575; A. Michel, *DTC* 15:1, 1235-39; W. Maguire, *John of Torquemada, The Antiquity of the Church* (Washington, 1957).
20. Cf. J. Schwane, *DGS* 3,575; P. Mandonnet, *DTC* 1:2, 1450-54.
21. *Summa* 3, 22, 3, 1.
22. DS 1375.
23. Cf. H. Oberman, *The Harvest of Medieval Theology* (Cambridge, 1963) 412-419.
24. *Apol.* c. 12, no. 721.
25. *De comp.* c. 9, no. 137.
26. *In summ.* 2-2, 1, 10.
27. *De comp.* c. 14, nos. 230-231.
28. DS 1445.
29. Cf. B. Tierney, *o.c.* 68-84, 206-212; G. Alberigo, *o.c.*

VI. THE REFORMATION AND COUNTER-REFORMATION

THE REVOLT OF THE PROTESTANTS

THE CATHOLIC REVIVAL

The Dominican, Savonarola, had predicted the approaching chastisement and renewal of the Church. For his outspokenness and other reasons too he paid with his life (1498). Nevertheless, the words of the prophet were soon verified. In 1517 Martin Luther (1483-1546) began to teach his doctrine that sinners are justified by faith; that is, men are saved by confidence in the sufficiency of Christ's death on Calvary to reconcile men with God. Luther quickly won many followers, several factors favoring his cause: the doctrine of justification by faith, Luther's talent as a preacher and writer, the corruption of Catholic life, and the favor of powerful German princes. Pope Leo X condemned propositions drawn from Luther's teaching in the bull *Exsurge Domine* (1520). The result was the disruption of religious unity in Germany leading sometimes to armed conflicts between Catholics and Protestants. In 1555 a kind of peace was achieved at Augsburg, Germany. The people were enjoined to follow the religion of the prince in whose territory they lived. Dissenters were given the right to emigrate.

The Protestant revolt spread into Switzerland. Ulrich Zwingli (1484-1531), encouraged by the example and writings of Luther, established the new movement at Zurich. John Calvin (1509-64), a French Lutheran known for his doctrine of predestination, became the virtual ruler of Geneva. He founded a college in Geneva for the training of Protestant ministers. These ministers won many converts to Calvinism which eventually supplanted Zwinglianism in Switzerland.

The Scandinavian countries accepted Lutheranism in the same century (the 16th).

At first, Protestantism made no headway in England. The king himself, Henry VIII (1509-47), had written a book against Luther called *The Defence of the Seven Sacraments.* For this book Pope Leo X gave Henry the title of Defender of the Faith. However Henry wished to divorce his wife, Catherine of Aragon, and marry Ann Boleyn. In order to thwart papal opposition to the divorce, Henry cut himself loose from Rome. By the Act of Supremacy of 1534, the English parliament proclaimed the king head of the English Church. The saints, John Fisher and Thomas More, were beheaded in 1535 for their refusal to accept the new state of affairs. Lutheran and Calvinist ideas gained a hold under Henry's successor, Edward VI (1547-53). The break between the Church of England and Rome was finalized under Henry's daughter, Elizabeth (1558-1603), who published the Thirty-nine Articles of Religion. These Articles defined the position of the Church of England at that time.

John Knox was instrumental in establishing the Reformation in Scotland. It took the form of Calvinism with a presbyterian form of government. In France, Protestantism gained some adherents who came to be called Huguenots. On occasions Catholics and Huguenots went to war with each other. However, the religious question was settled by the Edict of Nantes (1598) which granted freedom of conscience and worship to both parties. Louis XIV revoked the Edict of Nantes in 1685 and made Catholicism the religion of the land. As a result, thousands of Huguenots migrated to other countries. In the Netherlands, the progress of Protestantism was furthered by political discontent with the rule of Catholic Spain. Eventually Calvinism was made the religion of the State and a condition for holding public office. Catholics retained the right of private worship.

The other countries of western Europe—Ireland, Spain, and Italy remained Catholic.

An important element of the Catholic response to the Protestant Reformation was the Council of Trent (1545-1563), the 19th ecumenical council. The council was concerned with the doctrinal questions raised by the Protestants and the reform of the Church. The council met for the first time between 1545 and 1549 under Pope Paul III. It published decrees on Scripture, tradition, original sin, justification, the sacraments in general, and baptism and confirmation in particular. At the same time, the council issued regulations for preachers, bishops and clerics.

The council met for the second time between 1551 and 1552 under Pope Julius III. In less than a year, the council issued decrees on the Holy Eucharist, penance, and extreme unction and a series of reform decrees. The council met for the third and last time from 1562 to 1563 under Pope Paul IV. It dealt with communion under both species, the sacrifice of the Mass, orders, marriage, purgatory, the invocation of the saints, relics and images, and indulgences. It passed laws regarding the preaching of indulgences, episcopal residence and consecration, the erection of seminaries, the holding of synods on a regular basis, and the visitation of ecclesiastical institutions. The effect of the council was to clarify the Church's teaching on doctrinal questions raised by the reformers, remove the worst scandals, and create a spirit of greater unity and confidence among Catholics.

Another important element of the Catholic revival of the 16th century was the establishment of new religious orders. The Theatines (founded in 1524) and the Barnabites (founded in 1532) labored in Italy. The Capuchins originated in 1528 and dedicated themselves to a strict observance of the rule of St. Francis. They provided the Popes with effective preachers who labored among the masses of Italy, France and Germany. St. Teresa of Avila (1515-1582) and St. John of the Cross (1542-1591) were responsible for a revival within the Carmelite order. The most famous and important of all the new orders, however, was the Society of Jesus, the Jesuits. Founded by the Spaniard, Ignatius of Loyola, the Society was formally approved by Pope Paul III in 1540. The Jesuits demanded of their members a long training including a superb education. They bound themselves to a kind of military discipline recognizing the will of God in the will of their superiors. They engaged in preaching, the education of youth, missionary activity, and any task imposed on them by the Holy See. The Society was an immensely effective instrument of the Counter-Reformation. Among its first and greatest saints were the founder, Ignatius, author of the *Spiritual Exercises;* Francis Xavier, the missionary; Peter Canisius, the apostle of Germany after Boniface; and Robert Bellarmine, the most influential Catholic theologian of the period.

While whole nations renounced their allegiance to the Catholic Church in Europe, the Church gained millions of converts elsewhere. The discoveries of the Spaniards and Portuguese in the East and the West aroused the Church to a burst of missionary activity. The missionaries, especially Jesuits and Capuchins, were most successful on the recently discovered continents of America. South America, Cuba, Mexico, California, and parts of Canada accepted the Catholic faith. Missions were also sent to India, Japan and China but with less success.

With the Treaties of Westphalia (1648), the Thirty Years War came to an end. The war had involved the Germans, French and Swedes. It was fought for religious and ultimately political considerations. The Treaties of Westphalia were made without respect to the wishes of the Pope even though the rights of the Church were at stake. The Church had ceased to be a force in the public life of Europe.

The student of European history will recall the momentous change in the political and social life of the continent somewhat before and during this period. The voyages of Columbus to America, Vasco da Gama to India (1497-98), and Magellan around the world (1519-22) stimulated trade and the spread of European civilization. A new middle class emerged, dwelling in the cities and engaged in the production of goods and trade. This development and the use of gunpowder in firearms led to the final dissolution of feudal society which was tied to the land. The invention of printing by Gutenberg (ca. 1439-54) was the greatest single medium for the spread of knowledge among

mankind after the 15th century. Copernicus (1473-1543) established the fact that the earth and planets revolve around the
sun, and that the earth rotates daily on its axis (1543). The
Copernicon theory supplanted the Ptolemaic system which
placed the earth at the fixed center of the universe. Galileo
(1564-1642) conducted experiments with gravity and made
several important astronomical discoveries with the newly in-
vented telescope. The Renaissance, now at its height, gained
new energy by the flight of Greek savants from Constantinople
to the West after the city had been captured by the Turks in
1453. The colonization of North America by European settlers
was just beginning. The Spanish made their first settlement at
St. Augustine in Florida in 1565; the English, at Jamestown,
Virginia, in 1607; the French, at Quebec in 1608 and even earlier
at other sites.

THE CATHOLIC FAITH

At the beginning of the 16th century, the Catholic faith
was accepted by all in western Europe as the religion of
Christ. What Catholics believed or at least what they were
supposed to believe is known to us from an abundance of contemporary literature—learned Latin treatises composed by the
theologians connected with the universities of Italy, Spain,
France, England and Germany together with popular explana-
tions of the faith written in the vernacular for the benefit of
the layman. This literature presents a unified picture of the
Catholic faith.[1]

God created all things including man, the crown of visible
creation by reason of his spiritual and immortal soul. However,
Adam, the parent of the human race, rebelled against his
Maker. The result of his rebellion was a state of hostility between God and the sons of Adam. In His mercy, God sent His
only Son into the world to become man. By his sacrificial death
on Calvary, the incarnate Son of God made salvation available
to sinful men once more. What Adam had broken down, Christ
had repaired.

The Church of Christ is the instrument by which men are

associated with the saving death of Christ. The preaching of
the Church's ministers arouses the sinner to belief and repentance. The symbolic act of washing, baptism, has the effect
of cleansing the sinner and initiating him into the Church. The
Church is a mysterious unity, a body whose head is Christ.
The members of the Church participate in the life of Christ.
To be separated willfully from the Church is to be separated
from Christ. The ritual meal, the Holy Eucharist, serves to
cement the union between Christ and the faithful.

The faith of the Church is regarded as indefectible; that is,
what the whole Church believes to be the teaching of Christ
is, as a matter of fact, the teaching of Christ.

Good order within the local Church is the responsibility
of the bishop. It is he who preaches with authority to command
acceptance. It is he who presides over the liturgical celebrations.
It is he who governs the local community of believers. Union
with the bishop, recognition of his office, is a clear sign of
union with the Church.

There is one bishop, however, who decides with authority,
not only for his local flock, but also for others. He is the bishop
of Rome. His authority rests upon an act of Christ. Christ
founded the Church upon Peter, the prince of the apostles.
The bishop of Rome is the successor of Peter in his capacity as
the visible head of the Church.

MARTIN LUTHER

To the Roman Catholic conception of the Church Luther
opposed his own. In his *Brief Explanation of the Ten Commandments, the Creed, and the Lord's Prayer,* he explained the
article of the creed dealing with the Church in this way:

> I believe in. . .a Holy Christian Church, a communion of
> saints, a forgiveness of sins.
> This means—
> I believe that there is on earth, through the whole wide
> world, no more than one holy, common, Christian Church,
> which is nothing else than the congregation, or assembly
> of the saints, i.e., the pious, believing men on earth, which
> is gathered, preserved, and ruled by the Holy Ghost, and

daily increased by means of the sacraments and the Word of God.

I believe that no one can be saved who is not found in this congregation, holding with it to one faith, word, sacraments, hope and love, and that no Jew, heretic, heathen or sinner can be saved along with it, unless he become reconciled to it, united with it and conformed to it in all things.

I believe that in this congregation, or Church, all things are common, that everyone's possessions belong to the others and no one has anything of his own; therefore, all the prayers and good works of the whole congregation must help, assist and strengthen me and every believer at all times, in life and death, and thus each bear the other's burden, as St. Paul teaches.

I believe that in this congregation, and nowhere else, there is forgiveness of sins; that outside of it, good works, however great they may be or many, are of no avail for the forgiveness of sins; but that within it, no matter how much, how greatly or how often men may sin, nothing can hinder forgiveness of sins, which abides wherever and as long as this one congregation abides. To this congregation Christ gives the keys, and says, in Matthew xviii, 'Whatever ye shall bind on earth shall be bound in heaven.' In like manner He says, in Matthew xvi, to the one man Peter, who stands as the representative of the one and only Church, 'Whatever thou shalt loose on earth shall be loosed in heaven.'[2]

For Luther, then, the Church is an assembly of holy people, a congregation of believers on earth, a community of those who have been saved by faith. Participation in this community involves a sharing of goods and burdens. The goods of Christ and my fellow-believers are mine; my sins, burdens and troubles are theirs. The righteousness of Christ atones for my sins; the faith and prayer of the Christian community help me in my own weakness. My assistance to others means (in an ascending order of importance) the sacrifice of my temporal goods, physical service, teaching, consolation, intercession, and bearing with the weakness of my brother.

The Church or congregation of believers is one because of its faith. It is catholic in a temporal sense because it includes all the just from the time of Adam until the end of the world. It is holy because it has been redeemed by Christ; it "is gathered, preserved and ruled by the Holy Spirit;" and it possesses the sacraments and the word of God. The Church is apostolic because it lives by the apostolic gospel.

Outside the Church there is no salvation. Within the Church there is the forgiveness of sins. It is sufficient to confess one's sins to God to obtain the forgiveness of sins. Nevertheless, one may confess his sins privately to his brother in order to hear a word of comfort from him. It is a brotherly service to share the burden of sin by hearing the confession of another, to say to a sinner: "Take heart, your sins are forgiven." In this way, the whole community shares in the power to bind and loose (Mt 16:19; 18:18).

A passage from Luther's work on *The Papacy at Rome* explains his conception of the Church as an invisible and visible reality:

> For the sake of brevity and a better understanding, we shall call the two churches by different names. The first, which is the natural, essential, real and true one, let us call a spiritual, inner Christendom. The other, which is man-made and external, let us call a bodily, external Christendom: not as if we would part them asunder, but just as when I speak of a man, and call him, according to the soul, a spiritual, according to the body, a physical, man; or as the Apostle is wont to speak of the inner and outward man. Thus also the Christian assembly, according to the soul, is a communion of one accord in one faith, although according to the body it cannot be assembled at one place, and yet every group is assembled in its own place. This Christendom is ruled by Canon Law and the prelates of the Church. To this belong all the popes, cardinals, bishops, prelates, monks, nuns and all those who in these external things are taken to be Christians, whether they are truly Christians at heart or not. For though membership in this communion does not make true Christians, because all the orders mentioned may exist without faith; nevertheless this communion is never without some who at the same time are true Christians, just as the body does not give the soul its life, and yet the soul lives in the body and, indeed, can live without the body. Those who are without faith and are outside of

the first community, but are included in this second. community, are dead in sight of God, hypocrites, and but like wooden images of true Christians.[3]

For Luther, therefore, the Church is primarily and even essentially invisible because it is the congregation of believers. Believers are those who have been justified by faith. Faith is, in itself, a purely interior act or quality. Where faith is, there is the Church. The Church thus understood is no more visible than the faith which makes one a member of it. However, the Church is not entirely invisible; it has a visible side and can be recognized by external marks:

"The external marks whereby one can perceive where this Church is on earth, are baptism, the Sacraments, and the Gospel" (*The Papacy at Rome*).[4]

According to Luther, faith is the response to the preaching of the Gospel. One who has accepted the preaching of the Gospel in faith submits to baptism in accordance with the command of Jesus (Mt 28:19; Mk 16:16). The believer takes part in the Lord's Supper which is the sacrament of the Church's unity. The preaching of the Gospel, baptism and the Lord's Supper are external events. They are points where the invisible and visible aspects of the Church meet. They are the marks or signs of the Church on earth.

Luther maintained that all the baptized have the same power with respect to the word and the sacraments. All are priests for this reason. However no one may make use of this power without the consent of the community or the call of a superior. Luther put the matter in this way:

Let every one, therefore, who knows himself to be a Christian be assured of this, and apply it to himself,—that we are all priests, and there is no difference between us; that is to say, we have the same power in respect to the Word and all the sacraments. However, no one may make use of this power except by the consent of the community or by the call of a superior. For what is the common property of all, no individual may arrogate to himself, unless he be called ... The priesthood is properly nothing but the ministry of the Word, mark you, of the Word—not of the law, but of the Gospel (*The Babylonian Captivity of the Church*).[5]

Hence, the public ministry of the word is an office and function undertaken at the behest of the community. One administers this office as the representative of the community.

It seems to follow from Luther's conception of the Church that Church organization, while necessary for the sake of order, has not been divinely fixed but depends upon the decisions of local congregations. Moreover, visible unity among these congregations, even though it may be desirable, is not absolutely demanded by the nature of the Church.

It was Philip Melanchton (1497-1560), a younger colleague, who gave systematic expression to Luther's teachings. He did so in his *Loci communes rerum theologicarum*[6] which was revised by him several times between 1521 and 1555. For Melanchton as for Luther, the Church is the assembly of those embracing the gospel of Christ and rightly using the sacraments. Through these God regenerates many unto eternal life, although in this assembly there are many unregenerated who nonetheless assent to the true doctrine.[7]

Melanchton was also the principal and final author of the Augsburg Confession of 1530 and 1540, the earliest and principal confession of Lutheranism. The 7th and 8th articles of this confession are concerned with the Church. Once more the Church is defined as the "congregation of saints in which the gospel is rightly taught and the sacraments rightly administered... Yet seeing that in this life many hypocrites and evil persons are mingled with it, it is lawful to use the sacraments administered by evil men...; and the sacraments and the word are effective by reason of the institution and commandment of Christ though they be delivered by evil men."[8] This creed reflects the belief of Melanchton that there always has been and always will be a true visible Church despite the presence of wicked men and hypocrites in its midst.

JOHN CALVIN

John Calvin (1509-64) was a younger contemporary of Luther and deeply indebted to him for his theological ideas.

Calvin is widely known for his doctrine of predestination.

> Predestination we call the eternal decree of God by which
> He has determined with Himself what He would have to
> become of every man. For they are not all created with a
> similar destiny; but eternal life is foreordained for some,
> and eternal damnation for others. Every man, therefore,
> being formed for one or the other of these ends, we say
> he is predestined either to life or to death.[9]

For Calvin, the members of the Church were those predestined to eternal life. Predestination, however, is a matter
known only to God. Hence, the Church is invisible to us and
known to God alone. Nevertheless, "by a judgement of charity"
we regard as members of the Church those who by confession,
example, and participation in the sacraments profess God and
Christ. Calvin stated the matter in this way:

> The word *Church* is used in the sacred Scriptures in two
> senses. Sometimes, when they mention the Church, they
> intend that which is really such in the sight of God, into
> which none are received but those who by adoption and
> grace are the children of God, and by the sanctification
> of the Spirit are the true members of Christ. And then it
> comprehends not only the saints at any one time resident
> on earth, but all the elect who have lived from the be-
> ginning of the world. But the word *Church* is frequently
> used in the Scriptures to designate the whole multitude,
> dispersed over the world, who profess to worship the one
> God and Jesus Christ, who are initiated into his faith by
> baptism, who testify their unity in true doctrine and
> charity by a participation of the sacred supper, who con-
> sent to the word of the Lord, and preserve the ministry
> which Christ has instituted for the purpose of preaching
> it... As it is necessary, therefore, to believe that Church,
> which is invisible to us, and known to God alone, so this
> Church, which is visible to men, we are commanded to
> honor, and to maintain communion with it... We ought to
> acknowledge [by a judgment of charity] as members
> of the Church all those who by a confession of faith, an
> exemplary life, and a participation of the sacraments,
> profess the same God and Christ with ourselves. But the
> knowledge of the body itself being more necessary to our
> salvation, he has distinguished it by more clear and certain
> characters.

Hence, the visible Church rises conspicuous to our view. For wherever we find the word of God purely preached and heard, and the sacraments administered according to the institution of Christ, there, it is not to be doubted, is a Church of God; for his promise can never deceive— 'where two or three are gathered together in my name, there I am in the midst of them.'[10]

The visible Church of which Calvin spoke comprises those who profess God and Christ. It is marked by the preaching of the gospel and the administration of the sacraments according to the institution of Christ. The visible Church is aptly described as the communion of saints which means that "whatever benefits God confers upon the saints, they should mutually communicate to each other."[11] The visible Church is our mother "since there is no other way into life unless we are conceived by her, born of her, nourished at her breast, and continually preserved under her care and government till we are divested of this mortal flesh."[12]

One who withdraws from a Church which preserves the true ministry of the word and sacraments is a traitor and apostate from religion. The true ministry of the word means fidelity to such essential principles as, There is one God, Christ is God and the Son of God, Our salvation depends upon the mercy of God, and the like.[13]

The members of the Church are said to be holy, not as if they are without blemish, but because they aspire to holiness, and the goodness of God attributes to them that sanctity which they have not yet fully attained. The power of the keys was given to the Church to be continually exercised for the forgiveness of sins. Sins are continually remitted to us by the ministry of the Church when the presbyters or bishops, to whom this office is committed, confirm pious consciences by the promises of the gospel, in the hope of pardon and remission.[14]

For the government of His Church, the Lord uses the ministry of men whom He employs as His delegates. Those who preside over the government of the Church are the pastors and teachers. "Teachers have no official concern with the discipline, or the administration of the sacraments, or with admonitions and exhortations, but only with the interpretation of the Scripture, that pure and sound doctrine may be retained among the believers; whereas the pastoral office includes all these things."[15] In order that anyone be accounted a true minister of the Church, it is necessary, in the first place, that he be called to it, and, in the second place, that he answer his call.

The ministers of the Church have no other office than to teach what is revealed and recorded in the Scripture. If, however, the preaching of doctrine is to be effective, it must be accompanied by private admonitions, reproofs and other means of enforcement. The maintenance of discipline in the Church is an exercise of the power of keys and spiritual jurisdiction.[16]

Connected with the preaching of the gospel as a support to our faith is the administration of the sacraments. There are two of them. Baptism is a kind of entrance into the Church and an initiatory profession of faith. It is never repeated. The Lord's supper is a continual nourishment with which Christ spiritually feeds his family of believers. The supper is frequently distributed, that those who have once been admitted into the Church, may understand that they are continually nourished by Christ. The use of these two sacraments has been enjoined on the Christian Church from the commencement of the New Testament until the end of time. Besides these two sacraments no other sacraments have been instituted by God and no others ought to be acknowledged by the Church of believers.[17]

Two other fathers of Reformed Protestantism—Swiss and French Protestantism—must be mentioned. One is Ulrich Zwingli (1484-1531), the reformer of Zurich who was killed in a battle between Catholics and reformers. For Zwingli, Christ alone is the foundation of the Church which is the congregation of all those who are founded and built up in one faith upon the Lord Jesus Christ. This Church as the communion of saints is invisible and it is scattered throughout the world. That is the true Church which clings to the word of God and follows only the shepherds who bring that word. Later Zwingli modified his view of the Church so that it became the totality of the predestined. The separate congregations are the visible Church in which the

invisible or predestined Church is contained. There is no necessary connection between the two Churches.[18]

Martin Bucer (1491-1551) was the leader of the Reformed
community in Strasburg and a link between Lutheranism, Calvinism and Anglicanism, having influential contacts with members of all these groups. Bucer spoke of the kingdom of Christ
in which the Lord gathers His elect to Himself and incorporates
them in Himself and His Church so that, freed from their sins,
they may live well and blessedly. The elect allow themselves to
be guided and governed by the ministry regularly constituted.
The true Church is characterized by fidelity to Scripture in
teaching and administering the sacraments, discipline and care
of the poor.[19]

HENRY VIII AND ELIZABETH

The king of England, Henry VIII, wished to put aside his
wife, Catherine of Aragon, and marry another, Ann Boleyn. In
order to frustrate papal opposition to the divorce, Henry repudiated the authority of the Pope in England. By the Act of
Supremacy of 1534, the English parliament recognized the king
rather than the Pope as the head of Christ's Church in England.
The text of the Act is this:

> Albeit the King's majesty justly and rightly is and ought to
> be the supreme head of the church of England, and so is
> recognized by the clergy of this realm in their convocations;
> yet nevertheless, for corroboration and confirmation there-
> of, and for increase of virtue in Christ's religion within
> this realm of England, and to repress and extirp all errors,
> heresies, and other enormities and abuses heretofore used
> in the same: be it enacted by the authority of this present
> parliament, that the king our sovereign lord, his heirs and
> successors, kings of this realm, shall be taken, accepted
> and reputed the only supreme head on earth of the Church
> of England, called 'Anglicana Ecclesia,' and shall have
> and enjoy, annexed and united to the imperial crown of this
> realm, as well the title and style thereof, as all honors,
> dignities, pre-eminences, jurisdictions, privileges, authori-
> ties, immunities, profits and commodities to the said digni-
> ty of supreme head of the same church belonging and
> appertaining. And that our said sovereign lord, his heirs

and successors, kings of this realm, shall have full power and authority from time to time, to visit, repress, redress, reform, order, correct, restrain, and amend all such errors, abuses, offences, contempts, and enormities, whatsoever they be, which by any manner of spiritual authority or jurisdiction ought or may lawfully be reformed, repressed, ordered, redressed, corrected, restrained, or amended most to the pleasure of Almighty God, the increase of virtue in Christ's religion, and for the conservation of the peace, unity, and tranquillity of this realm: any usage, custom, foreign laws, foreign authority, prescription, or any things to the contrary hereof, notwithstanding.

From 1534 to 1547, the year of Henry's death, there were imposed, under Henry's authority, a number of official statements about what Christians ought to accept as the teaching of Christ: the Ten Articles of 1536, the Bishops' Book of 1537, the Six Articles of 1539, and the King's Book of 1543.

Under Henry's successor, the First Prayer Book of King Edward VI appeared in 1549. A single volume, the Prayer Book presented the ancient rites of the Church in English with, however, substantial revisions. The Prayer Book was intended to supplant all other books in the public worship of the English Church. The Second Prayer Book of King Edward VI, a revision of the first one, appeared in 1552. The archbishop of Canterbury, Thomas Cranmer (1489-1556), was, with others, the author of these Prayer Books.

In 1553, Cranmer drew up the Forty-two Articles of Religion which were sanctioned by Edward VI shortly before his death. These Forty-two Articles became, with some important changes, the Thirty-nine Articles of Religion still printed in the Book of Common Prayer. The Thirty-nine Articles were drawn up by the English bishops in 1562 and received the approbation of the queen, Elizabeth (d. 1603), in 1571. The nineteenth article gave a definition of the Church:

XIX. OF THE CHURCH

The visible Church of Christ is a congregation of faithful men, in the which the pure Word of God is preached, and the Sacraments be duly administered according to Christ's ordinance, in all those things that of necessity are requisite to the same.

As the Church of Jerusalem, Alexandria, and Antioch, have erred; so also the Church of Rome hath erred, not only in their living and manner of Ceremonies, but also in matters of Faith.

This definition of the Church could be understood in the Catholic tradition to mean that acceptance or rejection by the Church is the test of Christian doctrine and due administration of the sacraments. The definition can also be understood in the Protestant tradition to mean that the doctrine which a Church teaches and the sacraments which it administers are the touchstone of its legitimacy.

Other articles dealt with the authority of the Church, its sacraments and traditions:

XX. OF THE AUTHORITY OF THE CHURCH

The Church hath power to decree Rites or Ceremonies, and authority in Controversies of Faith: and yet it is not lawful for the Church to ordain anything that is contrary to God's Word written, neither may it so expound one place of Scripture, that it be repugnant to another. Wherefore, although the Church be a witness and a keeper of Holy Writ, yet, as it ought not to decree anything against the same, so besides the same ought it not to enforce any thing to be believed for necessity of salvation.

XXV. OF THE SACRAMENTS

Sacraments ordained of Christ be not only badges or tokens of Christian men's profession, but rather they be sure witnesses, and effectual signs of grace, and God's good will towards us, by the which he doth work invisibly in us, and doth not only quicken, but also strengthen and confirm our Faith in him.
There are two Sacraments ordained of Christ our Lord in the Gospel, that is to say, Baptism, and the Supper of the Lord...

XXXIV. OF THE TRADITION OF THE CHURCH

It is not necessary that Traditions and Ceremonies be in all places one, or utterly like... Whosoever, through his private judgement, willingly and purposely, doth openly break the Traditions and Ceremonies of the Church, which be not repugnant to the Word of God, and be ordained and approved by common authority, ought to be rebuked openly...

Every particular or national Church hath authority to ordain, change, and abolish, Ceremonies or Rites of the Church ordained only by man's authority, so that all things be done to edifying.

Despite the Articles, religious controversy continued in the English Church. The Puritans, a name applied to English Protestants after 1563, desired to reform or "purify" the Anglican Church. They hoped to impose their Calvinist views on the English nation through the established Church. They rejected the episcopacy of Anglicanism. The episcopacy, they maintained, is not of divine institution but only the creation of the Church. Elizabethan divines (that is, clergymen, theologians) of the Anglican Church, such as Richard Bancroft, Hadrian Saravia and Richard Hooker, defended the divine origin of the episcopacy. Hooker (1554-1600), in his great work, *The Laws of Ecclesiastical Polity*, was the first to present Anglicanism as a *via media*, a middle ground, which preserved traditional Christianity in contrast to (what he regarded as) the errors of the Puritans on the one hand and Roman Catholics on the other.

The Caroline (Anglican) divines of the first half of the 17th century stressed the need for conformity with the teaching, institutions and customs of the undivided Church of the first few centuries. They interpreted the Scriptures in the light of the Church Fathers. There was a strong tendency among them to admit the inerrancy of the universal Church which is formed of all the Churches which have preserved apostolic doctrine through apostolic (episcopal) succession. Eminent among the divines of this period was William Laud, archbishop of Canterbury from 1633 to 1645 when he was executed by the Puritans for treason.

From 1640 to 1649 there were religious and civil disorders in England. Anglican churches were desecrated; a number of bishops were imprisoned by the parliament; Laud was executed; the *Book of Common Prayer* was suppressed; Charles I was beheaded (1649). A commonwealth was declared the same year. England was ruled as a protectorate by the Puritan, Oliver Cromwell, and his son, Richard, from 1653 to 1659.

Anglicanism barely survived; but with the restoration of Charles II (1660-85) to the throne came the restoration of the Anglican Church.

The second half of the 17th century was marked by a vigorous attack of Anglican theologians on Calvinist theology. The Cambridge Platonists—Anglican clergymen associated with the university of Cambridge and under the influence of Plato— attacked (what they regarded as) the Calvinist denigration of human nature and human reason. The Platonists emphasized the compatibility of faith and reason and the ethical and practical character of religion. They came to be known as "Latitudinarians" because they took a tolerant and "broad" view of dogmatic differences. They considered these differences to be a matter of secondary importance: the essence of Christianity was to be found in a moral life. The Latitudinarians came to be the most influential party in Anglican theology of the period. From them is derived, at least partially, that spirit of openness that characterizes Anglicanism even today.

The Reformation, then, questioned everything including the nature of the Church and its authority. The continental Reformers emphasized the invisibility of the Church, for they conceived the Church of Christ to be the body of true believers. These, however, are known to God alone; hence, the Church is essentially invisible. As for man's relationship to God, only the authority of God and conscience can govern this relationship. Ecclesiastical authority has no bearing upon it. Ecclesiastical authority is necessary, but only for the good order of the community.

THE COUNCIL OF TRENT

An important part of the Catholic response to the Reformation was the Council of Trent (1545-63); but this council avoided questions of ecclesiology. The council did not speak about the Pope at all for fear of fanning the embers of conciliarism and deciding issues which remained doubtful. Nevertheless, in the twenty-third session on July 15, 1563, the council did define the teaching of the Church about the sacrament of holy orders and the hierarchy of the Church. The council said this among other things:

> Moreover, in the sacrament of orders, just as in baptism and in confirmation, a character is imprinted which can neither be blotted out nor taken away... If anyone says that all Christians without exception are priests of the New Testament or are endowed with equal spiritual power, it is apparent that he upsets the ecclesiastical hierarchy... Therefore the holy council declares that, besides other ecclesiastical grades, the bishops, who have succeeded the apostles, belong in a special way to the hierarchical order; and placed (as the Apostle says) by the Holy Spirit to rule the Church of God (Ac 20:28) they are superior to priests, and confer the sacrament of confirmation, can ordain ministers for the Church, and they have the power to perform many other functions that those of an inferior grade cannot. Moreover, the holy council declares that in the ordination of bishops, of priests, and of other grades, the consent, call, or authority, neither of the people nor of any secular power or public authority is necessary to the extent that without it the ordination is invalid. Rather it decrees that all those who have been called and appointed merely by the people or by the secular power or ruler, and thus undertake to exercise these ministries, and that all those who arrogate these ministries to themselves on their own authority, are not ministers of the Church but should be considered as thieves and robbers who have not entered through the door (Jn 10:1).[20]

By this declaration the Council of Trent reacted to the Reformers' conception of the priesthood of all believers. According to the Reformers, all are priests having the same power with respect to the word and the sacraments. However, no one may make use of this power without the consent of the community. One exercises the ministry of word and sacrament as the delegate of the community. Trent conceived the matter differently. Christ committed the ministry of word and sacrament to the apostles and their successors, the bishops, and not to all indiscriminately. Hence, no one may undertake such a ministry without episcopal authorization or ordination.

THE CATECHISM OF THE COUNCIL OF TRENT

In 1563 the Council of Trent ordered the composition of a
catechism which "the bishops will take care to have faithfully
translated into the vernacular language and expounded to the
people by all pastors."[21] A commission undertook the work which
was completed in 1566 and published by the authority of Pope
Pius V. The catechism was used throughout the Catholic world
for centuries. The four parts of the catechism are devoted to an
explanation of the articles of the creed, the sacraments, the
decalogue, and prayer. The catechism speaks of the Church in
connection with the 9th article of the creed.

The catechism adopts Augustine's definition of the Church
as the faithful dispersed throughout the world. It recalls the
Biblical images of the Church. The Church consists of two
parts, the Church triumphant and the Church militant. The
Church militant is composed of good and bad persons as the
chaff is mingled with the grain. Infidels, heretics and schismatics,
and excommunicated persons are excluded from the Church. A
distinctive mark of the Church is unity under Christ and His
vicar, the successor of Peter: "the unity of the Spirit in the bond
of peace: one body and one Spirit, even as you were called in
one hope of your calling, one Lord, one faith, one baptism, one
God and Father of all" (Ep 4:3-6).

Another distinctive mark of the Church, according to the
catechism, is holiness. The Church is called holy because she
is dedicated to God by baptism and faith, because, as the body,
she is united to her head, Christ Jesus, the fountain of all
holiness, because, finally, she possesses the efficacious means of
divine grace in the sacraments.

The third mark of the Church is that she is catholic, that is,
universal. "Unlike republics of human institution, or the con-
venticles of heretics, she is not circumscribed within the limits
of any one kingdom, nor confined to the members of any one
society of men; but embraces, within the amplitude of her love,
all mankind." To this Church belong all the faithful who have
existed from Adam to the present day, or who shall exist to the

end of time. All who desire eternal salvation must cling to and embrace her as the ark of salvation.

The Church is apostolic because she originated with the apostles and her doctrines were handed down by them. The Church is governed by apostolic men. Under the Holy Spirit it cannot err in faith and morals. Reason, it is true, and the senses are competent to ascertain the existence of the Church; but they cannot arrive at a knowledge of the origin, privileges and dignity of the Church; these we can contemplate only with the eyes of faith. Only faith can recognize the Church's power to remit sins, excommunicate, and consecrate the real body of Christ. In conclusion, we profess to believe the holy, not *in* the holy, catholic Church.

ROBERT BELLARMINE

The theological response to the ecclesiological questions raised by the Reformers was the *Disputationes de controversiis christianae fidei* of Robert Bellarmine (1542-1621), a series of lectures delivered in Rome between 1576 and 1588 and published between 1586 and 1593. These lectures countered the Reformers precisely in those areas where the Reformers attacked the Church. Because the Reformers rejected the visible structures of the Church, Bellarmine was intent on defending them.

According to Bellarmine, Christ is the head of the universal Church which includes the Church militant on earth, the Church suffering in purgatory, and the Church triumphant in heaven. The Church on earth is an ecclesiastical monarchy, that is, it is governed by an individual. It is not an aristocracy or a democracy. In this respect, the Church reflects the reign of God over the universe and the sovereignty of Christ over the entire Church. Christ placed Peter at the head of His Church on earth as is evident from Mt 16 and Jn 21, the change of Simon's name to Peter, and other privileges which Christ conferred on Peter. The primacy of Peter is confirmed by certain statements of the Greek and Latin Fathers.[22]

Furthermore, according to Bellarmine, Peter became and remained the bishop of Rome until his death at Rome. By divine

right the Roman Pontiff succeeds Peter as the bishop of Rome
and the visible head of the Church. Bellarmine supported the
latter point with arguments based upon the implications of the
Petrine passages in the Scriptures, the nature of the Church as a
visible and permanent entity, the declarations of councils, the
statements of Greek and Latin Fathers, and the historical role
of the papacy in the Church.[23]

Bellarmine discussed the spiritual and temporal power of
the bishop of Rome. As far as his spiritual power is concerned, the
bishop of Rome is the supreme judge in matters of faith and
morals. Indeed, his judgment in these matters is infallible when
it is directed to the whole Church. The Roman Pontiff can legislate for the whole Church in such a way that papal laws oblige
the members of the Church in conscience. Even though the apostles received jurisdiction immediately from Christ, the bishops,
their successors, receive it from the Pope, the bishop of Rome.[24]
The Pope has no temporal authority directly and immediately;
nevertheless, he does have temporal authority indirectly by reason
of his spiritual authority; that is to say, the Pope has no authority
generally in purely temporal affairs. These are the concern of
the civil authority. Where, however, the civil authority acts
against the best interests of souls, the Pope can and must intervene in the most effective way possible.[25]

Having described the position and role of the Pope, Bellarmine turned his attention to the Church militant on earth. The
Church on earth, as he defined it, "is the congregation of persons
bound together by profession of the same Christian faith and
participation in the same sacraments under the government of
legitimate pastors and especially of the one vicar of Christ on
earth, the Roman Pontiff."[26] Accordingly, Jews, Turks, pagans,
and heretics are not members of the Church because they do not
profess the true faith. Catechumens and excommunicated persons
are not members of the Church because they are excluded from
the sacraments of the Church. Schismatics are not members of
the Church because they do not submit to the legitimate pastors
of the Church.

A number of conclusions follow from Bellarmine's definition
of the Church, conclusions which he expressly drew. Membership

in the Church is not based on predestination, grace and charity. Moreover, the Church is a "congregation of persons which is just as visible and tangible as a group of the Roman people or the kingdom of France or the republic of Venice."[27] The profession of the same faith, the reception of the same sacraments, and the recognition of the same pastors entail such visibility.[28]

Bellarmine appended an important note to his definition of the Church:

> It must be noted as Augustine indicated *in breviculo colla-tionis, collat.* 3 that the Church is a living body in which there is a soul and body. The internal gifts of the Holy Spirit, faith, hope and charity, etc., are the soul. The external profession of faith and reception of the sacraments are the body. As a result, some belong to the soul and body of the Church; hence, they are united to Christ the head interiorly and exteriorly. These belong to the Church in the most perfect way. They are, as it were, living members, although even among them some possess life to a greater or lesser degree. Indeed, some have only the beginning of life, sensation, as it were, without activity, namely, those who have faith alone without charity. Again, some belong to the soul and not to the body, namely, catechumens and excommunicated persons, provided they have faith and charity as they can have. Finally, some belong to the body but not to the soul, namely, those who are without interior virtue but on account of hope or some temporal fear profess the faith and communicate in the sacraments and submit to the government of the pastors... Our definition includes the last mode of existence in the Church, because this is required as a minimum for being a part of the visible Church.[29]

Bellarmine taught that the visible Church of which he spoke is indefectible because of the promise of Christ.[30] This visible Church cannot err; that is, what all the faithful believe and all the bishops teach as a matter of faith is necessarily true and actually a matter of faith.[31]

Bellarmine elaborated an apologetics which defended the divine origin of the Catholic Church on the basis of fifteen notes or characteristics. (The four classical notes—unity, catholicity, apostolicity and sanctity—had not yet received particular attention.) The notes proposed by Bellarmine were the very name *Catholic* Church; the antiquity, perpetuity, and universality of the Catholic Church; the succession of bishops from apostolic times; the harmony between the doctrine of the ancient Church and Catholic doctrine; unity and sanctity; the presence of miracles and prophecies; the admission of the Church's adversaries; the unhappy end of those who have opposed the Church; and the temporal prosperity of those who have defended the Church.[32]

The writings of Bellarmine secured a kind of official and obligatory character in the Church. They became an arsenal out of which everyone took what he needed to defend the Catholic Church against the attacks of the Protestants. They exercised and continue to exercise an enormous influence upon ecclesiology. Bellarmine's ideas were frequently cited in opposition to Gallicanism, a theory, often reduced to practice, which developed in France in the 17th century and tended to restrict the authority of the Church and Pope unduly. The First Vatican Council (1870) accepted from Bellarmine its conception of the papal role in the Church. Bellarmine's position on the relationship of the Church and State was incorporated in statements of Pius IX and Leo XIII. His enumeration of the conditions for membership in the Church was repeated by Pius XII in the encyclical, *Mystici corporis* (1943).[33]

Nevertheless, the emphasis placed by Bellarmine and other Catholic theologians of the period upon the visible side of the Church, understandable as it is, led to an unfortunate result. The mystery of the Church received proportionately little attention.

MELCHIOR CANO

The Spanish Dominican, Melchior Cano (d. 1560), is the author of the important work, *De locis theologicis*, published posthumously (1563). The work is a systematic and critical study of the different sources from which the theologian must draw his arguments and conclusions, sources which Cano calls *loci*. He enumerates ten sources, namely, Holy Scripture, tradition, the faith of the Catholic Church, councils, the faith of the Roman Church, the Fathers of the Church, scholastic theologians, human reason, philosophy and history. Cano was unable to complete his work.

Cano defined the Church as the assembly or congregation of Catholics. He did not regard the unbaptized and heretics as members of the Church.[34] Membership in the Church is not based on predestination to glory (as Wycliffe and Hus held) nor on justification (as the Lutherans held).[35] The faith of the Church cannot fail; it cannot err in what it believes. The ancient Church could not err in faith; the Church of the present and future cannot and will not err in faith. The princes and the pastors of the Church have the spirit of truth. Cano based these conclusions upon the abiding presence of Christ and the Holy Spirit in the Church.[36] Therefore, the theologian may appeal to what the Catholic faithful believe and their pastors teach as evidence of Christian truth.

Speaking of the faith of the Roman Church, Cano adopted a traditional line of argumentation. The apostle Peter had been selected by Christ as shepherd of the universal Church. When Peter taught the Church and confirmed it in faith, he could not err (Lk 22; Mt 16). By divine right there are successors to Peter in his capacity as shepherd of the universal Church. The perpetuity of the Church demands such a succession.[37] *Deo auctore* the authority of Peter now rests with the Church at Rome and its bishops. Cano established this conclusion by appealing to the statements of many ancient writers and councils. It follows, according to Cano, that the Roman Pontiff cannot err when he puts an end to controversies about matters of faith.[38] Therefore, the faith of the Roman Church as defined by its bishop is also a criterion of Christian truth.

Cano's work, *De locis theologicis*, was a creative and important contribution to theological methodology.

DENIS PETAU (DIONYSIUS PETAVIUS)

Petau (1583-1652), a French Jesuit, is sometimes called the "Father of Positive Theology" or the "Father of the History of Dogma." In his great work, *Dogmata theologica* (1643-50), he employed in an original way the theological sources studied by Cano. Petau's work is characterized by its collection of patristic passages and historical approach to the dogmas of the Church.

In order to reply to heresies, Petau was intent on showing the conformity of the Church's dogmas with the position of early Christianity.

According to Petau, Christ is the head of the Church, as Paul taught. The union of Christ with His Church is so close, Petau noted, that Paul called the Church by the name of Christ (1 Cor 12:12). Christ guides, governs and vivifies the Church which is His body.[39] Christ has given the Holy Spirit, the Spirit of truth, to the whole Church so that what is believed throughout the Church proceeds from the Spirit.[40] The members of the Church are united by their faith in Christ and social unity.[41] The virgin Church begets Christians just as the virgin Mary begot Christ. It is the responsibility of the Church to determine the meaning of Holy Scripture.[42] The Church is the best interpreter of its own faith and dogmas.[43]

For Petau, the authority of bishops is not human but divine since it has been derived from Christ through the apostles and not from the faithful.[44] Ecclesiastical authority is twofold: the power of orders and the power of jurisdiction. The power of orders enables bishops and priests to consecrate the Holy Eucharist and administer the other sacraments. The power of jurisdiction is exercised in the internal forum, that is, in the sacrament of penance, and in the external forum where it has social effects including the right to inflict penalties.[45] The infliction of penalties pertains to a bishop's judicial authority. The Roman Pontiff has full authority throughout the Church without any restriction as to place or individuals.[46] As the visible head of the Church, the Roman Pontiff is the successor of the apostle Peter. Papal primacy has been recognized from the beginning.[47] While the Church has no authority to change or invalidate the liturgical prescriptions of divine institution, the details of sacramental administration rest with the Church.[48]

FRANCIS SUAREZ

The Spanish Jesuit, Francis Suarez (1548-1617), made an important contribution to ecclesiology by his study of the relationship between Church and State. Suarez' conclusions were published in two works, *De legibus* (1612) and *Defensio fidei catholicae* (1613). According to Suarez, the Church and the State are perfect, that is, self-sufficient, societies. Each society is capable of enacting laws for its members. However, the Church and the State exist for different reasons and on different levels: the Church exists for the good of souls and its mission is supernatural; on the other hand, the State exists for the temporal good of its citizens and its purpose is earthly, material and transitory. As a consequence, Church and State are independent of each other. The Church has no authority to enact laws of a civil nature. This is the function of the State. The Church asks only that the State place no obstacle to the salvation of souls.

What is to be done in the event of a conflict between ecclesiastical and civil laws? The conflict is to be resolved by the subjection of the temporal to the spiritual. Civil authority must yield to ecclesiastical authority in view of the latter's superior goal, the good of souls. Hence, the authority of the Church over civil society is indirect: it is the authority to change or abrogate civil laws which impede the salvation of souls.[49]

Suarez maintained that his position on this matter was common among the theologians of his day, having been defended before him by Cajetan, Vitoria, Soto, Bellarmine and others.

IGNATIUS OF LOYOLA

Ignatius (1491-1556), the founder of the Society of Jesus (Jesuits), contributed significantly to the development of a specific ecclesial climate in wide sections of the Church. He impressed upon the members of his society the necessity of thinking with the Church and obedience to the Holy See. Through the Jesuits he influenced a huge number of the faithful under their direction.

Ignatius was convinced there could be no conflict between the Spirit and the Church. By the Spirit he understood God's illumination and inspiration of the soul; by the Church he understood the Scriptures, virtue, the teaching and direction of the hierarchy, and right reason. Christ was incarnate in the Church; the decision of the vicar of Christ was a means of discerning the

will of Christ and the prompting of the Spirit. This conviction
prompted Ignatius to include in the constitutions of his society
a fourth vow for the professed: that of unconditional obedience
to the Holy See. For Ignatius, the Spirit behind personal inspiration is the Spirit behind the hierarchical Church. In his rules
of the orthodox faith which are a part of the *Spiritual Exercises,*
Ignatius counselled readiness "to obey with mind and heart,
setting aside all particular views, the true spouse of Jesus
Christ, our holy mother, our infallible and orthodox mistress, the
Catholic Church, whose authority is exercised over us by the
hierarchy of its pastors." The Society of Jesus was to follow the
Spirit beneath the standard of the cross, laboring for the
Church, the bride of Christ, under the Roman Pontiff, the vicar
of Christ on earth. The society has always been characterized
by a papal mentality.

THE ROMAN LITURGY

In order to deal with certain abuses and superstitions which
had crept into the worship of the Church during the medieval
period, the Council of Trent called for the revision of liturgical
books. Since the council was unable to undertake the task itself,
it was left to the Popes. Under the aegis of the Popes, new and
revised editions of the liturgical books appeared after the conclusion of the council: the Roman breviary in 1568, the Roman
missal in 1570, the Roman pontifical in 1596, the ceremonial of
bishops in 1600, and the Roman ritual for the administration of
the sacraments in 1614. The invention of printing made the
production of uniform copies possible. These liturgical books
were prescribed for the whole western Church. Only those
dioceses and religious orders which had their own liturgical
books for 200 years were exempted. Despite this exemption
most of them adopted the Roman books. In 1588 Pope Sixtus V
founded the sacred Congregation of Rites to implement the
reforms and settle difficulties.

The creation of a clear and stable liturgy in the western
Church made an enormous contribution to Catholic piety. No
institution in the Church other than the papacy could have ac-

complished the task as well. At the same time, the adoption of the Roman liturgy throughout the Church had an important consequence for ecclesiology: it encouraged the idea that Rome was the norm of ecclesiastical life in all areas, that one must go to Rome for the solution of all problems.

GALILEO GALILEI

The unfortunate case of Galileo (1564-1642) belongs to this era. By his observations with the telescope, Galileo confirmed the truth of the Copernican hypothesis of heliocentrism. When confronted with the idea that the Scriptures seem to teach the mobility of the sun and the immobility of the earth (see, for example, Jos 10:13), Galileo replied that the Scriptures cannot err, that sometimes they present natural phenomena as they appear to the senses and not as they are in reality.[50] Galileo was denounced to the Holy Office at Rome for his Copernican view with its alleged implication of biblical error. In 1616 the Holy Office condemned as heretical the statement that the sun is the center of the universe and altogether without motion. It condemned as an error in faith the statement that the earth is not the center of the universe but moves. When the condemnation of the Holy Office was communicated to him by Robert Bellarmine at the order of Pope Paul V, Galileo promised to abstain from defending the Copernican theory as a fact. He was permitted to discuss the theory as an hypothesis.

In 1632 Galileo published his great work, *Dialogue concerning the Two Great World Systems: Ptolemaic and Copernican.* In this book he defended heliocentrism openly as an established fact. A year later (1633) he was summoned to Rome before the Holy Office. After three appearances before that body, Galileo abjured the opinion that the earth goes round the sun. He was imprisoned in pleasant surroundings for holding the condemned opinion. Nonetheless, Galileo continued his studies. He died after receiving the last sacraments of the Church to which he remained ever faithful.

The theologian will observe that the condemnation of a scientific fact by the Holy Office in no way discredits the infallibility of the Church. The universal Church and the Pope when he speaks *ex cathedra* are infallible in matters of faith and morals. The Holy Office is not, and has never claimed to be, infallible. The Catholic must regret, however, the basically erroneous notion which the condemnation of Galileo fostered—that science and religion are in fundamental opposition. On the contrary, as Galileo himself recognized,[51] they are in fundamental accord since both proceed from one and the same divine source.

NOTES TO CHAPTER VI

1. Cf. P. Hughes, *A Popular History of the Reformation* (Garden City, 1957) 13-17.
2. *Works of Martin Luther* (Philadelphia, 1915-32) 2, 372-374.
3. *Ibid.*, 1, 355f.
4. *Ibid.*, 1, 361.
5. *Ibid.*, 2, 282f.
6. Trans. *On Christian Doctrine* (New York, 1965).
7. *Ibid.* c. 29.
8. P. Schaff, *Creeds of Christendom* (New York, 1877) 3, 12-13.
9. *Institutes of the Christian Religion* (Philadelphia, 1909) 3, 21, 5.
10. *Ibid.* 4, 1, 7-9.
11. *Ibid.* 4, 1, 3.
12. *Ibid.* 4, 1, 4.
13. *Ibid.* 4, 1, 10-12.
14. *Ibid.* 4, 1, 22.
15. *Ibid.* 4, 3, 4.
16. *Ibid.* 4, 12, 1.
17. *Ibid.* 4, 18, 19.
18. *THD* 2, 315. *DTC* 15/2, 3842-56.
19. *THD* 2, 392.
20. *CT* no. 843.
21. *Sess.* 24, *de Reform.* c. 7.
22. *III Controv. Generalis* 1.
23. *Ibid.* 2.
24. *Ibid.* 3.
25. *Ibid.* 5.
26. *Controv. Generalis de Conciliis et Ecclesia*, 3, 2.
27. *Ibid.*
28. *Ibid.* 3, 12.
29. *Ibid.*
30. *Ibid.* 3, 13.

31. *Ibid.* 3, 14.
32. *Ibid.* 4, 1-18.
33. No. 22.
34. *De locis theologicis* 4, 2, 1.
35. *Ibid.* 4, 3, 1.
36. *Ibid.* 4, 4.
37. *Ibid.* 6, 3.
38. *Ibid.* 6, 4-7.
39. *Dog. theolog., De incarn.* 12, 17, 1-3.
40. *Ibid.* 11, 4, 8.
41. *Ibid.* 12, 17, 5; 12, 7, 7.
42. *Ibid.* 13, 18, 2.
43. *Ibid.* 14, 12, 1.
44. *Dog. theolog., De eccl. hierarchia* 3, 14, 9.
45. *Ibid.* 3, 13, 9.
46. *Ibid.* 2, 2, 11.
47. *Ibid.* 3, 7, 11.
48. *Ibid.* 3, 3, 9.
49. *De legibus* 3, 6-11; *Defensio* 3, 5, 11; 3, 22, 1-5.
50. Letter to Castelli, Dec. 21, 1613. Quoted by J. Brodrick, *Galileo* (London, 1964) 76-78.
51. *Ibid.*

VII. THE 17th & 18th CENTURIES

The 17th century is notable for the revival of Catholic life in France, a revival stimulated by the saints of the period and accompanied by the establishment of new religious orders. St. Francis de Sales (1567-1622), the bishop of Geneva, Switzerland, made thousands of converts to the Catholic faith and was the author of two popular spiritual books, *An Introduction to the Devout Life* and a *Treatise on the Love of God*. With St. Jane Francis de Chantal he founded the nuns of the Visitation at Annecy, France, in 1610. The cardinal Pierre de Bérulle (1575-1629) founded the French congregation of the Oratory at Paris in 1611. The Oratorians established many seminaries for the training of priests. St. Vincent de Paul (1576-1660) founded the Vincentians (1624) for missionary work and the education of the clergy. With St. Louise de Marillac he founded the Sisters of Charity in 1633. St. John Eudes (1601-80) founded the Eudists and the Sisters of Refuge. Jean Jacques Olier (1608-57) founded a congregation of secular priests in 1641 to staff the famous church and seminary of St. Sulpice in Paris. St. John Baptist de la Salle (d. 1719) founded the Brothers of the Christian Schools at Reims, France, in 1680. St. Margaret Mary Alacoque (1647-90), assisted by the Jesuits, Claude de la Colombiere and Jean Croiset, fanned the flame of devotion to the Sacred Heart of Jesus. The devotion served to remind the Church of Jesus' love for sinners and His justice.

Three saints in particular must be noticed in the 18th century. St. Paul of the Cross (1694-1775) was remarkable for

his devotion to the passion of Jesus; and he founded the Passion-
ists to preach it. St. Alphonsus Liguori (1696-1787) was the
founder of the Redemptorists (1732) and a consummate moral
theologian. St. Clement Hofbauer (1751-1820) was the leader
of the Catholic revival in Austria.

The 17th century especially witnessed heated controversies
about the doctrine of grace. Michael de Bay (1513-89), a professor at Louvain, took the position that, as a result of Adam's
sin, human nature had been corrupted intrinsically and all the
actions of a sinner are sinful. Grace is necessary for every good
work and is irresistible. In 1567 Pius V condemned the substance of de Bay's teaching. However the ideas of de Bay were
taken up by Cornelius Janssens (d. 1638) and published in a
posthumous work, *Augustinus* (1640). The Jansenists—many of
them quite influential persons—compounded the mischief of
Janssens' errors by their opposition to the practice of frequent
communion. Pope Innocent X condemned Jansenism in 1653.
But Jansenism died a slow death reappearing in disguise in the
Reflexions morales of Paschase Quesnel published in 1693. This
book received a papal condemnation in 1713.

The Molinist controversy about grace was waged entirely
within the limits, of orthodoxy. The Portuguese Jesuit, Luis
Molina, published a book *Concordia* (1588), in which he employed the "middle knowledge" of God to reconcile human freedom with the infallibility of efficacious grace. Dominic Banez, a
Dominican professor at Salamanca, Spain, took issue with the
Concordia of Molina. Banez spoke of a divine premotion to explain the infallibility of efficacious grace. The disagreement between Molina and Banez gave rise to a sharp controversy between the Jesuits and Dominicans which is still unresolved.

In 1773 Pope Clement XIV suppressed the Society of Jesus.
The society had been an ardent defender of the Church's interests; it had assumed control of nearly all the schools in the Catholic world; and its members served as advisers and confessors to
many Catholic princes. In these circumstances it acquired many
powerful enemies—in Portugal, the king's minister, Pombal; in
France the encyclopaedists, the Jansenists and the mistress of the
king; in Spain and Naples, the kings themselves, Charles III and

Ferdinand. For the sake of peace, without judging the society, the Pope dissolved it, although it continued to function in Russia and Prussia. The society was reestablished by Pius VII in 1814.

There was an important development in the Russian Church, the most populous Church of the Orthodox faith. Russia had accepted the Christian faith from Constantinople in 988. The first metropolitan (archbishop) was appointed at Kiev in 1037. After the beginning of the 14th century Moscow became the capital of Russia. The metropolitan left Kiev and made Moscow the center of the Russian Church. In 1550, Ivan IV, who had himself crowned as the first czar of Russia three years earlier, drove out the Tartars and secured Russian independence. Shortly thereafter, the Russian Church secured its independence of Constantinople. With the consent of his eastern brethren, the patriarch of Constantinople created a new patriarchate at Moscow (1589). In 1721 the czar abolished the position of patriarch and replaced it with the Holy Synod consisting of representatives of the Church and State. The Russian constitution of 1918 separated the Church from the State; the Synod was abolished and replaced by a patriarchate.

Several religious groups well-known in America emerged at this time. The Congregationalists were founded by Robert Browne in England in 1581. To secure religious freedom they came to America where, as the Mayflower Pilgrims, they landed at Plymouth, Massachusetts, in 1620. The Baptists originated in England under the influence of John Smyth (1570-1612). They migrated to America; and under the leadership of Roger Williams, founder of Rhode Island, the first Baptist church was established at Providence in 1639. The Quakers originated in England about 1649 as the result of the preaching of George Fox (1624-91). They came to America, as early as 1655. A Quaker, William Penn, founded the colony of Pennsylvania in 1681. John Wesley (1703-91) founded the Methodists in England in 1783. The movement reached America in the same century.

The 18th century is the century of the "Enlightenment." The Enlightenment was marked by a rejection of traditional doctrines and values, a tendency towards individualism, a cult of the natural sciences, confidence in the possibility of universal human progress, and the free use of reason. The growing enlightenment prepared the way for religious tolerance and freedom of conscience; but it had regrettable consequences too. In England, Lord Herbert of Cherbury (d. 1648) suggested the establishment of a purely natural religion based on human reason rather than revelation (deism). In France, the principles of the Enlightenment were embodied in the famous *Encyclopedie* (1751-80) edited by Diderot and d'Alembert. The French movement, led by Voltaire (d. 1777), Rousseau (d. 1778) and the Encyclopaedists, was animated by a hatred of the Church and Christianity. In Germany, rationalism was defended from the preacher's pulpit and the professor's chair; the greatest German writers of the day, Lessing, Goethe and Schiller, were infected with it; and French free thinkers found a home at the court of Frederick II of Prussia (1740-86). The result was widespread apostasy from traditional Christianity in the countries affected.

GALLICANISM

The term, Gallicanism, designates a number of theories sustained for the most part in the French or Gallican Church and the theological schools of that country. These theories tended to restrict papal authority in favor of the authority of the king (political Gallicanism) or the bishops (episcopal Gallicanism).

The roots of Gallicanism go back at least to the reign of King Philip the Fair of France (1285-1314) who claimed the right to dispose of vacant ecclesiastical benefices in virtue of concessions made by previous Popes. The Frenchmen, D'Ailly (1350-1420) and Gerson (1363-1429), were ardent advocates of the conciliar theory which was adopted by the Council of Constance (1414-18) and asserted the superiority of a general council over the Pope. The *Pragmatic Sanction* of Bourges (1438) drawn up by the French clergy and approved by Charles VII of France reaffirmed the position of Constance and claimed for the French Church the right to administer the ecclesiatical temporalities under the king's patronage independently of the Pope. In the 16th and 17th centuries Peter Pithou (d.

1596) and Peter Dupuy (d. 1651) compiled lists of the privileges of the French Church to which they added learned commentaries. Then in 1681 King Louis XIV called a general assembly of the French clergy which issued the classical statement of Gallicanism in four articles (1682). The articles were actually formulated by Bossuet, the bishop of Meaux:

(1) Peter and his successors have authority over spiritual matters. They have no authority over civil and temporal affairs. In the latter area, therefore, princes are subject to no ecclesiastical authority; they cannot be deposed directly or indirectly by the Church's power of the keys; nor can their subjects be released from their allegiance to them.

(2) The authority of the Holy See must be understood in the light of the decrees of the Council of Constance about general councils. These decrees were approved by the Holy See and confirmed by the practice of the Popes themselves and the whole Church.

(3) Papal authority must be regulated by the canons of the Church. The usages of the Gallican Church must be respected. It is the duty of papal authority to maintain and support laws and customs established with the consent of the Holy See.

(4) While the Pope has the chief responsibility in questions of faith, his judgment is not final until the Church has consented to it.[1]

In support of these articles, the Gallican party appealed to history. The Popes of the early Church, it was said, had never attempted to depose rulers, even the most wicked of them. The attempt on the part of the Popes to do so began with Gregory VII. Moreover, history taught that the highest authority in the early Church for the regulation of faith and discipline was the general council, not the Pope. Finally, history also taught that individual Popes could err in faith; hence, the correctness of their doctrinal decisions had to be determined by the acceptance of the Church.

Louis XIV sanctioned the Gallican articles by royal authority. Professors of theology and candidates for academic degrees were compelled to accept them. No one was allowed to write anything against them. At Rome, however, the articles encountered great opposition. Both Innocent XI (in 1682) and Alexander

VIII (in 1690) protested vigorously against them. In 1693 the same king who had promulgated them, Louis XIV, withdrew them.

The royal withdrawal of the Gallican articles did not mean though the demise of the Gallican spirit. One of the most influential of all Gallican works, the *De Ecclesia Christi* of Honore Tournély, appeared in 1729. This work was widely used in the theological formation of French candidates for the priesthood. The arguments employed by Tournély were the very arguments used by the opponents of papal infallibility at Vatican I. Tournély accepted Bellarmine's definition of the Church with its divinely established hierarchy. The Church is a monarchy with the Pope at its head; but it is not merely a monarchy; it is also an aristocracy. The episcopacy is also of divine institution; the bishops also have received from Christ the authority to judge in matters of faith; the government of the Church rests with the bishops too. Indeed, the Pope is bound to observe the canons of the general councils of the Church. Just as Peter, even though he was its head, was nonetheless a member of the apostolic college and, as a consequence, inferior to it, so the Roman Pontiff, the successor of Peter, is superior to individual bishops but inferior to them as a body.

According to Tournély, a papal pronouncement *ex cathedra* is irreformable only after it has been accepted by the universal Church. The privilege of infallibility belongs to the entire Church and not to Peter or any other individual: Jesus promised that the gates of hell would not prevail against the *Church;* He promised to be with *all* the apostles and their successors to the end of time. The promises made by Christ to Peter were made to him as the representative of the universal Church.

According to Tournély, the Church has no temporal authority even of an indirect nature. In temporal affairs, princes are entirely independent of the Church. The Church cannot depose princes or release their subjects from obedience to them. Jesus conferred upon the Church the power to preach, baptize, bind and loose consciences, consecrate the Eucharist, and impose spiritual penalties; but He gave the Church no temporal authority. The Church cannot depose princes because princely authority is derived from God and the Church cannot suppress what is of divine origin. The Church wields only a spiritual sword to recall the faithful to their religious duties. Princes wield a material sword. Neither power may trespass upon the domain of the other. In this matter Tournély was reacting against the position of Bellarmine who conceded to the Church at least an indirect authority in temporal affairs.[2]

Gallicanism was sustained in French seminaries and—through the influence of Sulpician professors—in American seminaries to the middle of the 19th century. It was dealt a mortal blow at Vatican I.

FEBRONIANISM

The teacher of Febronius at Louvain was Zeger Bernard Van Espen (1646-1728) who taught canon law for a long period. He published a huge work, *Jus ecclesiasticum universum,* in 1728 defending the thesis that all the bishops of the Church are basically equal. Jurisdiction rests with the whole Church, the ministers simply exercising it. The approval of both bishops and the civil authority is necessary for a papal decree to take effect.

Febronianism appeared in Germany. The term refers to the ideas of John Nicholas von Hontheim, auxiliary bishop of Trier, which he expressed in a book written under the pseudonym of Justinus Febronius. The name of the book was *Febronii de statu ecclesiae et legitima potestate Romani Pontificis* (1763). The book was occasioned by certain complaints of German Catholics against the Holy See, the spread of Gallicanism, and, ostensibly on the part of the author, the desire to effect the reunion of Protestants with the Catholic Church. As Gallicanism did, so Febronianism questioned the role of the papacy as it actually functioned at that time.

According to Febronius, the power of the keys was given radically to the whole Church. By divine institution the Church exercises the power of the keys through its ministers, the chief of whom is the Pope. The function of the Pope is to secure the observance of the canons, the preservation of the faith and the

rightful administration of the sacraments. By their union with
the Pope individual Churches maintain their unity with each
other. The first eight centuries offer an example of the legitimate
exercise of papal responsibility. Since the 9th century, however,
under the influence of the Pseudo-Isidorian decretals, the administration of the Church had been unduly concentrated in the
hands of the Pope. Such matters as the selection of bishops and
the erection of new dioceses are properly the business of metropolitans and provincial synods and not of the Pope.

The Pope is not infallible, according to Febronius. He is inferior to a general council. His decisions about matters of faith
and discipline need confirmation by a general council before they
bind the Church. The Pope does not have 'the exclusive right
to summon a general council nor does its decrees require his
confirmation. All bishops have the same rights; consequently, the
Pope may not intervene in the affairs of a diocese other than
his own.

As a means of recovering the rightful state of affairs,
Febronius recommended the education of the people, the holding
of a general council and national synods, resistance to papal
decrees by civil rulers, and open disobedience where the Pope
had exceeded his authority.

The book of Febronius caused a great commotion. It went
through a second and third edition and was translated into
several European languages. Pope Clement XIII placed it on
the Index of Forbidden Books (1764). Supporters of the Pope
wrote refutations. The Protestants denied that the papacy was
the only obstacle to Christian unity. Eventually Hontheim or
Febronius came to deplore the strident tone of his book; but he
refused to retract the principles expressed in it.

JOSEPHINISM[3]

Josephinism refers to the ideas and practical measures implemented by the emperor, Joseph II (1741-90), with respect
to the Church in his Austrian domain. Joseph was a Hapsburg,
the son and successor of the empress, Maria Theresa. Josephinism
was a form of political Gallicanism and Febronianism.

Joseph had good intentions. He wished to root out abuses in the Church and make it function more efficiently. Joseph and his councillors sustained the point of view that the Church is an agency of the State, the latter being chiefly responsible for the spiritual and material welfare of its citizens. The State or prince, therefore, is empowered to intervene in ecclesiastical affairs to the degree these have a bearing upon the interests of the State. The prince can dispose of the resources of the Church when these are needed elsewhere. The clergy have a social role above all. By encouraging morality, they make an important contribution to the welfare of the State. Because of their important role, the State is vitally concerned with the training the clergy receive. The civil government need not consult the Holy See as it carries out its projected reforms. Indeed it must oppose those ecclesiastics who maintain the superiority of the spiritual over the temporal. The obedience given by the faithful and clergy to their religious superiors is a danger to the State and lessens its authority. The will of the prince must be supreme even where the Church is concerned.

The ideas of the emperor Joseph and his councillors were reflected in the practical measures taken in the empire. Diocesan seminaries were supplanted by central seminaries for both secular and religious clergy. Clerical studies were to include canon law (as it was understood by Joseph and his ministers), patristics, pastoral theology, and history (the latter being taught with a Protestant bias). Bishops were empowered to grant certain matrimonial dispensations previously sought from Rome. Papal and episcopal documents required the approval of the State before they took effect. Monasteries of contemplative orders were closed on the grounds that they were useless. Full civil rights were granted to religions other than the Catholic religion. The boundaries of dioceses were redrawn. New parishes were established from the resources of the closed monasteries.

In 1782 Pius VI, fearful of a schism, traveled to Vienna to meet with the emperor. The Pope gained some concessions; but, for the most part, the changes made by Joseph remained in effect. The spirit of Joseph's changes influenced Austrian policy toward the Church until World War I (1914-18).

ALPHONSUS LIGUORI

In the controversy with the Gallicans and Febronians, the Holy See was not without its defenders. Not the least was Alphonsus Liguori (1696-1787)—lawyer, priest, teacher, theologian, bishop and founder of the congregation of Redemptorists (1732). He wrote a number of works dealing with papal authority, among them, *Dissertatio de Romani Pontificis auctoritate* (1748), which was incorporated into his classic work on moral theology, *Theologia moralis,* and *Vindiciae pro suprema Romani Pontificis potestate adversus Justinum Febronium* (1768), a work written under a pseudonym against Febronius.

In his *Vindiciae* Alphonsus argued that upon the departure of the Savior from this world, it was necessary for some visible head and supreme judge to take His place to preserve the unity of faith. A primacy of jurisdiction was given to Peter and his successors, the Popes. This jurisdiction means among other things to have authority over general councils and ordinary power over the faithful.

The infallibility of the Pope is a consequence of his supreme authority in the Church. The Pope would not be supreme if he were not infallible. In terms suggestive of Vatican I, Alphonsus claimed infallibility for the Pope when he speaks as the teacher of the whole Church, defining *ex cathedra* a matter of faith or morals. To the Gallicans who declared the judgment of the Pope to be irreformable only after it had been accepted by the Church, Alphonsus put this question: How was the acceptance to be manifested? By the consent of the greater part of the bishops? In this case, Alphonsus reasoned, all Catholics were bound to accept papal definitions even before their acceptance by the Church. The greater part of the bishops, with the exception of the French bishops, were teaching and had always taught that papal definitions did not require acceptance by the Church for infallibility.

According to Alphonsus, the supremacy and infallibility of the Pope imply authority over general councils. Christ's prayer for the faith of Peter who was to strengthen his brethren (Lk 22:31) manifests the relationship between Pope and council.

It was wrong to suggest, as some Gallicans did, that Peter represented the whole Church on this occasion. The whole tenor of the prayer indicates that it was directed primarily to Peter.[9] A general council, convoked under the presidency of the Pope, cannot err since it takes the place of the universal Church. In case of the doubtful election of the Pope, the faithful must follow the judgment of a general council which has supreme authority from God in this instance. If the Pope as a private person falls into heresy, he is deprived of his position—not by a council as his superior, but by Christ.[10]

BLAISE PASCAL

Pascal (1623-62), the French philosopher, mathematician and scientist, was also an apologist for the Christian faith. In 1654 he underwent a profound religious conversion and entered the Jansenist community of Port Royal. His *Pensées*,[11] first published posthumously in 1669, present a summary ecclesiology. Tradition, according to Pascal, is the rule of faith. Tradition is the belief of the ancient Church as handed down to Christians by the Fathers:

> If the ancient Church was in error, the Church fell. It is not the same if the Church erred today, for it always has the higher norm of ecclesiastical tradition; so this submission and conformity to the ancient Church prevails and rectifies all. But the ancient Church did not presuppose or take into account the Church of the future as we presuppose and take into account the ancient Church.[12]

Pascal acknowledged the Pope to be the first of all. "Who else is recognized by all, being able to make his influence felt throughout the entire body... Yet how easy it was to let this degenerate into tyranny."[13]

If the Church is considered as one, the Pope is its head and is all. If the Church is considered as a multitude, the Pope is only a part. The Fathers used to consider the Church in both ways. Plurality without unity is confusion while unity without plurality is tyranny. With the exception of France there is no other country where one may say a council is above the Pope.[14]

The Pope hates and fears the learned who have not vowed obedience to him.[15] It is possible for the Pope to err and condemn the truth. In such a case the aggrieved must protest until a just Pope hears both sides and consults antiquity.[16] In these *Pensées* of Pascal, one hears a reaction to the papal condemnation of Jansenist teaching.

While Pascal seemed to have maintained his Jansenist views to the end, his confessor reported his last words a declaration of loyalty to the vicar of Christ in the person of the Pope.

ROBERT BARCLAY

Robert Barclay (1648-90) was an English Quaker. The Religious Society of Friends (Quakers) was founded by George Fox (1624-91) in England. Quakers are a third way of Christianity, being neither Catholic nor Protestant but accepting Fox' doctrine of the Inner Light. The contribution of Barclay was to give systematic expression to Fox' teaching in his (Barclay's) *Apology for the True Christian Divinity* and other works. In the years following its publication, the *Apology* was looked upon as the standard exposition of the Quaker faith.

According to Barclay, the catholic Church is "no other thing but the society, gathering or company of such as God hath called out of the world and worldly spirit to walk in his light and Life."[17] The Church is the body of Christ. Outside this Church there is no salvation; but even the heathen, Turks, Jews and Christians of all sorts are members of this Church if they are upright in their own hearts before the Lord.[18] Barclay recognized, however, that the word, Church, is often used in a narrow sense to signify a gathered and visible fellowship. In this sense, the Church

> is to be considered as it signifies a certain number of persons gathered by God's Spirit, and by the testimony of some of his servants raised up for that end, unto the belief of the true principles and doctrines of the Christian faith, who through their hearts being united by the same love, and their understandings informed in the same truths, gather, meet, and assemble together to wait upon God, to worship Him, and to bear a joint testimony for the truth

against error, suffering for the same, and so becoming through this fellowship as one family and household in certain respects, do each of them watch over, teach, instruct, and care for one another, according to their several measures and attainments: such were the churches of primitive times gathered by the apostles; whereof we have divers mentioned in the holy scriptures. And as to the visibility of the church in this respect, there hath been a great interruption since the apostles' days, by reason of the apostasy.[19]

Therefore, to be a member of the catholic Church it suffices for one to have turned from unrighteousness to righteousness whether he be a Christian or not. To be a member of the Church in the narrow sense of the term, as it is widely used in the New Testament, one must have forsaken iniquity and at the same time professed Christ and the holy truths delivered in the Scriptures. To be a member of the Church in either sense, outward profession of the Christian faith without interior conversion does not suffice.[20]

In other works, especially *Truth Triumphant*, Barclay expanded upon his conception of the Church. The Church has a single head, Christ Himself. One of the primary duties of the Church is the care of the poor, instruction of the young, and reproof of sinners. The Church is entirely independent of the State in the conduct of its own affairs. In reaching a decision the Church should not listen to one man but seek the will of God as a group. The Christian Church has the authority to expel erring members. One of the advantages of Church membership is the joy and encouragement which true fellowship brings. Apostolic succession is of no consequence because it has no necessary relationship to Christian life.

JOHN WESLEY

John Wesley (1703-91), the founder of the Methodists, was ordained an Anglican priest in 1728; and he remained within the Anglican communion until his death. In virtue of his ordination Wesley believed he had received an extraordinary ministry to revitalize the established Church. His program for revitalization included preaching in the open air, praying extemporaneously, forming "Methodist" societies and employing the services of lay preachers. One might think of him as the superior-general of an evangelical order dedicated to the service of the Church in a particular country. While Wesley wished his Methodist societies to serve the Church of England, they received no encouragement from the bishops of that Church; and after Wesley's death, they went into schism.

Wesley's repeated statements that he would never leave the Church of England furnish considerable evidence of his ecclesiological views; but his ideas about the Church can also be learned from references scattered throughout his written works. In his sermon *Of the Church* first published in *The Arminian Magazine* in 1786, Wesley took Paul's letter to the Ephesians 4:1-6 as his point of departure. The word, Church, Wesley wrote, is used in the New Testament to designate a group of Christians either in a family or a particular city or dispersed throughout a province or the entire world. Who are those who are properly the Church of God? The Apostle answers the question for Wesley in the text cited: they who are one body and have one Spirit, one Lord, one hope, one faith, one baptism, one God and Father of all. That part of the great body of the universal Church which inhabits any one kingdom or nation is properly termed a "national" Church, as the Church of France or the Church of England. Wesley believed his conception of the Church agreed perfectly with the 19th article of the Thirty-nine Articles of Religion of 1562. He went on to speak of the Church as holy because every member thereof is holy, though in different degrees. One who is not holy—the common swearer, the Sabbath-breaker, the drunkard, the whoremonger, the thief, the liar, one living in any outward sin or under the power of anger or pride, the lover of the world—cannot be a member of this Church.[21]

In a letter to a Roman Catholic written in 1749, Wesley described the Church as gathered by Christ through the apostles, extending to all nations and all ages, and holy in all its members.[22] In a letter to Gilbert Boyce, a Baptist minister, written in 1750, Wesley denied that the Church of England or the Methodists are the one true Church of Christ. On the contrary, every society of true believers is a branch of the one true Church. Wesley also believed in a succession of pastors and teachers. In his *Journal* for Feb. 14, 1761, he spoke of those who convert sinners to God as divinely appointed and assisted and as the successors of those who have delivered the faith once delivered to the saints.[23]

NOTES TO CHAPTER VII

1. DS 2281-84.
2. *DTC* 6/1, 1096-1122.
3. Cf. M. Goodwin, *The Papal Conflict with Josephinism* (New York, 1938).
4. 1, 2, 1, 2, 110-133.
5. 1, 3.
6. *Vindiciae, finis operis* 8.
7. *Theol. Mor., l.c.* 110.
8. *Ibid.* 115.
9. *Ibid.* 123.
10. *Ibid.* 121.
11. (New York, 1950).
12. *Pensées* (New York, 1950) p. 403, no. 58.
13. *Ibid.* no. 62.
14. *Ibid.* no. 61.
15. *Ibid.* no. 63.
16. *Ibid.* p. 411, no. 70.
17. *Apology* 10, 2.
18. *Ibid.*
19. *Ibid.* 10, 3.
20. *Ibid.* 10, 4-5.
21. Wesley's Works (New York, 1826) 6, 373-380.
22. *Ibid.* 9, 533.
23. *Ibid.* 3, 37.

VIII. THE 19th CENTURY

THE FIRST CENTURY OF THE MODERN ERA

The French Revolution (1789-99) was a violent reaction against the absolute monarchy and the Church allied with it. The revolutionaries wished to grant the people a share in the government and to distribute the burden of taxation more equitably. To meet the demand for funds, the revolutionary government confiscated the lands of the Church; and it also undertook the reorganization of the Church, dissolving certain religious orders, reducing the number of dioceses, and providing for the election of bishops and parish priests. The Pope, Pius VI, two-thirds of the clergy, and the mass of the people opposed these measures, but to no avail.

Between 1792 and 1795 the revolution reached a new intensity. The Legislative Assembly and the Convention caused the banishment or death of thousands of people including many clergy. The king, Louis XVI, and his queen, Maria Antoinette, were executed in 1793. A republic was proclaimed. The clergy were obliged to marry. The Christian method of reckoning time was replaced by another. The goddess of reason in the person of an actress was enthroned on the altar of Notre Dame. The cry of "Liberty, Equality, Fraternity" rang throughout the land.

With the ascendancy of Robespierre there was some hope of relief for the Church. While hating the Church, he believed in a Supreme Being; and he broke the hold of atheism on the French government. In 1795 the government granted a slight measure of toleration to Catholics; nevertheless, under the Directory (1795-99) there were more executions and deportations of the clergy to Guiana. The Pope, Pius VI, lost certain territories to a French army under Napoleon Bonaparte and was himself taken prisoner. The terror did not abate until Napoleon made a concordat with Pius VII in 1801.

Napoleon became the First Consul of France in 1799 as the result of a coup d'etat. To consolidate his position he made peace with the Church and the Pope. The reason was that the great majority of the French people remained Catholic. To the concordat of 1801 and without the consent of the Pope, Napoleon added the so-called Organic Articles which resurrected the Gallican Articles of 1682 and imposed restrictions on the Church's freedom. In 1804, despite personal misgivings, Pius VII traveled to Paris to officiate at the coronation of Napoleon as emperor. Eventually, though, papal opposition to Napoleon's political ventures caused him to imprison the Pope (1809). The release of the Pope came only after Napoleon's power was broken (1813).

After' the Congress of Vienna (1815) monarchies, mostly absolute in character, were restored throughout Europe. Rome, grateful for the peace that was generally maintained until the revolutionary year 1848, accepted the situation by entering into concordats with the existing governments. The alliance of the Church with the absolute monarchies aroused the opposition of the Liberals to the Church everywhere. What is more, the Liberals denied in principle the right of the Church to speak about the morality of public affairs.

The year of revolutions, 1848, witnessed the triumph of a Liberal revolution in almost every capital of Europe. That year Pius IX (1846-78) was driven from Rome and the Papal States by Mazzini and Garibaldi who set up a republic. Two years later, however, with the help of a French army, the Pope regained his temporal sovereignty. It was not to endure. In 1860 King Victor Emmanuel of Piedmont captured the Papal States; and in 1870 he took Rome itself. The Italian government introduced the Law of Guarantees to regulate the position of the papacy and the relations between Church and State. The Pope refused to recognize the Law of Guarantees because recognition would have been tantamount to renunciation of papal sovereignty over the Papal States. The Pope became the "Prisoner of the Vatican."

There were also important doctrinal developments during the pontificate of Pius IX: the definition of Mary's Immaculate Conception (1854), the Syllabus of Errors (1864), and the definition of papal infallibility by the First Vatican Council (1870).

In America, the first amendment to the constitution of the United States forbade the Congress to make any law respecting an establishment of religion or prohibiting the free exercise thereof. In 1789 John Carroll was appointed bishop of Baltimore which became an archdiocese in 1808 with four suffragan dioceses, New York, Philadelphia, Boston, and Bardstown. Soon afterwards the dioceses of Cincinnati (1821) and St. Louis (1826) were set up. At the beginning of the 19th century the American Catholic community was quite small, being numbered in the thousands; but it expanded rapidly in the 1830s and 1840s as the result of immigration. The immigration, largely Irish, raised the Catholic population to two or three million by the middle of the century. The number of bishoprics increased correspondingly. The rapid growth of the Catholic population aroused a violent anti-Catholic reaction centered in the "Know-Nothing" movement. The national emergency of the Civil War (1861-65), however, drew Catholics and their compatriots together. Catholics fought side by side with their Protestant brethren, while priests and nuns did admirable work in ministering to the wounded and dying. In the second half of the century waves of German and Italian immigrants poured into the country so that there were approximately ten million Catholics in the United States by the turn of the century. Bigotry reasserted itself from time to time —one thinks of the American Protective Association, for example; but it did not reach the intensity of the Know-Nothing campaign.

The successor of Pius IX was Leo XIII (1878-1903), one of the greatest Popes of modern times. He was notable for his clear perception of the wave of the future: democracy and unionism. He wrote a series of remarkable encyclical letters on a variety of topics: the importance of Thomas Aquinas for Catholic philosophy and theology, the relationship between the Church and the secular State, the condition of the working classes, the Holy Spirit, the Eucharist, the rosary, and biblical studies. Leo consecrated the human race to the Sacred Heart of Jesus, encouraged

Eucharistic congresses, established the Biblical Commission, and opened the secret archives of the Vatican to historians. During his pontificate new Catholic universities were founded at Washington and Fribourg, Switzerland; the Thomistic institute of philosophy was opened at Louvain; the hierarchy was expanded considerably; and missionary activity received a new impulse.

Leo's diplomacy on behalf of the Church was only partially successful. He did witness the end of the *Kulturkampf* in Germany. The *Kulturkampf* (1871-87) was waged by the chancellor Bismarck against the Church. It involved the expulsion of the Jesuits and other religious orders and the interference of the State in ecclesiastical affairs such as the training of the clergy and the bishop's relations with his priests. The unified resistance of German Catholics, the unwillingness of Leo to compromise on essential points, and other factors led ultimately to the revocation of the offensive laws by the government.

In France Leo's efforts did not succeed—at least in his own lifetime. In 1880 a government hostile to Catholics dissolved or expelled the religious orders, prohibited religious instructions in the schools, suppressed chaplaincies in State institutions, and took other measures to secularize French life. Leo counseled French Catholics to seek redress, not by working for the restoration of the monarchy, but by employing the legal machinery set up by the republic. French Catholics were so divided among themselves, however, that they were able to achieve very little; and Leo's remonstrances to the French government were ignored. In Italy, Leo had no greater success. The Italian government, provoked because the Pope refused to accept the Law of Guarantees (mentioned earlier), had enacted anti-Catholic laws similar to those in force in France. Violent anti-papal demonstrations took place with the connivance of the Italian government. Leo even thought of leaving Rome. The situation did not improve while he was Pope.

The 19th century saw the establishment of new religious orders: numerous Benedictine congregations (including the one at Solesmes founded by Dom Guéranger), the Oblates of Mary Immaculate (1816), the Marists (1816), the Sisters of the Good Shepherd (1835), the Little Sisters of the Poor (1840), the

Salesians (1868) founded by St. John Bosco, and the Trappists (1892). The Church-wide reestablishment of the Jesuits (1814) has already been mentioned. The Dominicans gained new life and inspiration from Lacordaire and Jandel. The apparitions of our Lady to St. Bernadette at Lourdes took place in 1858. The Curé of Ars, St. John Mary Vianney, a model of parish priests, died in 1859.

ULTRAMONTANISM

After the French Revolution, two ecclesiological currents emerged. One current, ultramontanism, represented in France by the traditionalists, de Maistre and La Mennais, and in Italy by Cappellari (later Pope Gregory XVI) and others, pressed for the reestablishment of papal authority. In doing so, it tended to resist both Gallican and liberal tendencies within the Church. Ultramontanism prepared the way for the First Vatican Council. The other ecclesiological current, to which the German theologian, J.A. Möhler, gave a powerful impetus, stimulated the renewal of the Church by viewing it as a communion with an inner life of its own. The ideas of Möhler eventually found expression in the first draft of the constitution on the Church submitted to the First Vatican Council, then in the encyclical, *Mystici corporis* (1943) of Pope Pius XII, and finally in the constitution on the Church (1964) published by the Second Vatican Council.

Joseph de Maistre (1753-1821), the father of ultramontanism in France, was a layman. As a pupil of the Jesuits, he had been inspired with an intense love of the Church and the papacy. His book, *Du Pape* (*The Pope*), published in 1819, was the result of his reflection upon the relationship between religion and the social order. He came to this conclusion: Christianity cannot exist without the Pope, and without Christianity the social order cannot endure. The book has four parts. In the first part, the author demonstrates the sovereignty of the Pope over the Church which has a monarchial constitution. The absolute sovereignty of the Pope demands that he be infallible when he teaches since it is by his teaching that he exercises his sovereignty. The distinction between the see of Rome and its occupant is without foundation. History testifies that no Pope has erred in a matter of faith in accordance with the divine promise of infallibility. The doctrine of papal sovereignty has undergone a legitimate development over the centuries. In the remaining parts of his book de Maistre discusses the relations between the papacy and the State, civilization, and the schismatic Churches. De Maistre's book on the Pope had the effect of bringing the question of papal primacy and infallibility to the attention of the public.

Felicité de La Mennais (1782-1854), a French priest, also promoted the cause of ultramontanism. He was convinced that the Church should lend full support to democratic movements everywhere. He called for those civil liberties that are now taken for granted in modern democratic countries: freedom of the press, freedom of speech, freedom of education, freedom of assembly and universal suffrage. La Mennais believed that a clergy which was totally independent of the State could be a powerful bulwark against political tyranny. Such a clergy, however, had to be led by an infallible Pope who was the undisputed master of the Church. For this reason La Mennais was a proponent of ultramontanism and a vigorous opponent of Gallican tendencies in the Church. He criticized severely those French bishops who, in his judgment, maintained the Church in subjection to the State. It seems that La Mennais supported ultramontanism not so much because he believed in the spiritual primacy of the Pope, but because he saw in it a valuable political tool. La Mennais propagated his ideas especially in his newspaper, L'Avenir (*The Future*). Having gained a reputation as an apologist for the Church in his *Essai sur l'indifférence en matiére de religion,* he attracted a number of enthusiastic disciples for his ultramontane campaign, among them Guéranger, the abbot, and Rohrbacher, the historian. La Mennais abandoned the Church after Pope Gregory XVI (1831-46) condemned his liberal views in the encyclical, *Mirari vos* (1832).

Prior to his election as Pope Gregory XVI, Mauro Cappellari had written a book *Il Trionfo della Santa Sede e della Chiesa (The Triumph of the Holy See and the Church)* published in

1799. In this book, the future Pope asserted the identity between the Church and its juridical structure. In opposition to Febronius, Cappellari denied that the original collegial constitution of the Church had been illegitimately supplanted by a monarchial constitution under the influence of the false decretals. Since the Church does not change, he argued, the Church has always had a monarchial constitution such as it had in Cappellari's day. He discussed the monarchial government of the Church in terms of the *Politics* of Aristotle for whom a monarchy was the ideal form of government. Because Cappellari identified the Church with its juridical structure, he concluded that the Church is infallible since the Pope, its ruler and foundation, is infallible. Cappellari's book attracted considerable attention especially after he was elected Pope. His election and the book furthered the ultramontanist cause.

During the pontificate of Leo XII (1823-29), the Gregorian University, which had been reopened at Rome in 1818, was once again placed under the direction of the Jesuits in 1824. The teaching of the Jesuit professors was marked by balance. While they forcefully defended the visible side of the Church and the prerogatives of the Roman Pontiff, they did not neglect the invisible aspects of the Church as the body of Christ. Their balanced presentation was the result of study of the writings of the Greek Fathers and contact with the writings of Petau, the great positive theologian of the 17th century, and Möhler, their contemporary.

Among the Jesuit professors at the Gregorian University several stand out. John Perrone served successively as professor, rector, and prefect of studies from 1824 until 1876, the year of his death. He exercised an enormous influence in Catholic theological circles throughout Europe and the rest of the world thanks to an ever-growing number of students and the success of the manuals he composed. His *Praelectiones theologicae* (1835-42) in nine volumes went through 34 editions; and a *Compendium* (1845) in two volumes went through 47 editions. Charles Passaglia (1812-87) published his *De Ecclesia Christi* (2 vols.) in 1853-56. In this work he inaugurated a new method

of theologizing about the Church, taking as his point of departure
the Scriptural and patristic images of the Church and not the
nature and laws of a human society. He recognized the analogy
between the hypostatic union and the union between Christ and
His Church. His balanced treatment and methodology represented a considerable advance over the many contemporary (almost exclusively) juridical treatises on the Church.

John Franzelin (1816-86), the student of Perrone and
Passaglia, then professor, papal theologian at Vatican I, and
cardinal, composed *Theses de Ecclesia* which appeared posthumously in 1887. He too began his study of the Church with
the Scriptural data, defending the visible and monarchial character of the Church. The Church is the spouse of Christ and His
mystical body; it is the extension of the Incarnation. At the
end of his work, Franzelin discussed membership in the Church
much after the manner of Bellarmine. Clement Schrader (1820-
75), who was noted for his ultramontane views, was largely responsible for the first draft of the dogmatic constitution on the
Church of Christ presented to the First Vatican Council. In
this draft Schrader proposed to define the Church as the mystical
body of Christ—to the great astonishment of many conciliar
fathers who were accustomed to a more juridical definition of
the Church.

Two active proponents of ultramontanism among English-
speaking Catholics were W.G. Ward (1812-82), the editor of
the *Dublin Review,* and H.E. Manning (1808-92), the archbishop of Westminster.

With the First Vatican Council (1869-70), the ultramontane
campaign reached a successful conclusion. The council produced
a definition of papal primacy and infallibility. It had planned to
issue other definitions about the constitution of the Church; but
the deliberations of the council were interrupted by the threat of
war between Germany and France. The council had aroused
considerable excitement in Europe; and after its adjournment
there was a schism in Germany among those who refused to
accept the conciliar definitions. The historian, Ignaz Döllinger,
and other academics at Munich, Bonn, Braunsberg and else-

where were either excommunicated by their bishops or left the Church. Döllinger himself was never reconciled to the Church; but against his advice a number of schismatic clerics and laymen decided to form a separate Church, the "Old Catholics," at a congress held at Munich in 1871.

At the outset of his academic career at the university of Munich, Döllinger (1799-1890) had defended the monarchial constitution of the Church. The concept of tradition played an important role in his thinking. The consensus of the Fathers and Churches of the early centuries was the norm of faith for all ages to come. Yet Döllinger was prepared to admit the possibility of doctrinal development whereby that which was involved in facts, principles and dogmas was eventually disclosed. The principal object of theological effort was to show the unilinear continuity of dogma.

For a number of reasons, though, Döllinger became anti-Roman. He looked askance at the revival of scholastic theology by the Jesuits at Rome to the detriment, in his opinion, of historical theology. He came under attack for his frank discussions of papal failures in the course of history. A congress of theologians which met under his presidency at Munich in 1863 was the occasion of a critical letter, *Tuas libenter*,[1] from Pius IX to the archbishop of Munich. Döllinger began to call for national Churches ruled by a national metropolitan—a kind of Febronianism.

Döllinger was unable to accept the definitions of Vatican I. He could not reconcile in his own mind these definitions with the role of the papacy in the early Christian centuries. He could not understand how the council could define a doctrine as a dogma of faith when the opposite had been freely taught and believed in many dioceses. He felt too that the council had been deprived of its freedom by excessive pressure from the Pope. Finally, it seemed to him that the definition of papal supremacy had robbed the episcopal office of meaning.[2]

The other ecclesiological current of the 19th century which looked at the Church as a communion with an inner life of its own was inaugurated by the German theologian, J.A. Möhler.

JOHANN ADAM MOHLER

Möhler (1796-1838) was born at the beginning of the romantic era, roughly 1800 to 1850. Romanticism was the reaction against the cold intellectualism of the Enlightenment with its rejection of traditional values and its tendency towards individualism. Romanticism reawakened an interest in the past and an awareness of human solidarity. The influential German theologian Friederick Schleiermacher (1768-1834), was faithful to the romantic trend when he pictured the community of mankind as a living organism, each individual making a specific contribution to the life of the greater organism. In this context it was easy for philosophers and writers to speak about the soul of a community or nation. The romantic movement was not without effect upon German Catholic theologians. It encouraged them to undertake a study of the Scriptural and patristic sources of the past. It stimulated in them a renewed consciousness of the Church as a communion and social organism with a life of its own whose soul is the Spirit of Christ.

The principal precursor of Möhler was Johann Michael Sailer (1751-1832) who taught pastoral and moral theology, pedagogy, homiletics, liturgy and catechetics at the university of Landshut, Germany. Sailer saw in the Church a society which contributed to the religious development of the individual by its liturgical rites and hierarchical directives. The Church is the living norm of faith. Apostolic tradition is preserved in the Church under the active assistance of God. The Church is the mystical body of Christ, a spiritual organism which is both visible and invisible. Before Möhler, Sailer had been the moving spirit in the Catholic restoration in Germany, attracting large crowds of students to the university of Landshut—the former university of Ingolstadt which was eventually moved to Munich.

Johann Adam Möhler was ordained to the priesthood in 1819. He taught at the university of Tübingen from 1823 until 1835 and then taught at the university of Munich until his premature death in 1838. Möhler's theological reflection upon the mystery of the Church evolved through several stages. The first stage is represented by his lectures on canon law (1824-25) at Tübingen and by articles and reviews published by him in the *Theologische Quartalschrift* (1823-24). At this stage Möhler saw the Church principally as a visible and hierarchical society. Very quickly, however, under the influence of romanticism and in opposition to the principles of the Enlightenment, he came to look at the Church differently. He began to stress the "mystical" side of the Church—the action of the Holy Spirit and the union of the faithful in faith and charity. Sometimes his regard for the influence of the Spirit seemed to render the external structures of the Church superfluous. In his lectures on canon law Möhler defended the basic equality of bishops and priests in order and jurisdiction. Priests and bishops differ only because the fullness of jurisdiction is reserved to bishops. The Pope is subordinate to the whole body of bishops but he is the supreme executor of the canons.

The second stage of Möhler's reflection upon the mystery of the Church is represented by his book, *Unity in the Church or the Principle of Catholicism Expounded in the Spirit of the Fathers of the Church of the First Three Centuries* (1825). In this book Möhler reconciled more successfully the visible and social aspects of the Church with the vivifying influence of the Holy Spirit. The book is divided into two parts. The first part which is concerned with the unity of the Spirit of the Church speaks of the Spirit as the One who fashions believers into a community. Only in the community do we become conscious of Christ (ch. 1). Christian doctrine is the conceptual expression of that which the Spirit accomplishes in the Church. Both Scripture and tradition reflect the life of the Church which is animated by the Spirit (ch. 2). The fact that heretics are guilty of unorthodox doctrines is a sign that they are not animated by the Spirit of the Church (ch. 3). Even though the Church is a communion, each member preserves his individuality. The members complement each other in virtue of their differences (ch. 4).

The second part of Möhler's book, *Unity in the Church,* is concerned with the unity of the body of the Church. The Church is the visible form of the love imparted to believers by the Holy Spirit. The center of each diocese is the bishop who is the image of the love in the community; indeed, he is the personification of

the community's love. Ordination is a testimony that the Spirit
is present in a member of the faithful and makes him capable of
representing the love of a certain number of believers (ch. 1).
Neighboring dioceses quite naturally seek a close association.
Their bishops form a unity which finds expression and a center
in the metropolitan (archbishop). The bishop must not undertake
any important project without the consultation of the metropolitan (ch. 2). The tendency toward visible unity affects the whole
Church. The visible unity of all the believers in the Church corresponds to their invisible unity in the Spirit. The unity of the
whole Church is centered in, and personified by, the successor
of Peter, the bishop of Rome (chs. 3-4). It is evident that
Möhler explains the role of the hierarchy by appealing to the
community's impulse toward unity. He pays less attention to
the historical link between the hierarchy and the apostles.

The third stage of Möhler's reflection upon the mystery of
the Church is represented by his *Symbolik*[4] which went through
five editions between 1832 and 1838. The *Symbolik* is a study of
the doctrinal differences that separate Christian confessions. The
fifth chapter of the first section is devoted to the Church. In the
Symbolik Möhler no longer stresses the organic and pneumato-
logical aspects of the Church. Instead he turns to the incarnate
Son of God as the appropriate analogue of the Church. The human and the divine are distinct but not separated in the Church
as in the hypostatic union. The Church is the extension of the
incarnation in space and time. The incarnation is the ultimate
reason for the visibility of the Church.

> By the Church on earth Catholics mean the visible com-
> munity of all the believers founded by Christ. In this com-
> munion the acts of Christ performed by Him during His
> earthly life for the forgiveness and sanctification of men
> are continued to the end of the world by an enduring ap-
> ostolic ministry commissioned by Him. . . .
>
> The ultimate reason for the visibility of the Church lies in
> the incarnation of the divine Word. If the Word had de-
> scended into the hearts of men without assuming the form
> of a slave and appearing in a visible manner, He would have
> established an invisible, inner Church. But the Word be-
> came flesh; He spoke in a manner perceptible to men; He

suffered and worked in a human manner in order to win men for the kingdom of God. Hence, He chose that means which was most appropriate for the instruction of men. After His departure from this world.., the preaching of His message required a visible, human agency [the Church] whereby men spoke to men and dealt with them in order to bring them the word of God....

The visible Church is the enduring presence of the Son of God in human form among men... It is His continual incarnation; hence, the faithful are called the body of Christ in the Scriptures. From this it is clear that the Church is not merely human although its members are human beings. What is more, just as the divine and human are to be distinguished in Christ but not separated, so Christ is continued in the Church in an undivided manner. The Church which is His continuing appearance among men is both divine and human at the same time; the Church is the union of both. It is Christ, hidden in earthly and human forms, who works in the Church..; the Church is infallible.

In the Church and through it the redemption proclaimed by Christ through the Spirit has become real, for in the Church His truths are believed, His institutions are carried out and become alive... When the word spoken by Christ—word being taken in its widest sense—enters with His Spirit into a community and is accepted by it, the word takes shape, it becomes flesh and blood, and this shape is the Church....[5]

What is the origin and role of the hierarchy according to this conception of the Church? In the *Unity in the Church* the communion of believers engenders the bishop, the metropolitan and the Pope under the impulse of the Holy Spirit. In the *Symbolik* the Church derives its origin from the incarnate Son of God with the selection of the apostles. In turn, the apostles chose the bishops as their successors who continue the mission of the apostles to the present. The episcopacy, therefore, is of divine institution. The succession of bishops is an external sign of the Church founded by Christ. The papacy too is of divine institution. The Pope is the successor of Peter and the visible head of the visible Church. The Pope is the center and chief of the episcopacy. Papal primacy is necessary in order to coordinate the activity of the universal Church.[6]

Möhler's writings were well-known to the Jesuit professors at the Gregorian University. In their own writings, these professors—Perrone, Passaglia, Schrader, Franzelin—presented a more or less balanced view of the Church as a visible, yet spiritual society which is the body of Christ. Schrader and Franzelin proposed this view of the Church in the first draft of the constitution on the Church submitted to the fathers of the First Vatican Council; but the council was unable to complete its work. Later, the encyclical, *Mystici corporis* (1943) of Pope Pius XII and *Lumen gentium*, Vatican II's constitution on the Church (1964), incorporated certain ideas of Möhler.

JOHN PERRONE

John Perrone (d. 1876), a Jesuit who taught at the Gregorian University in Rome, was possibly the most influential of all the theologians associated with that institution in the 19th century. His students were many; and the theological manuals he composed were extremely successful by reason of their clarity and erudition. His principal work was the *Praelectiones theologicae*. In this work the treatise on the Church is a part of the treatise, *De locis theologicis,* which studies the sources from which the theologian draws his arguments and conclusions. Hence, Perrone was more concerned with the role of the Church as the rule of faith and action than with the inner life of the Church. In the first section on the Church, Perrone speaks of the foundation of the Church by Christ, its constitution (which he compares to the union of soul and body), its marks, and its characteristics (indefectibility, infallibility, and authority). In the second and final section on the Church, Perrone speaks exclusively of the Roman Pontiff who is the successor of Peter and the visible head of the Church. The authority of the Roman Pontiff extends to all the faithful including the bishops, singly and collectively. The Roman Pontiff is infallible when he speaks *ex cathedra.*[7]

One notes in Perrone's discussion of the Church few references to the office of bishops or the role of the laity. There is no extended examination of many important biblical and patristic images of the Church. The life of the Church as a communion receives comparatively little attention. It must be said, however, that Perrone did recognize the analogy between the Church and the human person with his soul and body and the analogy between the Church and the incarnate Son of God.[8]

PIUS IX

THE FIRST VATICAN COUNCIL

Prior to his confirmation of Vatican I's definition of papal infallibility, Pope Pius IX revealed his mind about the teaching authority of the Church in several documents. In the encyclical, *Qui pluribus* (1846), he spoke of the infallibility of the Roman Church and the Pope:

> Since the Church is where Peter is, since Peter speaks through the Roman Pontiff and always lives and judges in his successors and affords the truth of faith to those who seek it, therefore what God has said must be plainly understood in the sense which the chair of Peter at Rome has held and holds. As the mother and teacher of all the Churches, it has always kept whole and inviolate the faith handed down by Christ the Lord. . .[9]

In a letter to the archbishop of Munich (1862), Pius IX remarked about the duty of philosophers to teach nothing contrary to what divine revelation and the Church teach.[10] In a second letter to the same archbishop (1863), the Pope insisted on the obligation of Catholic academics to accept not only the dogmas of the Church but also the doctrinal decisions of papal congregations and teachings commonly held by Catholics.[11]

During the pontificate of Pius IX, the Holy Office rejected (1864) the so-called "branch theory" of the Church in a letter to the bishops of England. The branch theory supposed that the true Church of Christ consists of three branches: the Roman Catholic, Orthodox and Anglican Churches. In its rejection of the branch theory, the Holy Office made this statement about the Church of Jesus Christ:

> . . . The true Church of Jesus Christ is constituted by divine authority and is known by four notes. We lay down these notes as matters of faith in the Creed. And any one of these notes is so joined to the others that it cannot be separated

from them. Hence it is that the Church that is really catholic, and is called Catholic, must, at the same time, shine with the prerogative of unity, sanctity, and apostolic succession. Therefore, the Catholic Church is one by a conspicuous and perfect unity of the whole world and of all peoples, by that unity, indeed, whose principle, root, and never-failing source is in the supreme authority and 'greater sovereignty' of St. Peter, the Prince of the Apostles, and of his successors in the Roman Chair. Nor is any other Church catholic except that which has been built upon Peter alone and which rises into one body closely joined and knit together (Ep 4:16) in the unity of faith and love....[12]

The same year (1864) Pius IX issued the encyclical *Quanta cura* to which he attached the famous Syllabus of Errors. The syllabus was a compilation and condemnation of eighty current religious errors. The errors had been condemned in earlier papal documents such as encyclicals, apostolic letters and allocutions; but the condemned errors were enumerated once more in the syllabus for the benefit of those bishops who might have been unaware of them. The errors were concerned with pantheism, naturalism, rationalism, indifferentism, latitudinarianism, the Church, civil society, natural and Christian ethics, Christian matrimony, the temporal authority of the Roman Pontiff, and liberalism.[13]

It would be misleading simply to recount the errors about the Church included in the syllabus. Catholic interpreters of the syllabus point out that the errors condemned must be understood in the context of the document in which they were originally examined. As an illustration, take the very last error noted in the syllabus:

"The Roman Pontiff can and should reconcile and harmonize himself with progress, liberalism, and recent civilization."[14]

This error was originally examined in the allocution *Jamdudum cernimus* of March 18, 1861. From the context of the allocution, it is clear that the Pope is unwilling to reconcile himself to the notions of progress, liberalism and civilization sustained by the anti-clerical government of Piedmont. This government's conception of progress, liberalism and civilization entailed an infringement of the Church's rights. Hence, the

Pope's condemnation did not necessarily mean a condemnation of progress, liberalism and civilization as these terms were understood elsewhere. The misunderstanding surrounding the Syllabus of Errors underscores the necessity of reading papal pronouncements in their historical context.

Pius IX summoned the First Vatican Council (1869-70), the 20th ecumenical council, to deal with the contemporary onslaught against the foundations of revealed religion and the authority of the Church to teach. On April 24th, 1870, the Pope solemnly proclaimed the constitution, *Dei Filius*, drawn up by the council. This constitution treats of God, revelation, faith and reason in four chapters. In the chapter on faith (c. 3), the council described the Church as a perpetual motive of credibility and an irrefutable proof of its own divine mission:

> For all the many marvelous proofs that God has provided to make the credibility of the Christian faith evident point to the Catholic Church alone. Indeed, the Church itself, because of its marvelous propagation, its exalted sanctity, and its inexhaustible fruitfulness in all that is good, because of its catholic unity and its unshaken stability, is a great and perpetual motive of credibility and an irrefutable proof of its own divine mission.[15]

On July 18, 1870, the Pope solemnly proclaimed the constitution, *Pastor aeternus,* drawn up by the council. This constitution defined the primacy of the Pope and his infallibility in matters of faith and morals. Originally, the subject of papal infallibility had not been on the council's agenda. The first draft of the constitution on the Church submitted to the council contained 15 chapters none of which referred specifically to papal infallibility. The first draft spoke of the Church as the body of Christ, a visible and spiritual society outside of which there is no salvation. This Church is indefectible and infallible, infallibility being ascribed to the Church as a whole and to the magisterium without further explicitation. In the first draft there were also chapters on papal authority and the relationship between the Church and the State.[16] The Pope thought it would be improper for him to introduce the subject of papal infallibility, although he was agreeable to its introduction if the council wished to consider it.

Under the leadership of Manning, the archbishop of Westminster, the ultramontanes pressed for consideration of papal primacy and infallibility. They were successful. At the direction of the Pope, the council took up the subject. The result was the constitution, *Pastor aeternus.*[17] The constitution covers familiar ground in four chapters: Christ conferred the primacy of jurisdiction over the Church of God upon the apostle Peter. The council cited three gospel passages in support of this thesis: Jn 1: 42; Mt 16:17-19; Jn 21:15-17 (ch. 1). According to the institution of Christ, Peter has perpetual successors in the primacy since the Church will endure until the end of time. These successors are the Roman Pontiffs (ch. 2). The Roman Pontiff has full and supreme power of jurisdiction, not only in matters of faith and morals, but also in matters that pertain to the discipline and government of the Church. His jurisdiction is ordinary and immediate over every Church and every shepherd and individual faithful (ch. 3).

The final chapter of the constitution (ch. 4) deals with the infallible teaching authority of the Roman Pontiff. The primacy of the Pope includes the supreme power of teaching. The practice of the Church and its ecumenical councils confirms this fact. The charism of truth was conferred on Peter and his successors that the Church might be secure in the teaching of Christ and preserved as one. Hence, the definition of papal infallibility:

> The Roman Pontiff, when he speaks *ex cathedra*, that is, when, acting in the office of shepherd and teacher of all Christians, he defines, by virtue of his supreme apostolic authority, doctrine concerning faith or morals to be held by the universal Church, possesses through the divine assistance promised him in the person of St. Peter, the infallibility with which the divine Redeemer willed his Church to be endowed in defining doctrine concerning faith or morals; and that such definitions of the Roman Pontiff are therefore irreformable because of their nature, but not because of the agreement of the Church.[18]

The constitution, *Pastor aeternus*, laid to rest the theory of Gallicanism which held, among other things, that the judgement of the Pope in matters of faith is not final until the Church has consented to it. The constitution, however, led to a certain narrowing of perspective. The office of teaching and governing tended to be seen more and more by Catholics as concentrated in the hands of the Pope. The episcopacy was allotted and actually exercised a diminishing role in the government of the Church and the formulation of Christian teaching. It was this constitution which more than any other factor determined the terms and context of the debates of Vatican II on episcopal collegiality.

MATTHIAS JOSEPH SCHEEBEN

M.J. Scheeben (1835-88) studied at the Gregorian University under Perrone and Passaglia from 1852 to 1859. He taught dogmatic theology at the episcopal seminary of Cologne (1860-88). He was unable to complete his most extensive work, the *Manual of Catholic Dogma;* consequently, he did not write his projected treatise on the Church. At the beginning of this work, however, he dealt with the *Lehrapostolat* (teaching mission) of the Church. Moreover, in *The Mysteries of Christianity*, the second edition of which was his last scientific work, Scheeben gave us a comprehensive view of the whole of his theology. In this latter work he devoted part 6 to the mystery of the Church.

Scheeben included the Church among the mysteries of Christianity because it is impossible to understand fully the supernatural grandeur and sublimity of the Church even after it has been revealed by God. "To the eyes of faith the Church is not merely a society founded and approved by God or a divine legate; but it is built upon the God-man, it is made an organic part of Him, it is raised to His level, it is upheld by His divine power and it is filled with His divine excellence."[19] Faith and baptism truly initiate us into the Church which is the body of Christ; but faith and baptism are only preliminaries for the coming together of man and the God-man in one flesh by a real communion of flesh and blood in the Eucharist. The Holy Spirit dwells in the Church as the soul in its own body. The Spirit reigns in the members of the Church by guiding, assisting and healing them, by elevating and transfiguring man beyond his nature, by pervading him with divine life.[20]

With all this we are still far from appreciating the mystery of the Church. Scheeben explains why. The God-man willed further to appoint some members of the ecclesiastical community as representatives and organs of His own activity. These members are the priesthood of the Church. Through the priesthood, the Church, the bride of Christ, exercises her maternity. The Church is a loving mother toward her members by imparting to them a new birth, by caring for them, nourishing them, instructing them and rearing them like children. The Church accomplishes all this through the priesthood which functions as an intermediary between Christ and His children much as a mother does between father and children.[21]

The maternity of the Church which is represented by a specially favored number of its members comprises two functions: the power to confer grace and the power to direct the use and acquisition of grace. This distinction coincides with the distinction between the power of orders and the power of jurisdiction. By the power of jurisdiction is meant not only external legislative power but especially the power by which the Church authoritatively directs and regulates the activity of her subjects and by which it establishes and enforces the norms for that activity. The unity of the Church in its social life depends in a special way on the unity of the pastoral power. The unity of pastoral power is guaranteed by the fact that the entire social structure of the Church rests on the foundation of the supreme pontiff. The pastoral power passes from him to other pastors of the Church as rays emanate from the sun. He who has the pastoral power in its plenitude must possess infallibility; otherwise, he could not guide those subject to that power with absolute reliability.[22]

Scheeben wrote about the teaching mission of the Church in the first volume of his *Handbuch der katholischen Dogmatik*[23] (*Manual of Catholic Dogmatics*). According to Scheeben, the proclamation of God's revealed word comprises three elements: exposition of its content and meaning, certification of its authenticity, and imposition of the obligation to accept it as the object of faith.[24] The first two elements pertain to the hierarchy's power of orders while the third element pertains to its power of jurisdiction.[25] In virtue of their fulness of orders, bishops are independent and authentic teachers while other orders, such as priests and deacons, are their helpers.[26] The jurisdiction of bishops, however, is restricted to a particular flock and is subordinate to that of the Pope; hence, the doctrinal pronouncements of bishops do not have the force of papal pronouncements.[27]

The Pope and the bishops constitute a body of teachers, the *Ecclesia docens*. The faithful constitute a body of learners and believers, the *Ecclesia discens*. Together both constitute one bodily organism,[28] related to each other as an active principle to a receptive principle.[29] Infallibility belongs radically to the Holy Spirit which animates the body of the Church in its entirety. In virtue of the assistance of the Holy Spirit, the hierarchy is infallible in an active sense so that it cannot lead the Church into error by its teaching. The faithful are infallible in a passive sense so that they cannot be misled by the teaching of the hierarchy. Infallibility has been given to the hierarchy for the benefit of the faithful.[30] The Holy Spirit effects the unity of those who teach and those who believe. The belief of the faithful reflects the teaching of the hierarchy, reinforces it, and prepares the way for doctrinal decisions.[31]

Scheeben belonged to no theological school nor did he found one; but he expressed a number of ideas about the Church which gained a new currency after the Second Vatican Council.

JOHN HENRY NEWMAN

J.H. Newman was born in London in 1801. After studies at Oxford, he was ordained an Anglican priest in 1824. He entered the Catholic Church in 1845 and was named a cardinal in 1879. He died in Birmingham, England, in 1890.

Newman did not write a monograph on the Church. He wrote about it when and as circumstances demanded. Prominent in his mind was the dynamic union of Christians with Christ in His mystical body in virtue of which they share in the threefold office of Christ as prophet, priest and king. Christ exercised his prophetical office in teaching and foretelling the future, His priestly office in sacrificing Himself on Calvary and at the Last Supper, His kingly office in rising from the dead and in the glorious events following thereupon. When Christ withdrew from this earth, He left behind Him those who would take His place, a ministerial order, who were His representatives and instruments; and these show forth the prophetical, priestly and regal character of Christ. Indeed, all the followers of Christ in some measure bear all three offices, as Scripture[32] is not slow to declare.[33] In accordance with the three offices of Christ, holy Church, the body of Christ, has a triple office—teaching, ruling, and sacred ministry.[34]

For Newman, Christianity is a *revelatio revelata,* a message from God to man distinctly conveyed by chosen instruments and to be received as such a message. It is to be maintained as true and certain because it comes from God who can neither deceive nor be deceived.[35] A revelation, however, is not given if there is no authority to decide what it is that is given. There is no such authority except the Church. Hence, we must yield to the authority of the Church in questions of faith. Scripture expressly calls the Church "the pillar and ground of truth."[36] Both the hierarchy and the faithful are involved in the teaching office of the Church. The hierarchy has received the divine mandate to teach while the faithful render testimony to the faith they have received. All the faithful including the hierarchy have the duty and the privilege of meditating upon the faith handed down in order to gain a better understanding of it. The theologian has a special responsibility for furthering a better understanding of it by reason of his training. Both the hierarchy and the laity are charged with the apostolate of spreading the faith. The laity can carry on this apostolate by personal contacts, by study, and by being Christians to the core.[37]

The members of the Church, each in his own way, participate in the office of Christ as priest by prayer and suffering.

> Christ died to bestow upon the Christian that privilege which implies or involves all others, and bring him into nearest resemblance to Himself, the privilege of intercession... As an heir of eternity, full of grace and good works, as walking in all the commandments of the Lord blameless, such a one, I repeat it; is plainly in his fitting place when he intercedes. He is made after the pattern

and in the fulness of Christ—he is what Christ is. Christ intercedes above, and he intercedes below.[38]

The Church participates in the office of Christ as priest in order to reconcile the soul to God.

The one object of the Church, to which every other object is second, is that of reconciling the soul to God... Her one object, through her ten thousand organs, by preachers, by confessors, by parish priests and by religious communities, in missions and retreats, at Christmas and at Easter, by fasts and by feasts, by confraternities and by pilgrimages, by devotions and by indulgences, is this unwearied, ever-patient reconciliation of the soul to God and obliteration of sin.[39]

Finally, the Church participates in the office of Christ as king.

As the kingdom of heaven upon earth, the Christian Church is a universal empire without earthly arms; temporal pretensions without temporal sanctions; a claim to rule without the power to enforce; a continual tendency to acquire with a continual exposure to be dispossessed; greatness of mind with weakness of body. What will be the fortunes of such an empire in the world? Persecution. Persecution is the token of the Church, perhaps the most abiding note of all. The world is strong: men of the world have the arms of the world, they have swords, they have armies, they have prisons, they have chains, they have passions. The Church has none of these, and yet it claims a right to rule, direct, rebuke, exhort, denounce, condemn. It claims the obedience of the powerful; it confronts the haughty; it places itself across the path of the wilful; it undertakes the defence of the poor; it accepts the gifts of the world, and becomes involved in their stewardship; and yet it is at the mercy of these said powerful, haughty, and wilful men, to ill-treat and to spoil.[40]

Newman was always the defender of the prerogatives of the hierarchy. He was simultaneously the defender of the important role which the laity must play in the life of the Church.

LEO XIII

Pope Leo XIII (1878-1903) frequently employed the encyclical letter in order to express his mind. His encyclical letter,

Immortale Dei (1885), dealt with the Christian constitution of States. According to the Pope, man's natural instinct moves him to live in civil society. Every civilized community must have a ruling authority. The right to rule is not necessarily bound up with any special form of government. Government exists solely for the welfare of the State. All authority, civil and religious, is from God. There are two perfect (self-sufficient) societies, the Church and the State. Each is independent and sovereign in its own sphere. Church and State should cooperate. The Church is superior to the State in virtue of its spiritual and higher goal. The Church is competent in all matters of morality, natural law and revelation.

From these principles the Pope drew certain conclusions:

No one of the several forms of government is in itself condemned, inasmuch as none of them contains anything contrary to Catholic doctrine, and all of them are capable, if wisely and justly managed, to insure the welfare of the State. Neither is it blameworthy in itself, in any manner, for the people to share, to a greater or lesser degree, in the government: for at certain times, and under certain laws, such participation may not only be of benefit to the citizens, but may even be of obligation... The Church, indeed, deems it unlawful to place the various forms of divine worship on the same footing as the true religion, but does not, on that account, condemn those rulers who, for the sake of securing some great good or of hindering some great evil, allow patiently custom or usage to be a kind of sanction for each kind of religion having its place in the State. And in fact the Church is wont to take earnest heed that no one shall be forced to embrace the Catholic faith against his will, for, as St. Augustine wisely reminds us, 'Man cannot believe otherwise than of his own free will."[41]

Furthermore, the Church cannot approve that liberty which refuses obedience to lawful authority. This is not liberty so much as license. For individuals genuine liberty means freedom from error and passion. For the State it means the capacity for greater benefits and freedom from foreign intervention.

In his encyclical, *Satis cognitum* (1896), Pope Leo wrote about a different aspect of the Church, namely, its unity. The Church continues the mission of Christ until the end of time.

The Church is the body of Christ endowed with supernatural life.

As Christ, the head and exemplar, is not wholly in His visible human nature, which Photinians and Nestorians assert, nor wholly in the invisible divine nature, as the Monophysites hold, but is one, from and in both natures, visible and invisible; so the mystical body of Christ is the true Church only because its visible parts draw life and power from the supernatural gifts and other things whence spring their nature and essence.[42]

The Church of Christ is one; but it is not one in the sense that it is comprised of several communities similar in nature, but in themselves distinct and lacking those bonds which render the Church unique and indivisible. The Church is one because it is characterized by unity of faith. To insure the unity of faith Christ established a living, authoritative and permanent teaching authority. The magisterium rests with the Pope and bishops. The Church is one because it is characterized by unity of worship and social authority.[43]

The Church is a society divine in origin, supernatural in its end and in the means proximately adapted to the attainment of that end; but it is a human community inasmuch as it is composed of men. It is a perfect, that is, self-sufficient, society. As a society, the Church requires a supreme authority which effects a unity of communion. Christ established the Church on Peter and made him the supreme authority in His Church. The Popes have succeeded Peter in this capacity. The unity of the episcopacy is maintained by their communion with the chair of Peter.[44]

In the encyclical letter, *Divinum illud* (1897), Pope Leo wrote about the Holy Spirit and the Church. On the day of Pentecost the Holy Spirit began to manifest His gifts poured out on the Church. The descent of the Spirit was the fulfillment of a promise made by Christ. The Spirit continues to dwell in the Church for its increase and preservation. The Spirit acts through the bishops who minister the gifts of the Spirit to their flocks. As Christ is the head of the Church, so the Spirit is its soul. The Spirit will abide with the Church until the end.[45]

Finally, in his encyclical letter on the Holy Eucharist, *Mirae* caritatis (1902), Pope Leo wrote about the place of the Holy Eucharist in the Church. The Eucharist is a symbol and cause of unity among the faithful on earth. The Eucharist is a sacrifice which may be offered in honor of the saints in heaven and for the expiation of those being purified in purgatory. This sacrament is, as it were, the very soul of the Church. From this source the Church draws all her strength; therefore, the Church is intent on preparing the hearts of the faithful for an intimate union with Christ in this sacrament.[46]

Pope Leo was the last Pope of the 19th century. The 19th century had witnessed a determined effort on the part of the Popes and others—an effort that was not always successful— to reassert and exercise the legitimate authority of the Church and the Holy See. Simultaneously, the invisible and spiritual aspects of the Church received increased attention especially from theologians in German-speaking countries. This attention was the beginning of a doctrinal development that was to culminate in Vatican II's constitution on the Church.

THE OXFORD MOVEMENT

The 18th century was the age of the Enlightenment. The rationalism and deism of the period did not leave the Church of England untouched. As a reaction against the encroachment of the Enlightenment two strong movements arose within the Church of England—the Methodist (founded by John Wesley) and the evangelical. For the most part, the Methodists separated themselves from the Anglican Church. The evangelical movement did not break with the Anglican Church, but it emphasized those elements associated with Protestantism—preaching, salvation through faith, hymn singing, and less attachment to the sacramental and ceremonial aspects of religious life. The adherents of the evangelical movement are sometimes called Low Churchmen. The High Churchmen of Anglicanism, less numerous than their evangelical brethren at the end of the 18th century but not without influence, continued to stress the importance of episcopal succession and the authority of the Fathers along with other Catholic elements.

The most prominent event in the life of the English Church of the 19th century was the Oxford movement, an effort by Anglican clergymen of the university of Oxford between 1833 and 1845 to renew the Church of England by a revival of Catholic doctrine and practice. For the supporters of this movement, the Gospel was the story of God's real intervention in human history; and the Church and its sacraments were the tangible link between the historical incarnation of God's Son, Jesus Christ, and believers in every age. The Church was a pledge and proof of God's never-dying love and power from age to age (Newman). The Church was a divinely established community with its own authority, its own life and its own self-determination which ought to be free of interference from the State. The subjection of the English Church to the liberal and secular government in England was a calamity. The bishops of the Church rightly claimed apostolic succession and the dogmas of the Church were of apostolic origin. As long as the divisions within the Christian Church persisted, it was the duty of the Anglican Church to remain absolutely faithful to the teaching of the undivided Church of antiquity. The Oxford movement was characterized by a rejection of Protestant principles and a sympathy with many of the traditional ideas of High Churchmen.

John Keble (1792-1866) inaugurated the movement in a sermon preached at Oxford on "National Apostasy" in 1833. The immediate occasion of the sermon was the reorganization of Anglican bishoprics in Ireland by the English parliament. Keble was joined by Hurrell Froude (1802-36), his pupil, who "professed openly his admiration of the Church of Rome and his hatred of the Reformers. He delighted in the notion of a hierarchical system, of sacerdotal power, and of full ecclesiastical liberty . . . . He gloried in accepting Tradition as a main instrument of religious teaching."[47] Froude was in the closest and most affectionate friendship with John Henry Newman. Newman was the vicar of St. Mary's, the university church of Oxford. He was the movement's dominant figure and clearest voice. As an Anglican, he looked upon the English Church as a *via media*, a middle ground, between the extremes of papal corruptions and Protestant heresies. At this point in his life, he was vigorously anti-Roman. The English Church, he felt, was the Catholic Church in England because it preserved episcopal succession, the faith of the Fathers, and the use of the sacraments. An important convert to the Oxford movement was E.B. Pusey (1800-82), a distinguished professor of the university, after whom its adherents were sometimes called "Puseyites."

The views of the Oxford movement were systematically propounded in a series, *Tracts for the Times*, whence its advocates were called Tractarians. One of the most notable tracts was Tract 90 (1841) in which Newman attempted to show that the Thirty-nine Articles of Anglicanism were susceptible of a Catholic interpretation, that they did not condemn the Council of Trent. The controversy that followed upon the publication of Tract 90 forced Newman to retire from his ministry in Oxford to Littlemore. Four years later (1845) he was received into the Roman Catholic Church. Newman's conversion had been preceded by the conversion of another erstwhile partisan of the movement, W.G. Ward, the author of *The Ideal of the Christian Church* (1844). Others who submitted to Rome were F.W. Faber, J.D. Dalgairns, and H.E. Manning, later cardinal and archbishop of Westminster.

Newman's departure marked the end of one phase of the Oxford movement which, under the leadership of Pusey and Keble, evolved into the Anglo-Catholic movement. Keble and Pusey continued to stress Catholic elements such as fidelity to the faith of the undivided Church of the Fathers, apostolic succession and the sacraments. They promoted the use of vestments, reservation of the Holy Eucharist, confession of sins, veneration of Mary and the saints, and the foundation of religious orders. Anglo-Catholicism sustains the branch theory of the Church according to which the Catholic Church of Christ has several branches—the Roman, Eastern and Anglican. This theory has encouraged Anglo-Catholics to seek reunion on a corporate level with Rome and the Orthodox Church. One of the great figures of the Anglo-Catholic movement was Charles Gore (1853-1932) who with his friends accepted the principles of the Tractarians and added a strong concern for humanity, the social order, and the future. In 1896 Pope Leo XIII rejected the branch theory of the

Church in his encyclical, *Satis cogitum.*[48] In the same year the Pope also declared Anglican ordinations as understood by Anglo-Catholics to be invalid.[49]

Of course, the evangelical and latitudinarian wings continued to exist side by side with the Anglo-Catholic wing of the Church of England.

METROPOLITAN PHILARET, A. KHOMIAKOV, V. SOLOVYOV

Possibly the greatest Orthodox theologian of the 19th century was the metropolitan (archbishop) of Moscow, Philaret (1782-1867). At Philaret's death, the patriarch of Constantinople described him as a light and teacher for the whole Orthodox Church. Philaret left no systematic work on ecclesiology but dealt with the subject in other works and above all in his sermons.

His ecclesiology was rooted in the Scriptures as interpreted by the Fathers. The word of God upon which the faith of the Church rests is to be found uniquely and sufficiently in the Scriptures. There is no article of faith which cannot be found in the Scriptures. No interpreter is absolutely necessary to discern their message. The Church in council has the authority to define articles of faith but ecclesial definitions must be proved by the Scriptures. (One detects the influence of Philaret's Lutheran preceptors in this position.)

According to Philaret, the Church came into existence at the beginning of the world which was created in view of the Church. In the garden of paradise God communed with man. The essence of the Church is the divinizing communion of God with man. Sin interrupted this communion which was restored by the cross of Christ. Philaret's ecclesiology was concerned with the implications of this restoration.

Philaret acknowledged Jesus Christ as the only head of the Church. The rock upon which the Church is built is not the apostle Peter himself, but his confession of faith: "You are the Christ." There can be no foundation other than Christ Jesus (1 Cor 3:11). Sustaining the independence of the local and national Churches, Philaret rejected the claims of the papacy to a universal jurisdiction. The Holy Spirit is the cause of the Church's unity which manifests itself in the unity of faith and sacramental life. The faith of the Orthodox Church remains undefiled because it preserved the ancient tradition of the universal Church without contamination of error. The Western Church is of God, Philaret acknowledged, because it confesses that Jesus Christ has come in the flesh (1 Jn 4:2); but it has separated itself from its sister, the Orthodox Church, because it has corrupted the Christian faith with human opinions. He compared the separation of the Eastern and Western Churches to the division between Judah and Israel after the death of Solomon. The Orthodox Church continues to recognize the first seven ecumenical councils; but it rejects the councils held subsequently in the West without the participation of the East. The promise of protection against the gates of hell was made by Christ to the universal Church and not to particular Churches. Philaret felt that only the universal Church was fully capable of judging the Western Church. For his part, he devoutly wished the reunion of all Christians.[50]

A contemporary of Philaret, Alexy Khomiakov (1804-60), was the intellectual leader of the so-called Slavophiles and a lay theologian. He expressed his views on the Church in an *Essay on the Unity of the Church*,[51] written about 1850. For Khomiakov, the Church is one because God is one. The unity of the Church is the unity of many members in a living body united by the grace of God. This unity includes men on earth, deceased members, the angels, and those yet to be born. The earthly Church has continued uninterruptedly from the creation of the world. The notes of the earthly Church are inward holiness and outward unchangeableness. Only one who remains in the Church and lives its life can understand the nature of the Church and see more than its external forms. The love which comes from the Holy Spirit is the eye which enables Christians to discern the nature of the Church.

The Church herself does not err. Within that Church false doctrines may be engendered, but then the infected members fall away into heresy or schism and no longer defile the Church. The whole Church is the custodian of the faith, and no single community of Christians or individual can impose his interpretation on other Christians. The Spirit of God who lives in the Church manifests Himself in Scripture, tradition, and works. There are no limits to Scripture, for every writing which the Church acknowledges as hers is Holy Scripture. Such preeminently are the creeds of the general councils, especially the Niceno-Constantinopolitan creed which is the full and complete confession of the Church. The addition of the *filioque* to this creed is a distortion of the faith.

The Church is the instrument and vessel of divine grace. She confesses sacraments through which God sends down His grace upon men. Through baptism a man enters into the unity of the Church. The Eucharist is Christ's true body and blood. It effects the spiritual and corporal union of the faithful with Christ. Through the sacrament of ordination the grace which brings the sacrament into effect is handed down from the apostles and Christ Himself. In confirmation with chrism the gifts of the Holy Spirit are conferred on the Christian, confirming his faith and inward holiness. Marriage is a true sacrament. In the sacrament of penance the Church justifies the sinner; and in the sacrament of the anointing she blesses the end of life.

The external unity of the Church is the unity manifested in the communion of the sacraments, while internal unity is unity of the Spirit. Many have been saved without partaking of the sacraments of the Church, but no one is saved without partaking of the inward holiness of the Church, of her faith, hope and love; for it is not works which save, but faith.

Khomiakov held the Orthodox Church to be the true Church of Christ. Catholicism and Protestantism had fallen away from the Church of Christ through rationalism. He believed it was the vocation of Russia to be the most Christian of all societies. He died while ministering to victims of the plague.

One of the most prominent figures in the religious and intellectual life of Russia at the end of the 19th century was Vladimir Solovyov (1835-1900). He was a mystic, prophet, moral teacher, philosopher and theologian. He dreamed of the unity of all mankind through a united Church headed by the Pope and a political entity headed by the czar. Hence, Solovyov desired the reunion of all Christians. Each group of them had a contribution to make to a united Church: the Christian East, a contemplative spirit

personified by the apostle John; Rome, a tradition of action and
leadership personified by the apostle Peter; and Protestantism,
the Pauline interpretation of the Gospel message. The lamentable
division of the Church was the fault of all parties: the Orthodox
failed to recognize the human aspect of the Church; Roman
Catholics exaggerated the role of the magisterium; and Protestants destroyed objective standards of right and wrong by appealing to personal opinion. In virtue of his self-sufficiency and devotion to technical progress, western man was well on his way
to becoming the anti-Christ. Solovyov prophesied Church reunion. He felt reunion would be achieved by a small group of
Christians of diverse confessions in the face of universal apostasy.
This reunion was to take place at the end of the world. It is
possible (but not established) that Solovyov was received into
the Catholic Church at the end of his life.[52]

An interesting phenomenon of the 19th century in Russia was
the role played by certain remarkable novelists in strengthening
the Orthodox faith. One of the novelists was Nikolay Gogol
(1809-52), the author of *Dead Souls* (1842). He believed the
Orthodox Church was of universal significance with the capacity
to solve the problems of mankind. Even more prominent than
Gogol was Fyodor Dostoyevsky (1821-81). In his novel *The
Brothers Karamazov*, he told the parable of the Grand Inquisitor
to express his understanding of Christ and his distrust of the
Catholic Church. The Inquisitor accuses Christ of demanding
too much of human nature by His gospel. The Inquisitor would
remove the burden of freedom from the shoulders of men and
thus make them happy. Throughout the passionate diatribe
against the gospel Christ maintains an eloquent silence. Dostoyevsky was convinced of the superiority of Russian civilization over the materialistic civilization of the West. This superiority lay in the influence of Christianity embodied in the Russian
Orthodox Church.

NOTES TO CHAPTER VIII

1. DS 2875-80.
2. *CE* 5, 94-99; *NCE* 4, 959-960; *LTK²* 3, 475.
3. Ed. J.R. Geiselmann (Cologne, 1956).
4. Ed. J.R. Geiselmann (Cologne, 1958).
5. *Symbolik* no. 36. The analogy between the Church and the incarnate Son of God was recognized by Vatican II, *Lumen gentium* no. 8.
6. *Ibid.* no. 43.
7. *Prael. theologicae* (Paris, 1870) 4, 1-328.
8. *Ibid.* 18-19.
9. DS 2781.
10. DS 2859-61.
11. DS 2879-80.
12. *CT* 181.
13. DS 2901-80.
14. DS 2980.
15. *CT* 66.
16. Cf. *CT* 189-200 which gives the contents of the first 10 chapters only.
17. *CT* 201-220.
18. *CT* 219.
19. *The Mysteries of Christianity* (St. Louis, 1947) 541.
20. *Ibid.* 542-545.
21. *Ibid.* 545-550.
22. *Ibid.* 550-557.
23. (Freiburg i. Br., 1927).
24. *Ibid.* no. 67.
25. *Ibid.* nos. 110-126.
26. *Ibid.* no. 115.
27. *Ibid.* nos. 121-122.
28. *Ibid.* no. 174.
29. *Ibid.* no. 173.
30. *Ibid.* nos. 181-182.
31. *Ibid.* nos. 170-173.
32. Ap 1:6; 1 Jn 2:20.
33. Sermon on The Three Offices of Christ, *Sermon Subjects of the Day* (London, 1898) 52-62.
34. *Via Media* (London, 1897) 1, xl.
35. *Grammar of Assent* (London, 1901) 386-387.
36. *Development of Christian Doctrine* (London, 1900) 89.
37. *Present Position of Catholics* (London, 1899) 381, 390.
38. *Parochial and Plain Sermons* (London, 1899) 3, 362-363.
39. *Difficulties of Anglicans* (London, 1897) 1, 242-244.
40. Sermon on *The Condition of the Members of the Christian Empire* in *Sermons on Subjects of the Day* (London, 1898) 260-261.

41. *The Great Encyclical Letters of Leo XIII* (New York, 1903) 126-127.
42. *Ibid.* 353.
43. *Ibid.* 354-370.
44. *Ibid.* 371-388.
45. *Ibid.* 429-430.
46. *Ibid.* 528-531.
47. J.H. Newman, *Apologia* (London, 1900) 24.
48. DS 3300-10.
49. DS 3315-19.
50. *DTC* 12/1, 1387-89; P. Evdomikov, *L 'Ecclésiologie Orthodoxe in L 'Ecclésiologie au XIXe Siècle* (Paris, 1960) 60-64.
51. Reprinted in W.J. Birkbeck (ed.), *Russian and the English Church* (London, 1895) 1, 192-222.
52. K. Latourette, *The Nineteenth Century in Europe* (New York, 1959) 2, 460-461; N. Zernov, *Eastern Christendom* (London, 1963) 199-201; B.M. Reardon, *Religious Thought in the Nineteenth Century* (Cambridge, 1966) 218-236.

IX. THE 20th CENTURY: THE AGE OF THE CHURCH

The successor of Leo XIII was Pius X (1903-14). At the beginning of his pontificate and thereafter the Pope was concerned with modernism. The Pope condemned the heresy in the decree of the Holy Office, *Lamentabili* (1907), and the encyclical letter, *Pascendi* (1907). The condemnation was aimed principally at the Frenchman, Alfred Loisy, and the Irishman, George Tyrrell. The Pope encouraged the use of Gregorian chant in liturgical services (1903); he undertook the codification of canon law (1904) which was promulgated by his successor (1917); he reformed the curia (1908) and established the Pontifical Biblical Institute (1909); he fostered the frequent reception of Holy Communion (1905) to which children were to be admitted at an early age (1910). A year later (1911) the Pope provided for the rearrangement of the prayers of the breviary.

In 1905 the French government revoked the concordat made by Napoleon with the Holy See in 1801. The government effected a separation of Church and State, transferring ecclesiastical properties to lay associations. The Pope forbade French Catholics to cooperate in any way with the new system. In Italy, the Roman question remained unsettled; but the Pope allowed Italian Catholics to take a limited part in the political life of the country. In Spain and Portugal anti-clerical governments were responsible for bitter persecutions of the Church. Grieved by the outbreak of the First World War (1914-18), the Pope died soon afterwards.

The next Pope, Benedict XV (1914-22), dedicated himself

to the restoration of peace and the alleviation of the horrors of
the war. Remaining neutral, the Pope protested atrocities per-
petrated by either side and exhausted his resources on behalf of
the victims of the war. He instituted an international bureau of
missing persons in the Vatican. His seven-point peace plan sent
to the heads of the Central and Allied Powers (1917) met with
little positive response. In the same year the Pope published
the code of canon law and established the Sacred Congregation
for the Oriental Church and the Pontifical Oriental Institute. In
1920 the Pope issued an encyclical on Holy Scripture, *Spiritus
Paraclitus.*

The successor of Benedict XV was Pius XI (1922-39). Possibly the most difficult task of the latter was to deal with the
totalitarian governments which emerged in central and eastern
Europe. In 1929 the Pope settled the Roman question with Musso-
lini in Italy: Vatican City became a sovereign state and the
Church received a monetary settlement for the losses it sustained.
Catholicism was made the state religion. In 1933 Pius entered a
concordat with the government of Adolph Hitler in Germany; but
in 1937 the Pope was compelled to issue an encyclical in which
he condemned the excesses of national socialism. He continually
protested the persecution of all religions in Russia. His encyclical,
Divini Redemptoris (1937), condemned atheistic communism.

Pius XI made concordats with other European governments.
He was able to reach an agreement with the French government
(1924) over many vexing issues raised by the Law of Separation
(1905). In Spain and Mexico the Church underwent bloody
persecutions although the situation improved gradually in both
countries. Pius XI is remembered for his concerted effort to
place missionaries under the direction of native bishops and
clergy and for a series of remarkable encyclical letters: *Ubi arcano*
(1922) on Catholic Action; *Divini illius magistri* (1929) on
Christian education; *Casti connubii* (1930) on Christian marriage; and *Quadragesimo anno* (1931) on the Christian social
order.

The first years of the pontificate of Pius XII (1939-58) were
darkened by the Second World War (1939-45). Unsuccessful in
his attempts to preserve the peace, the Pope devoted his energies

to reconciling the warring parties, assisting the victims of the catastrophe, and rescuing Jews from the minions of Hitler. After the war an "iron curtain" fell upon eastern Europe. Communist governments attempted to withdraw the isolated Catholics from their loyalty to the Church of Rome. The "Church of silence" suffered and still suffers terribly at the hands of the tyrant. Pius XII supported the foundation of the United Nations at San Francisco in 1945 as an important means of maintaining world peace.

The Pope was an indefatigable teacher. He addressed himself to social questions, war and peace, and government. He wrote numerous encyclicals of great importance: *Humani generis* (1950) on doctrinal questions; *Mystici corporis* (1943) on the mystical body of Christ; *Divino afflante Spiritu* (1943) on Holy Scripture; *Mediator Dei* (1947) on the liturgy; *Musicae sacrae* (1955) on lay participation in liturgical functions; and *Miranda prosus* (1955) on radio, television and motion pictures. In 1947 the Pope clarified the conditions for the valid ordination of bishops, priests and deacons; and in 1950 he solemnly defined the assumption of Mary after he had consulted the entire episcopacy.

John XXIII (1958-63) summoned the Second Vatican Council (1962-65) to renew the Church and thereby further the cause of Christian unity. He established a pontifical commission (1962) for the revision of canon law. He wrote a number of encyclicals, among them *Mater et magistra* (1961) on social questions and *Pacem in terris* (1963) on peace among nations. He founded the Secretariat for Promoting Christian Unity (1960) with Cardinal Bea at its head. In 1962 the Pope received the peace prize from the International Balzan Foundation. The successor of John XXIII, Paul VI, took the initial steps leading to the canonization of both his immediate predecessors, Pius XII and John XXIII.

MODERNISM

Modernism is the name given to a conglomeration of ideas having to do with Biblical criticism and the philosophy of religion. These ideas emerged at the beginning of the 20th century among certain Catholic scholars in France, England and Italy who wished to bring Catholic teaching abreast of the times. These ideas were condemned by Pope Pius X in a number of documents. It must be noted, however, that the condemned ideas were not sustained in every instance by a particular individual.

Among the most prominent modernists was Alfred Loisy (1857-1940), a French priest. After he had been excommunicated in 1908, he gave up the Catholic faith and died without being reconciled to the Church. Possibly his most famous book was his *L' Évangile et L' Èglise* (1902) which was published in English as *The Gospel and the Church*.[1] The book was placed on the index of forbidden books (1903). The section on the Church is of immediate interest. Loisy wrote:

> It is difficul' to understand. . . how the Society of Christ was something less visible and external than the Roman Church. . . The Society was composed of certain faithful ones who persevered to the end, and met again after the Passion to form the nucleus of the first Christian community. They formed a circumscribed group, perfectly distinct, a very centralized, even a hierarchical fraternity. Jesus is the centre and the chief, the incontestable authority. Around Him the disciples are not a confused mass; the Saviour has distinguished among them the Twelve, and has associated them, directly and effectively, with His ministry; even among the Twelve there is one who stands first, not only by priority of conversion or the ardour of his zeal, but by a kind of designation by the Master. . .

> Christian communities were founded among the Gentiles, and soon became the Church, entirely distinct and even separated from the Synagogue. In these communities the apostles and early missionaries established a college of elders, or superintendents, to govern the societies as they themselves had governed the first community at Jerusalem. The organization of the body of elders, the affirmation of their rights, the pre-eminence of the bishop in the body and in the community, the pre-eminence of the bishop of Rome amongst the bishops, these changes are only defined and established in the course of time, according to the needs of the evangelical work. The Church became, at important moments, what it had become in order not to decline and perish, dragging the gospel down with it. Nevertheless, it created no essential portion of its constitution. . .

In proportion as the episcopate increased, the preponderance of the Church of Rome became evident... A central body was needed to give some kind of support to the force of the universal tendency, and to safeguard the concerted action of the Churches, by making its results visible and regular. This central point and capital of ecclesiastical unity was indicated by the grandest Christian memories, and by the political situation of the Empire. Incontestably it is owing to its rank as the capital that Rome owed the attraction that brought to it the two most important personages of the Apostolic Church. Peter and Paul both came to Rome...

We may imagine also, that when they died, they little thought that they were bequeathing a master to Caesar, or even that they had given a supreme chief to the Church. The thought of the great Advent was too strong in their minds, the questions of creed and of government too little familiar, for them to see in Rome and the Roman Church anything but the providential center of Christian evangelization... With full consciousness they made Rome the capital of the gospel. At the same time, all unknowing, they made the Roman Church the mother and queen of the Churches of the whole world...[2]

Loisy went on to analyze the evolution of the Church and the role of the papacy in the following centuries. He concluded:

The Church today resembles the community of the first disciples neither more nor less than a grown man resembles the child he was at first. The identity of the Church or of the man is not determined by permanent immobility of external forms, but by continuity of existence and consciousness of life through the perpetual transformations which are life's condition and manifestation. Setting aside all theological subtleties, the Catholic Church, as a society founded on the gospel, is identical with the first circle of the disciples of Jesus if she feels herself to be, and is, in the same relations with Jesus as the disciples were, if there is a general correspondence between her actual state and the primitive state, if the actual organism is only the primitive organism developed and decided, and if the elements of the Church today are the primitive elements, grown and fortified, adapted to the ever-increasing functions they have to fulfill.[3]

George Tyrrell (1861-1909) was born a Protestant in Dublin. As a young man, he became a convert to Catholicism and subsequently a Jesuit priest; but he was excommunicated for his modernist views in 1907. Under the pseudonym of Hilaire Bourdon, he wrote *The Church and the Future*[4] (1903) which is representative of his ecclesiological views during his modernist period. According to Tyrrell, Biblical criticism had undermined the traditional Catholic conception of the Church; and the history of dogma had shattered the Church's claim to infallibility. Tyrrell called for a new conception of the Church which regarded the Church as a way or manner of life, as a school of charity rather than a body of doctrine. Conceived in this fashion, the Church would be a community in which the spirit of Christ dwells and in which the individual Christian is the beneficiary of gathered experience and mutual support and encouragement. It is the task of certain heroic souls within the Church to work for its transformation in this direction. This transformation is completely dependent upon papal renunciation of any quasi-oracular power to speak as the mouthpiece of God not *through* the Church but *to* the Church. In this way papal headship could be reconciled with the fundamentally democratic character of the Church.

The true teacher of the Church is the Holy Spirit, Tyrrell maintained. The Holy Spirit acts immediately in and through the whole body of the faithful—lay and cleric. The function of religious doctrine is first of all to fix and embody the inward sentiment begotten of contact with the divine, to describe it as accurately as it can be described in the language of another world. The dogmas of the Church are only approximations of reality. They can be regarded as infallible only to the extent they stimulate life and action. They cannot be viewed as final and exhaustive nor can they be violently imposed on the future. The purpose of a central ecclesiastical authority such as papal authority is to gather up, formulate and propose (rather than impose), for the guidance of each, that truth which under the influence of the Holy Spirit has been worked out (up to its present stage of development) in the minds of all.

Tyrrell saw the shape of the Church emerging in the future as one based on selfless service. "There is a logic in ideas; and this is what, as far as that logic is concerned, the idea of Catholicism, (of institutional Christianity) ought to lead us to" (p. 104).

As a response to modernism, the Holy Office issued the decree, *Lamentabili* (1907). The effect of the decree was to insist (among other things) that faith cannot contradict history;[5] that the magisterium of the Church is able to determine the sense of Holy Scripture;[6] that the magisterium does more than merely ratify what the rest of the Church believes;[7] that public revelation, completed at the close of the apostolic period, comprises truths which come from God; that it is not a subjective interpretation of one's religious experience;[8] that Christ wished to establish the Church as an enduring society whose organic constitution is immutable; that Peter was made the primate of the Church by Christ; that the Roman Church was made the head of all other Churches by the ordinance of divine providence;[10] that truth is immutable and Christ taught a body of doctrine which has universal application;[11] that the principal articles of the creed do not vary in significance as time passes.[12]

The encyclical of Pius X, *Pascendi* (1907), analyzed modernism in a systematic way. Modernism, according to the encyclical, was based upon certain false philosophical systems, that is, agnosticism, immanentism and radical evolutionism. Hence, modernism led to a denial of the existence of God, the objectivity of revelation, the inspiration of the Bible and other fundamental Christian dogmas including the establishment of the Church by Christ and papal primacy.[13] The Pope was convinced that modernism was a heresy, indeed, "the poisonous juice of all heresies."

ECCLESIOLOGY AFTER THE FIRST WORLD WAR[14]

Immediately after the First World War (1914-18) there was a burst of theological activity. Much of the activity centered on the Church. The disastrous effects of divisions among nations (underscored by the devastation of the war) prompted a renewed interest in human solidarity. Statesmen formed the League of Nations. Theologians turned their attention to the Church as a community. Efforts to heal the divisions among Christians became more intense.

Interest in ecclesiology was also stimulated by the dissatis-

faction of some theologians with the ecclesiology of the past.
They noted the lack of systematic and comprehensive works on
the Church in the writings of the Fathers and earlier theologians.
Moreover, they said, since the time of the Reformation, Bellarmine's definition of the Church had been dominant. In their
judgment the result was a lack of balance. The visible, juridical
side of the Church had received a disproportionate amount of
attention; apologetical (rather than dogmatic) considerations had
been paramount; the invisible, communitarian, and "mysterious"
aspects of the Church had been neglected.

The post-war generation of theologians set itself to the task
of redressing the imbalance. They asked themselves where the
tract on the Church was to be inserted in the manuals of theology.
Some felt that an apologetical study necessarily preceded a dogmatic study of the Church since reason too had a place in theology. A second group combined an apologetical and dogmatic
study while a third group studied the Church exclusively from a
dogmatic point of view. There was a conscious effort on the part
of many theologians to dispense with scholastic and juridical concepts and terminology and employ images drawn from the Bible
and the Fathers. Renewed consideration of the Church as a
mystery raised the question whether the Church could be defined
and, if it could be, what its definition was. The tension between
the visible and invisible, the human and the divine, the transitory
and permanent, the earthly and heavenly, the horizontal and the
vertical, ideal and reality, the hierarchical and charismatic, community and individual, law and love was recognized and resolved
in various ways.

Renewed attention was paid to an idea which the Orthodox
Church had never forgotten: the Church is the coming down of
the heavenly Jerusalem. Do the angels belong to the Church? A
goodly number of theologians replied affirmatively while others
disagreed. Theologians spoke of the Church triumphant in
heaven, the Church suffering in purgatory, and the Church militant on earth. The teaching of the Fathers about the preexistence
of the Church was investigated and evaluated.

Theologians probed the relationship of Jesus to the foundation of the Church. Had Jesus intended to found a Church? Was

not the expression, "my Church" (Mt 16:18), unique in the New Testament? Did not Jesus' warning about the nearness of the kingdom preclude the intention to found a Church? Nevertheless, it was pointed out that Jesus as the Messiah was necessarily oriented to a messianic community. Moreover, the mind of Jesus for the Church was revealed in passages of the New Testament even where the word, Church, was not employed. When did Jesus found the Church? Various answers were given: when He gathered the apostolic college, or when He spoke to Peter at Caesarea Philippi, or at the Last Supper, or on the cross, or when He sent the Spirit, or—the answer most frequently given—by a series of actions including the ones mentioned.

Theologians inquired into the relationship of the Church to humanity in general and the cosmos. Is not Christ the redeemer of all men? Are not all men related therefore to the Church because they are related to Christ? Do not the letters to the Ephesians and Colossians suggest that the Church is, as a matter of fact, the totality of creation which has been redeemed by Christ? Yet the identification of the Church on the one hand and humanity and the cosmos on the other was not accepted by all.

What is the connection between the Church and the kingdom of God? Some theologians spoke of the kingdom of God as fully present; some, as a purely future reality; others, as a reality already present but not yet fully realized. Some denied any connection between the Church and the kingdom of God; others identified the Church and the kingdom of God; but these opinions did not gain much support. Mainly theologians spoke of the Church as the kingdom of Christ which would yield to the kingdom of God at the Parousia. The function of the Church is to prepare the way for the kingdom of God; but the two are not to be identified. The Church has an interim character.

The question of membership in the Church was reexamined. Bellarmine, it will be recalled, restricted membership in the Church to Roman Catholics, that is, those who were united in faith and worship under the government of the bishops in communion with the vicar of Christ, the Roman Pontiff. Such a view excluded pagans, heretics and schismatics from membership in the Church. For Bellarmine, membership in the Church was not based upon predestination, grace and charity. This idea was taken up by Pope Pius XII in his encyclical, *Mystici Corporis* (1943):

> Only those are really to be included as members of the Church who have been baptized and profess the true faith and who have not had the misfortune of withdrawing from the body or for grave faults been cut off by legitimate authority. . . One must not imagine that the body of the Church, just because it bears the name of Christ, is made up during the days of its earthly pilgrimage only of members conspicuous for their holiness, or consists only of those whom God has predestined to eternal happiness.[15]

Obviously Pius XII (along with Bellarmine) thought of the Catholic Church as a closely knit society. This society, comparable in many ways to other purely human societies, has a specific goal, the sanctification of its members and the evangelization of others. This goal is to be achieved by cooperation of the members under the authority of their leaders, the bishops and the vicar of Christ. Just as any society cannot achieve its goal unless its members subscribe to its principles and accept its leadership, so the Catholic Church cannot achieve its goal unless its members are united in a common faith and cooperate with each other under the Catholic bishops. According to this conception of the Church, a Baptist, for example, cannot be a member of the Catholic Church because he cannot subscribe to the Catholic faith or recognize its leaders.

Not all Catholic theologians, however, were satisfied with the Pope's conditions for membership in the Church. All persons, they said, who have been baptized must be reckoned among the members of the Church since baptism is the portal through which one enters the Church.

The axiom, "Outside the Church there is no salvation," was clarified. The clarification was the result of a controversy in which the Rev. Leonard Feeney, an American Catholic priest, was involved. He and other members of his circle took the position that only members of the visible and true Church, the Roman Catholic Church, could be saved. On August 8, 1949, the Holy Office rejected Father Feeney's position when it wrote:

To gain eternal salvation it is not always necessary that a person be incorporated in fact as a member of the Church, but it is required that he belong to it at least in desire and longing. It is not always necessary that this desire be explicit as it is with catechumens. When a man is invincibly ignorant, God also accepts an implicit desire, so called because it is contained in the good disposition of soul by which a man wants his will to be conformed to God's will.[16]

The document of the Holy Office pointed out that its teaching about this matter reflected the teaching of Pius XII in *Mystici Corporis*. In that encyclical the Pope spoke of those who "by an unconscious desire and longing have a certain relationship with the mystical body of the Redeemer." The Pope did not exclude them from eternal salvation; but he noted that "they still remain deprived of those many heavenly gifts and helps which can only be enjoyed in the Catholic Church."[17]

Some Catholic theologians suggested that the axiom, "Outside the Church there is no salvation," should no longer be repeated because it gives rise to misinterpretations such as Father Feeney's. The axiom should be replaced by another which means much the same thing without being misleading, namely, "The Church is the universal sacrament of salvation." The latter formula implies (as does the former one) that the (Roman Catholic) Church is the only institution created and mandated by God to provide men with salvation, the only one truly capable of gathering them together in a single and visible people of God, body of Christ, and temple of the Spirit. The latter formula implies further that the Church is the sensible, visible, public form of God's intention to bestow grace.

To what degree can non-Catholic Christian communities be regarded as Churches? One view saw in Protestant bodies visible, Christian, ecclesial, but juridically imperfect communities. A second view held that the Catholic Church was working through Protestant Churches which continued to baptize and arouse faith despite their separation from the Catholic Church. In this sense, the Catholic Church had never ceased to exist in countries such as Scandinavia and England. A third view recognized Protestant communities as Churches to the extent they retained the elements of truth and sanctification found fully in the

Catholic Church. Hence, some Catholic theologians in a more or less explicit manner tended to accept the ecclesial character of non-Catholic Christian communities. There were, of course, those who felt such acceptance was unjustified on Scriptural and historical grounds.

At the end of the 19th and the beginning of the 20th centuries, Catholic apologists employed the four marks of the Church—unity, catholicity, sanctity and apostolicity—to single out the Roman Catholic Church as the Church of Christ. The four marks appear in the Niceno-Constantinopolitan creed as properties of the Church: "We believe in one, holy, catholic and apostolic Church." Bellarmine, it will be remembered, had isolated fifteen marks of the true Church. The First Vatican Council had spoken of unmistakable marks of the Church by which it could be recognized by all as the guardian and teacher of the revealed word;[18] but it did not refer to the group of four marks as such.

After the First World War there was a reexamination of the four marks as signs of the true Church. In his book, *Les notes de l'Église* (1937), G. Thils stated the impossibility of reserving the four notes exclusively to the Catholic Church and denying them entirely to other Christian communities; but the Jesuit, T. Zapalena, in his *De Ecclesia Christi*[19] vigorously defended the validity of the four marks as an apologetical demonstration; and the debate continued. A number of Catholic apologists added other notes to the four traditional ones such as authority, visibility, infallibility, independence of the State, "Romanity," etc.

The notes of the Church received individual consideration. The unity of the Church was a matter of particular interest because of the ecumenical movement. The official documents of the Church and Catholic theologians tended to avoid such expressions as the "return" or "submission" of separated brethren to the Church; instead, they spoke of "reconciliation" with them. At the same time, the official Catholic position on Church unity remained unchanged: there is only one Church founded by Christ which is destined to be the Church in which all Christians are to be one in faith and authentic sacraments as well as in fidelity to legitimate pastors, and not only one in a vague faith in some invisible Church in which all Christians could remain in spiritual unity despite all their divisions.

The Church was described as holy for various reasons: because of the call of the holy God who established the Church as the people of the new covenant through His Son; because of its teaching, worship, and divinely appointed leadership; because of the indwelling of the Holy Spirit; and because of the presence of holy persons in its midst. The presence of sinners in the Church was acknowledged. Pius XII, it will be recalled, refused to exclude sinners from membership.

The catholicity of the Church was explained in various ways: the Church is catholic because it has a mission to all men (*catholicitas juris sive virtualis*); because it actually has a conspicuous number of members dispersed throughout the world who are one in faith, worship, and fidelity to legitimate pastors (*catholicitas facti*). One view went even further by extending catholicity to mean inclusion of all mankind and the entire cosmos as redeemed by Christ. This concept of catholicity was quantitative; but catholicity was also seen in a qualitative sense as the fullness of truth and the means of salvation. Some non-Catholics took the position that the "Romanity" and "Latinity" of the Roman Catholic Church rendered its catholicity questionable.

The Church was described as apostolic because it originated with the apostles, because it proclaims apostolic doctrines, and because it accomplishes its mission with apostolic authority.

Can the conception of the Church as a community of love be reconciled with the conception of the Church as a juridical society? The problem was raised anew by the publication of the Code of Canon Law in 1917. The significance of love or charity for the Church had been emphasized by the Fathers and Thomas Aquinas among many others; and no Catholic theologian was disposed to disagree with them. Moreover, Catholic theologians were not prepared to deny the authority of the Church to make laws. This authority was explained as a corollary of the pastoral office to bind and loose or as a necessary implication of the social character of the Church. Law, though, was seen as an instrument of Christian truth and love. It was not an end in itself, but a means to an end, namely, the love of God and neighbor.

The conception or rather denomination of the Church as a "perfect society" was reexamined. Theologians and canonists spoke of the Church and the State as perfect societies. A society is said to be perfect in this context when it has for its goal, within its own sphere and on its own plane, the supreme and total good of men, and when it possesses concomitantly, either actually or rightly, sufficient means to achieve its goal. In this sense a perfect society could be described as one that is self-sufficient. The denomination of the Church as a perfect society was for some too juridical, too bureaucratic, too mechanical, too capable of being misunderstood. Others, of course, defended the use of the phrase, perfect society, on the grounds that it does distinguish the Church (and the State) from other societies.

In what sense is the Church the communion of saints? The phrase appears in the Apostles Creed; and it was known and interpreted by many Fathers and medieval theologians. The Latin phrase, *communio sanctorum*, can mean literally either a congregation of holy people or a sharing in holy things; that is, it can refer either to persons or things. The phrase was understood in both senses in antiquity. Quite commonly, in the period after the First World War, Catholic theologians used the phrase, communion of saints, to designate the Church militant on earth, the Church suffering in purgatory, and the Church triumphant in heaven. Some also associated it with the Church as the mystical body of Christ.

The comparison of the Church to a living organism became more frequent. It was a common practice in antiquity to compare a group of persons to a living organism. According to some Catholic exegetes, Paul had incorporated this comparison in his conception of the Church as the body of Christ, especially in 1 Cor 12 and Rm 12. Of course, Paul viewed the Church as an organism not on the natural, but on the supernatural, plane. Undoubtedly the prestige of the biological sciences after the First World War contributed to the popularity of such a comparison. Moreover, renewed interest in human solidarity after the disastrous war and a desire to counterbalance a juridical concept of the Church had the same effect.

If the Church is a living organism, then it is subject to the possibility of development. What are the principles and what has been the actual course of this development? To what degree and in what sense is the collective teaching of the ecumenical councils, for example, identical with that of Christ or the ancient Church? Is this dogmatic development to be regarded simply as the explication of that which was implicit in the message of Christ? Is the development of dogma and the evolution of ecclesiastical structures to be compared to the development of the mature oak tree from the acorn—a kind of organic development? The question of development was particularly pertinent with respect to the papacy. To what degree was the role of the papacy in more recent centuries identical with the role of Peter as portrayed in the New Testament? After the publication of Cullmann's book on Peter, *Petrus*,[20] a kind of consensus emerged between Catholic and Protestant exegetes: Peter was the rock upon whom Christ built the Church (Mt 16:18), the prince of the apostles. The consensus disintegrated, however, when the issue of successors to Peter was raised. According to Cullmann and other Protestant exegetes, the principle of succession cannot be justified either from Scripture or the history of the ancient Church: the rock, the foundation for all churches of all times, remains the historical Peter. Catholic exegetes, on the other hand, defended the principle of succession. It was generally recognized that ancient writers often understood Mt 16:18 in a variety of senses, that the Christian Church of the earliest centuries did not see the Bishop of Rome in the same light in which the Catholic Church sees him today. Yet, the Catholic historian of dogma saw the development of the papacy as a legitimate outgrowth of the office conferred on Peter by Christ. Only time and historical circumstances, he said, could gradually reveal the full significance of the Petrine office for the Church.

The Code of Canon Law (1917) defined the role of the laity in the Church. According to the Code, by the institution of Christ the sacrament of orders distinguishes clerics from the laity for the purpose of governing the faithful and of providing a ministry for divine worship (c. 948). Laymen are forbidden to preach in church (c. 1342, 2). They have the right to receive from the clergy, in accordance with the provisions of ecclesiastical law, spiritual benefits, especially the means necessary for salvation (c. 682). The faithful owe the clergy reverence (c. 119). They are to be praised if they become members of associations established or recommended by the Church; but they must beware of societies with objectionable features (c. 684). They may share in the administration of ecclesiastical property (c. 1521, 2). Without the express consent of the bishop, no layman may have a seat reserved in church for himself and his family (c. 1263, 2). These comparatively few explicit references to the laity together with the frequent explicit references to the clergy reinforced the impression (where it already existed) of a clerically dominated Church.

Laymen were viewed sometimes in a purely negative fashion as those who did not share in the powers of orders and jurisdiction which were reserved to the clergy. The passage in 1 P 2:9—"You are a chosen race, a royal priesthood"—which was addressed to Christians in general, was understood in some circles as hyperbole or metaphor. In the minds of some clerics, the principal responsibility of the layman was obedience to the clergy. The liturgical movement helped to dispel this attitude toward the layman. The liturgical movement rediscovered the implications of the common priesthood of the laity for liturgical worship. Not only does the ministerial priest offer the Mass; but the laity actively offer it too. The priesthood of the laity is based upon the sacramental characters of baptism and confirmation. The recognition of the laity's role in liturgical worship led to an ever increasing desire for the use of the vernacular.

The rediscovery of the layman's role in the Church was furthered by recent Popes who summoned laymen to participate in "Catholic Action." As explained by Pope Pius XI, Catholic Action consists in this, that the laity participate in some measure in the apostolic work of the hierarchy. Catholic Action is a true apostolate in which the faithful seek not only Christian perfection for themselves, but also religious and social goals for the benefit of the entire community. Catholics, who are united and organized to engage in Catholic Action, receive from the hierarchy not only a mandate, but also incentive and encouragement. The possibilities for Catholic Action differ according to age and sex. Organizations of youth look chiefly to the training and preparation of their members for further undertakings, while adults have a wider field inasmuch as they can serve human society in innumerable ways. For its apostolate, Catholic Action employs those means suited to its goals. It does not preclude its members from access to public office. Pius XI regarded Catholic Action as a force which could unite Catholics throughout the world despite national boundaries.[21] His successor, Pius XII, was equally intent on promoting the movement. Many ideas of the two pontiffs were incorporated in Vatican II's teaching on the apostolate of the laity. Of course, neither the council nor the Popes restricted the lay apostolate to the formal structure of Catholic Action.

Questions about the hierarchy and apostolic succession were raised. No Catholic theologian was disposed to question the canon of Trent which stated: "If anyone says that in the Catholic Church there is no divinely instituted hierarchy consisting of bishops, priests, and ministers: let him be anathema."[22] No Catholic theologian was disposed to deny the Tridentine teaching that the hierarchy derives its power from Christ and not from the people.[23] What, however, is the collegial relationship between the Petrine office and episcopal office? What is the relationship between the episcopal office and the priestly office? Are priests essentially helpers and co-workers of the bishop? Is the power of bishops to confirm and ordain a matter of divine or ecclesiastical right? Is the imposition of hands absolutely necessary for the reception of a higher ecclesiastical office? Is insistence upon the imposition of hands in such a case similar to reliance upon physical descent from Abraham? In unusual circumstances could a "prophet" undertake a hierarchical function under inspiration of the Spirit and validly consecrate the Eucharist or forgive sins? What is the relationship between the hierarchy and the laity? In what sense does each share in the threefold office of Christ who is priest, prophet and king?

Catholic theologians continued to study the activity of the Holy Spirit in the Church. The Spirit is the soul of the Church, the principle of ecclesiastical unity, the guarantor of its mission.

8

Pentecost endures in the Church. The Church is a community assembled by the Spirit who has been sent by Christ. Christ and the Holy Spirit are not to be separated in their relationship to the Church. The role of the Spirit is not to be misunderstood to the extent that the Church ceases to be a visible communion.

The analogy between the incarnate Son of God and the Church was reaffirmed. The Church is the extension of the incarnate Savior; it is Christ extended in space and time. Protestant theologians, however, tended to shy away from such expressions because in their judgment such expressions obscured the differences between Christ and the Church. Yet it was pointed out that Christ had identified Himself with the Church when He spoke to Paul: "Why are you persecuting Me?" (Ac 9:4-5). The same identification is suggested by the image of the vine and branches in John's Gospel. Of course, the union between Christ and the Church is not so immediate that personal distinctions are obliterated.

The Scriptural image of bridegroom and bride, applied to Christ and the Church, clearly distinguishes Christ from His Church. At the same time, the image expresses the close union between the divine bridegroom and His spouse, the Church, which begets new children through the union. Moreover, the image of bridegroom and bride expresses the subordination of the Church to Christ.

The likeness between Mary and the Church continued to be recognized. Mary is the type, image and representative of the Church. Mary is the virgin mother of Christ; so is the Church which gives birth to Christ in a spiritual and sacramental manner. Mary is the mother of believers; so is the Church. Mary was preserved from original sin; the Church is protected from error. Mary is the mediatrix of graces; so is the Church. Mary was assumed into heaven; one day the Church will be freed of the bond of mortality. In a sense, what is said of Mary can be said of the Church; what is said of the Church can be said of Mary.

How is Christ present in His Church? Quite commonly Catholic theologians responded to this question by pointing to His presence in the sacrifice of the Mass, not only in the person of His minister, the priest, but also under the eucharistic species. He is present in the sacraments by His power and in His word embodied in the Scriptures. He is present when two or three are gathered together in His name (Mt 18:20). He dwells in those who have been regenerated by baptism and He is present in His Church through the Holy Spirit. Dom Odo Casel, a monk of Maria Laach, suggested another mode of presence: presence in mystery (*Mysteriengegenwart*). According to Casel, mystery means in this case a sacred action of worship in which a saving act of Christ becomes really present under the rite. As the worshiping community accomplishes the rite, it shares in the saving act and acquires salvation for itself. Casel's opinion encountered considerable opposition.

Pope Pius XII's encyclical letter, *Humani generis* (1950), contained significant statements about the Church's doctrinal authority. The Pope granted that the terminology employed by the magisterium is capable of being perfected; but he rejected the idea that the terms and concepts of dogmatic definitions distort the truth (nos. 15-16). The magisterium is the proximate and universal norm of truth for theologians (no. 17). Papal encyclicals expect assent for they are instances of the ordinary teaching authority of the Popes (no. 20). It is the task of theologians to point out how magisterial statements are found in Scripture and tradition (no. 21). Indifference to the magisterium has led some to deny that the mystical body of Christ and the Roman Catholic Church are one and the same thing—a doctrine taught by the Pope in his encyclical, *Mystici Corporis* (no. 27). The Pope recognized the bearing of sound philosophy upon doctrine—a philosophy which "safeguards the genuine validity of human knowledge, the unshakable metaphysical principles of sufficient reason, causality, and finality, and finally the mind's ability to attain certain and unchangeable truth" (no. 29).

A few months after the publication of *Humani generis,* the same Pope, Pius XII, defined the dogma of Mary's assumption in the bull, *Munificentissimus Deus* (1950). Leaving unresolved the question whether or not Mary died, the Pope declared: "The Immaculate Mother of God, Mary ever Virgin, after her life on

earth, was assumed, body and soul, to the glory of heaven".[24]
The reasons given by the Pope for defining the dogma mention the
doctrinal sources upon which he relied. The Pope wrote:

> The universal Church in which the Spirit of Truth dwells,
> and which he infallibly guides to perfect knowledge of
> revealed truths, has shown its faith many times in the course
> of centuries. Bishops from all over the world with almost
> perfect unanimity have petitioned that the truth of the
> corporal assumption of the Blessed Virgin Mary into heaven
> be defined as a dogma of the divine, Catholic faith. The
> truth of this dogma is based on Sacred Scripture and is
> deeply rooted in the hearts of the faithful. It is sanctioned
> by the worship of the Church from the most ancient times.
> It is completely consonant with all other revealed truths.
> It has been explained and proclaimed by the study, the
> knowledge, and the wisdom of theologians. In consideration
> of all these reasons, we judge that in God's providence
> the time has come to proclaim solemnly this wonderful
> privilege of the Virgin Mary...[25]

The explicit evidence for the assumption of Mary derived
from the earliest doctrinal sources is quite meager. Nonetheless,
the universal belief of the Church in Mary's assumption is
sufficient warranty for the papal definition. It is the task of
theologians to point out how magisterial statements are found
in Scripture and tradition.

The Church heard severe criticism of itself after the First
World War. The divine side of the Church, derived from its
Founder, is beyond criticism and change; the human side, how-
ever, is subject to criticism and change. The divine side of the
Church includes its apostolic structure, sacramental system and
the substance of its belief. The human side includes the life of
Catholics and certain ecclesiastical structures and practices.
Clergy and laity were reminded that penance and conversion are
necessary for Christians throughout their lives. The bad example
of many Catholics is a hindrance to the mission of the Church.
The Church is an *Ecclesia semper reformanda*, a Church in
need of constant renewal, always subject to temptation, sin, and
human weakness. The Church was accused of fidelity to out-
moded traditions, bureaucracy, unwarranted involvement in tem-

poral and political affairs, indifference to social problems, restriction of academic freedom and a concern for structures rather than people. There was a call for renewal of the liturgy, improvement of preaching, more relevant theology, upgrading of Catholic schools, modernization of ecclesiastical administration, professionalism in Catholic journalism, elimination of a defensive mentality, and greater interest in the restoration of Christian unity.

PIUS XII'S ENCYCLICAL MYSTICI CORPORIS (*1943*)

Immediately after the First World War, the mystical body of Christ became the dominant theme of Catholic theology—not only in ecclesiology but also in Christology and moral, ascetical and pastoral theology. Many a theologian described it as the center or heart of theology. Often enough the Church was defined simply as the mystical body of Christ. Not that objections to this development were lacking. It was noted, for example, that the apostle Paul never spoke of the *mystical* body of Christ, that the idea was not central to the ecclesiology of the Fathers or all the New Testament, that the bishops of the First Vatican Council had found the expression obscure, that other Biblical images expressed more clearly certain aspects of the Church. In some Catholic circles there was fear that a misunderstanding of the mystical body of Christ would lead to a denial of the visible side of the Church and a false mysticism.

In the introduction to his encyclical, the Pope gave his reasons for writing it: the nobility of the subject and current interest in it; the circumstances of the time in which men were caught up in a terrible war, the Second World War (1939-45); and the wish of the Pope to deal with certain errors, namely, a false rationalism, naturalism, and a false mysticism.

"If we would define and describe the true Church of Jesus Christ," the Pope wrote, "which is the one, holy, catholic, apostolic Roman Church, we shall find nothing more noble, more sublime, or more divine than the expression, 'the mystical body of Christ'" (no. 13). This Church is a body. It is one, undivided, and visible; "hence, they err in a matter of divine truth who imagine the Church to be invisible. . . by which many Christian communities, though they differ from each other in their profession of faith, are united by an invisible bond" (no. 14). The Church is constituted organically and hierarchically and endowed with sacraments. The members are those who share its social unity (nos. 16-23).

The Church is the body of Christ. He is its founder, head, support and savior (nos. 25-59). The Holy Spirit is its soul (no. 57). The Church is the *mystical* body of Christ. It is called the mystical body of Christ for two reasons: first, to distinguish it from the physical body of Christ now in heaven; and second, to distinguish the Church from other societies which are also bodies in a certain sense. That which unites the members of a society other than the Church is their cooperative pursuit of the same end under the direction of the officers of the society. Surely the members of the Church are united in this way too; but the unity achieved in this way is reinforced by the active presence of the Holy Spirit, the Spirit of unity (nos. 60-63).

The members of the Church are united to Christ and to each other by social and juridical bonds and the theological virtues (nos. 67-75). Christ is in us through His Spirit who dwells in us (nos. 76-80). The Holy Eucharist is a symbol of the unity of the mystical body with its head (nos. 81-84).

A false mysticism looks upon the divine redeemer and the members of His body as coalescing in one physical person. A false quietism attributes the whole spiritual life of Christians exclusively to the Holy Spirit while setting aside the collaboration which is necessary on our part. Furthermore, it is wrong to deny the value of frequent confession of venial sins or of private prayer; and it is quite proper to direct prayers to the person of Jesus Christ (nos. 86-90).

Finally, the Pope exhorted Catholics to love the Church with an undivided love. In order that they may love the Church in this way, Catholics must accustom themselves to see Christ Himself in the Church. The Pope urged Catholics to love the Church as Christ loved the Church—with an all-embracing love, by prayer and suffering on behalf of it (nos. 91-109).

The Pope concluded *Mystici corporis* with a prayer to Mary, the Mother of the head of the mystical body and the mother of all His members.

The encyclical bears a marked resemblance to the views of Father Sebastian Tromp, S.J., a professor at the Gregorian University, Rome, during the pontificate of Pius XII. Professor Tromp had devoted considerable study to the mystical body of Christ, for example, in his work, *Corpus Christi quod est Ecclesia*.[26] He too had identified the Roman Catholic Church with the mystical body of Christ.

MEDIATOR DEI (*1947*)

The most sublime activity of the Church is the celebration of the sacred liturgy. In his encyclical, *Mediator Dei*, Pius XII defined the liturgy as "the public worship which our redeemer as head of the Church renders to the Father as well as the worship which the community of the faithful renders to its founder and through Him to the heavenly Father. It is, in short, the worship rendered by the mystical body of Christ in the entirety of its head and members" (no. 20).

At the beginning of the encyclical, the Pope spoke of the honor and worship given by the incarnate Word on earth to His heavenly Father. In union with Christ, the Church continues to honor and worship God through the sacred liturgy. The liturgy includes the rites of Mass, the sacraments, the divine office, and other ceremonies and blessings found in the ritual books of the Church (nos. 17-22).

The worship rendered by the Church to God must be, in its entirety, interior as well as exterior. Interior worship is most important; but exterior worship is also necessary because, among other reasons, "exterior worship reveals and emphasizes the unity of the mystical body, feeds new fuel to its holy zeal, fortifies its energy, and intensifies its action day by day. . ."(no. 23).

The Church is a society and as such it requires an authority. This authority is the hierarchy consecrated by the sacrament of orders. The hierarchy is charged with particular responsibility for the celebration of the liturgy for two reasons: one, orders confer a unique capacity for performing the liturgy; and, two, the liturgy is an expression of doctrine which the hierarchy must teach and safeguard: *lex credendi statuat legem supplicandi* (nos. 38-48).

Just as the Church has divine and human sides, so the liturgy includes divine and human elements. The former, instituted by God, cannot be changed or suppressed; the latter admit of change as circumstances demand and the hierarchy permits (nos. 49-58).

The Mass is the crowning act of sacred liturgy. In the Mass the entire mystical body, head and members, offers worship to the Father. By an unbloody immolation Jesus offers Himself as a victim through the ministry of the priest (no. 68). Even though the faithful do not have the power to consecrate the bread and wine, they do offer the sacrifice of the Mass. They do so through Christ who acts in the name of His members. They offer the Mass by uniting their hearts with the prayers of the priest (no. 93) and by offering themselves as victims (no. 98). The Pope commended those who try to involve the Christian people more actively in the Mass (no. 105).

What is true of the Mass is true of other liturgical actions *mutatis mutandis*. The whole mystical body is engaged in the administration of the sacraments and sacramentals and in the recitation of the divine office. The liturgy is the Church at worship.

THE PEOPLE OF GOD

The Church is a mystery. The New Testament employs many images to illumine the mystery of the Church—images such as the body of Christ, the bride of Christ, the temple of the Holy Spirit and others. In his book, *Ekklesiologie im Werden*,[27] the German Dominican, M. D. Koster, studied the Church as the people of God. This, he felt, was the most fundamental conception of the Church. The Church must be seen within the history of salvation; hence, the starting point of ecclesiology must be the people of God, an idea so prominent in both the Old and New Testaments.

All the other Biblical images of the Church presuppose and clarify the nature of the Church as the people of God. The image of the Church as the family of God, for example, suggests that the hierarchical direction of the people of God must be familial and not lordly. The image of the Church as the body of Christ suggests the corporality of the people of God.[28] The designation, people of God, aptly summarizes the Church's understanding of itself.

During and after the Second World War, a number of other Biblical and patristic studies appeared which showed the central place the idea of the people of God occupies in Scripture and ancient Christian tradition. One of the best known of these works is L. Cerfaux' *La Théologie de l'Église suivant S. Paul*.[29] Cerfaux showed that the Jewish idea of "God's people" is basic to Paul's theology of the Church. God had given the Jewish nation privileges such as the covenant and promises. When Christ came, these privileges were automatically transferred to the Christian community. Paul recognized the Christians as God's true people, the real heirs of the promise. Such Pauline expressions as "Church of God," "the saints," and "the chosen," borrowed by Paul from the Old Testament and applied by him to the Christians, designated their status as the new people of God. Furthermore, the Christians regarded themselves as the new temple and as priests offering God a spiritual sacrifice. These ideas, according to Cerfaux, are fundamental to Paul's theology of the Church which begins as a theology of God's people.

In 1949, in an article in the *Benediktinische Monatsschrift*,[30] the Benedictine, A. Schaut, pointed out how frequently the prayers of the Roman Missal spoke of the Church as the people of God. He saw in this frequency an expression of the faith of the Church: *lex orandi est lex credendi*. He explained the significance of this idea for ecclesiology:

> To understand the Church as a people of God is an idea derived from the Old Testament which reveals the broad outlines of the plan of salvation. . . By this designation one's thought is turned to baptism and the Eucharist. Baptism makes one a member of the people of God while the Eucharist is the meal of the covenant. . . Therefore, this people is necessarily a community of worship. Furthermore,

the concept, "people," demands a juridical order and arrangement of this community which, as a consequence, must be essentially visible. Thus it appears to us that the designation, people of God, offers a starting point for the understanding of both the spiritual, invisible side as well as the visible, juridical side of the Church.[31]

The Redemptorist, J. Eger, in a doctrinal dissertation, *Salus gentium*[32], submitted to the University of Munich, proved how the ecclesiology of Ambrose of Milan is dominated by the idea of the people of God and people of Christ. Eger's dissertation also contained citations from the works of Cyril of Jerusalem and Leo the Great about the people of God. Eger's work (along with Koster's) drew the attention of German Catholic theologians (such as M. Schmaus) and canonists (such as Kl. Mörsdorf) to the importance of this concept. In France a similar development took place, the theologians, Y. Congar and L. Bouyer, for example, recognizing the significance of the idea of the people of God.

One particular aspect of the theme of the people of God merits particular attention. This is the idea of the Church as the *pilgrim* people of God, the new Israel on its way to the promised land. This idea has been current among Protestant theologians for a long time. One of the first Catholic theologians to study the theme was Robert Grosche of Cologne who published a collection of essays in 1938 under the title *Pilgernde Kirche* (*Pilgrim Church*). The theme was utilized comparatively early too by R. Guardini and Y. Congar. In *Mystici Corporis* (no. 23), Pius XII spoke of "the time of the earthly pilgrimage of the body of Christ." The idea of the pilgrim Church recalls, of course, the exodus of the Hebrew people from Egypt into the promised land; but it also recalls the earthly pilgrimage of the Redeemer who passed from the earthly conditions of this life through death to the glory of His heavenly Father.

THE CHURCH AS SACRAMENT

In a generic sense, a sacrament is a sign and instrument of

God's salvation. In this sense, the term is applicable to Jesus Christ above all. He is *the* sign and instrument of God's salvation. Preeminently He is the image of the invisible God. He is the Word made flesh for our salvation. Said Aquinas: "Our Savior and Lord Jesus Christ, in delivering His people from their sins, as the angel announced, revealed Himself to us as the way of truth by which we are able to come to resurrection and the blessedness of immortal life."[33] Therefore, Jesus is the fundamental sacrament of the Christian religion.

The analogy between the incarnate Son of God and the Church led to the recognition of the Church as a sacrament. At the beginning of the 19th century, J.B. Möhler employed the analogy to explain the union of the visible and invisible in the Church. In the Church too, he wrote, the human is the instrument and manifestation of the divine.[34] Even more explicitly, J.H. Oswald wrote:

> The Church is surely the universal means of sanctification and a saving institution already in its external and visible structure. Sustained by the invisible action of the Holy Spirit, it must be called not merely *a* sacrament, but rather *the* Christian sacrament. The Church is *the* sacrament because it is *the* means of salvation.[35]

The French Jesuit, Henri de Lubac, furthered the development:

> If Christ is the sacrament of God, the Church is for us the sacrament of Christ; she represents Him, in the full and ancient meaning of the term; she really makes Him present. She not only carries on His work, but she is His very continuation, in a sense far more real than that in which it can be said that any human institution is its founder's continuation.[36]

A German Jesuit, Otto Semmelroth, wrote a classical exposition of this idea in his work, *Die Kirche als Ursakrament*[37] (*The Church as Primordial Sacrament*), published in 1953. Other Catholic theologians, such as K. Rahner, E. Schillebeeckx, P. Smulders, and Y. Congar, also took up the idea.

The magisterium of the Church sanctioned the designation of the Church as a sacrament. In 1949 (in the Feeney case mentioned earlier), the Holy Office spoke of the Church as "a general help to salvation"[38] without explicitly calling the Church a sacrament. Vatican II, however, did not hesitate to do so. In the very first paragraph of *Lumen gentium,* its constitution on the Church, Vatican II said: "The Church is a kind of sacrament of intimate union with God, and of the unity of all mankind, that is, she is a sign and instrument of such union and unity." Further on in the same constitution, the council taught:

> Christ, having been lifted up from the earth, is drawing all men to Himself. Rising from the dead, He sent His life-giving Spirit upon His disciples and through this Spirit has established His body, the Church, as the universal sacrament of salvation. Sitting at the right hand of the Father, He is continually active in the world, leading men to the Church, and through her joining them more closely to Himself and making them partakers of His glorious life by nourishing them with His own body and blood.[39]

By reason of its relationship with Christ, therefore, the Church is a sign and instrument of salvation and, consequently, a sacrament.

KARL BARTH

Karl Barth (1886-1968), the Swiss Protestant theologian, exercised considerable influence during the period under consideration. His reputation was made by his commentary on Paul's epistle to the Romans, *Römerbrief* (1919); but he is best understood through his massive *Church Dogmatics.*[40] For Barth, there is no natural theology. Man cannot know or approach God by himself. God has revealed Himself decisively in Jesus Christ. In Jesus Christ God has revealed His purposes for man and chosen sinful man as the object of His love. Jesus Christ is both electing God and the elected man—both giver and recipient. Barth accepts the definitions of the Council of Chalcedon as a matter of faith. As God, Christ was in the beginning with God; through Christ all things were made that have been made. As God, Christ is the elector of man. As man, Christ is the elected one through whom all are chosen. To believe in Christ, to believe what God has done in Him is to share in the election of Christ.

By faith one shares in the exaltation of Christ into fellowship with God.

Included in the election of Jesus Christ is the election of the one community of God which has two forms, the people of Israel and the Church of Jesus and the Gentiles.[41] The Church is the community of those who have been reconciled to God through Jesus Christ, that is, it is "the gathering of the community of those whom already before all others He has made willing and ready for life under the divine verdict executed in His death and revealed in His resurrection from the dead."[42] The Church is an event, that is, an assembly which comes into existence in response to a call, in a definite place, its members sharing a common interest.[43] Since the Church involves the gathering and separation of certain men in a fellowship, an order and constitution are necessary. There must be worship, preaching, theology, and confession. In these ways, the Church is as genuinely and thoroughly visible as any other community.[44] The Church is also invisible: "the gathering and maintaining and completing of the community... is in the hands of God, and as His own work, a spiritual reality, its third dimension, it is invisible, it cannot be perceived but only believed."[45]

The Church as a community is the earthly-historical form of existence of Jesus Christ Himself, or, in the language of the New Testament, it is the body of Christ.[46] The Church is one: "the community as the gathering of the men who know and confess Him can only be one."[47] The Church is holy because it has been set apart and marked off by God as a being with its own origin, nature and direction.[48] The Church is catholic because "it is always and everywhere the same and always and everywhere recognizable in this sameness, to the preservation of which it is committed."[49] "Apostolic means in the discipleship, in the school, under the normative authority, instruction and direction of the apostles... because listening to them and accepting their message."[50] The Holy Spirit is the quickening power with which Jesus builds up Christianity in the world.[51] The Spirit is the enlightening power for the Church's ministry of the prophetic word.[52] The Church is the eschatological fact par excellence.[53]

RUDOLPH BULTMANN

Rudolph Bultmann (1884-   ) distinguished himself as a
New Testament scholar and Protestant theologian during his
tenure at the University of Marburg, Germany, from 1921 to
1951. Just as Barth's ecclesiology must be understood in relation
to his doctrine on election, Jesus Christ, and justification, so
Bultmann's ecclesiology must be understood in relation to his
doctrine on the word. According to Bultmann, even the unbeliever understands the claim of Jesus to be one who reveals
God. Even the unbeliever can recognize the crucifixion of Jesus
as the death of a noble individual. Only the believer though can
recognize the intervention of God in the life and death of Jesus.
How does the believer come to this recognition? Only by his positive response to the summons to believe what God has done in
Jesus. How is this summons delivered? Through the preaching of
the Church. Actually very little is known about the historical
Jesus. This ignorance is unimportant. What is important is man's
acceptance or rejection of the proclamation that God has acted
in Jesus. In proclamation the act of God in Christ is present to us.

This proclamation of the word must, of course, be understandable. It is understandable when it presents man with the
opportunity to understand himself according to the meaning of
the proclamation. To make the word or "kerygma" understandable, the preacher must proclaim the saving action of God in
Jesus Christ without the mythology of the first century. One
must "demythologize" the Biblical records in which the word or
kerygma was originally presented. One does so by taking an
anthropological approach. One must ask: what is the author
saying about his own existence? What does this mean for my
understanding of my life? In this way, one will be confronted by
a decision—to accept or reject the Christ event.

The Church is, so to speak, the "place of the word." The
word summons the Church into existence as the community of
salvation. The Church is the eschatological people of God, the
congregation of saints, those who are called out of the world and
divorced from it. In turn, the existence of the Church is also the

foundation of preaching. It is the Church which sends forth preachers to proclaim the word.

The Church has a double character: it is an eschatological congregation and, as such, it is invisible; nonetheless, it takes form in individual congregations within the world and so it is visible. "The *ecclesia* is just as ambiguous a phenomenon as the cross of Christ: visible as a worldly fact; invisible—yet to the eye of faith also visible—as a thing of the world to come." The eschatological congregation takes its purest form from time to time in the cultic gathering in which Christ is confessed as Lord. Christ is present in this gathering by the working of the Spirit. In this gathering all worldly distinctions are obliterated: "There is neither Jew nor Greek. . ." (Gal 3:28). "The negation of worldly differentiation does not mean a sociological program within the world; rather, it is an eschatological occurrence which takes place only within the eschatological congregation."[54]

As a matter of fact, the Church has never been at the center of Bultmann's theological reflection; but his ideas have stimulated others dealing with ecclesiological questions.

PAUL TILLICH

Paul Tillich (1886-1965), born in Germany and ordained a Lutheran minister, taught at German and American universities. From 1933 to 1955 he served as professor of philosophical theology at Union Theological Seminary and Columbia University, New York. He is known for his study of the relation of religion to culture.

For Tillich, God is being itself. God does not exist; He is. God is the ground of being, the abyss in which all finite being is swallowed up. (One might see an implied pantheism in this position; yet, Tillich himself rejected the implication.) God is living. God is more than a person; yet, He is personal in relation to a person. Men seek union with God, the ground of being. For this purpose they need new being. This new being is manifest in Jesus the Christ in whom there is a unity between the finite and the infinite—between man and God. (Tillich does not conceive

this union after the manner of traditional Christology but as the
actualization of essential humanity which is not eroded by the
conditions of existence.) This new being is available to others.
The community of those who receive Jesus Christ as the new
being is the Church.

The quest for life is common to all the religions of the world.
This quest would go unrewarded unless the divine Spirit chose
to enter the human spirit.[55] Tillich calls the indwelling of the
divine Spirit the Spiritual Presence. "The Spiritual Presence,
elevating man through faith and love to the transcendent unity
of the unambiguous life, creates the New Being above the gap
between essence and existence and consequently above the
ambiguities of life."[56] Those who have been grasped by the new
being constitute the spiritual community. The spiritual community is founded on the new being as it has appeared in Christ.[57]
The spiritual community exists in latent and manifest stages. The
spiritual community is latent in those groups such as youth alliances and political movements which have been gripped by an
ultimate concern and show the power of the new being without
recognizing Jesus as the Christ. The community is manifest in the
Churches who have accepted Jesus as the Christ and taken up the
cross of Christ. Hence, the spiritual community includes the
Churches and extends beyond them.[58]

The Churches are a paradox. "The paradox of the Churches
consists in the fact that they participate, on the one hand, in the
ambiguities of life in general and of the religious life in particular
and, on the other hand, in the unambiguous life of the Spiritual
Community."[59] The Churches as Churches relate themselves to
other groups in three ways: 1) by silent interpenetration through
radiation of the Spiritual Presence; 2) by critical judgment,
publicly exposing and energetically protesting the negativities of
society; and 3) by political establishment which is not always
harmful.[60]

Tillich had much to say about Protestantism. He defined the
Protestant principle as the "protest against any absolute claim
made for a relative reality."[61] No Church can be founded on a
protest; but Protestantism became a Church. The reason is the
Protestant Church is a *Gestalt* of grace, a structure involving both

form and negation of form, a structure through which grace comes but is not identical with it.[62] Nevertheless, the Protestant principle is not the exclusive possession of Protestantism. Secular movements and culture can express a religious protest more effectively than religion itself on occasions.[63] On the basis of the Protestant principle, Tillich protests against the Catholic Church which has been able to preserve a genuine substance within an ever hardening crust.[64] The crust is the assertion of a dogmatic authority and the claim to be above criticism. The substance is the sacramental and priestly elements which sanctify the community by preaching the forgiveness of sins.

YVES CONGAR

Possibly Yves Congar (1904-   ), a French Dominican priest, was (and is) the leading Catholic ecclesiologist of the day. He is remarkable for his ecumenical studies—of the true conception of the Church, the ecclesiological position of separated Churches, the causes of divisions among Christians, the nature of Church reform, the layman's place in the Church, and the problems of the Church in France and elsewhere.

Congar's book, *Chrétiens desunis*,[65] inaugurated the distinguished series of ecumenical studies, *Unam sanctam*. In this book, the author considers the significance of the divisions among Christians in historical perspective.[66] He reviews the Pauline conception of the Church as the body of Christ.[67] He examines the non-Catholic Christian communities with regard to the problem of ecclesiastical unity and the nature of the Church.[68] For Congar, the reunion of Christendom means the reintegration of all Christians into the *ecclesia catholica*. The Catholic Church is the union of the faithful with Christ in faith and charity. It is, moreover, a social unity, a visible organization with a vicar of Christ. Yet there are not two Churches, but only one in which the divine and human, the invisible and visible, are united in a manner comparable to the union of body and soul. Congar thinks of those who have been justified through Christ without visible membership in the Catholic Church as belonging to the Church in an imperfect way. To the extent separated communities have

preserved the Christian heritage, to that extent they have preserved the essence of the Church.[69] The goal of ecumenism is the
union of all Christians in the fullness of the mystical Christ.
Only when this fullness has been realized by all will the
catholicity of the Church be perfectly actualized.[70]

Congar's book, *Vraie et fausse réforme dans l'Église*,[71] is concerned with a subject of engrossing interest to him, namely, the
reform of the Church. Congar asks two questions: 1) Why and in
what sense does the Church admit of reform? 2) What are the
conditions which allow reform to be realized without prejudice
to Catholic communion? He answers: the means of salvation—
faith, sacraments and apostolic functions—are not subject to
change or suppression; the Church cannot be separated from
God and the Holy Spirit; the teaching and pastoral functions of
the Church are under the guidance of the Holy Spirit. When
reform is possible, four conditions must be met: the reformer
must not attempt to set up a different Church even though he
tries to make the Church different in a certain respect; the
reformer must retain membership in the Church so that there
will be a continual reaction between himself and the hierarchy;
cognizant of the human condition, the reformer will exercise
patience; finally, he will look to the sources of Christian truth
and practice—the scriptures, apostolic tradition and the Fathers.
Congar devotes the last section of his book to the question of
reform and Protestantism. He maintains that the reformers of
the 16th century, in their effort to make man's salvation totally
dependent on God, forgot what Jesus had placed in the hands
of the Church.

In the book, *Jalons pour une théologie du laïcat*,[72] Congar
anticipated the teaching of Vatican II about the laity. The
author notes that lay people do God's work in doing the world's
work. The Church is the collectivity of the faithful. The Church
is made the community of the faithful through the means of
salvation provided by Christ. Lay people are not solely the
object of hierarchical ministry; they have, each according to his
state, an active function of bringing the world and history to God
in Christ.[73]

Next, the author turns his attention to the priestly, kingly and prophetical functions of the laity. The laity are priests insofar as they offer an acceptable sacrifice. This may be the sacramental offering of the sacrifice of Christ or the sacrifice of oneself in a variety of ways such as virginity or marriage. The spiritual kingship of the laity is manifested by kingship over oneself and the world (although under the cross) and by the exercise of kingly powers (to a degree) within the Church. The laity are prophets in virtue of a teaching function. In the Church all are animated by the Holy Spirit—the hierarchy to teach, the laity to believe. By living the faith, the laity contribute to the doctrinal wealth of the Church. While the episcopal body teaches with authority, the laity are empowered to teach the faith in private and even publicly when they have received a mission.[74]

Finally, Congar discusses the responsibility of the faithful to be apostles largely in terms of Catholic Action: participation of the laity in the content of the apostolate, not in the hierarchy's apostolic mandate and its powers. The problem of lay holiness arises at this point. God calls the Christian to the city on high but also gives him the world as task and duty. The essential thing is to cooperate with what God wills to be done on earth as in heaven. Each one's place is providentially determined by his gifts. Laymen are God's stewards called to serve. Engagement and responsibility are characteristics of an adult Christian life. All this is to be under the sign of the cross. The laity are set at the junction of the Church and the world.[75]

In *Le Mystère du Temple*,[76] Congar is concerned with the presence of God among His people. God was present among the Hebrew people to reveal, guide, hear, judge, aid and punish. With the construction of the temple, God was present in a given place; but the prophets did not cease to preach that God wishes to reign in the hearts of men above all. After the incarnation of the Son of God, the reality of the divine presence is found in the Church. The author describes the Church in accordance with the texts of the New Testament which present her to us as the spiritual temple of God. No longer is God only present, but now He actually dwells among the faithful. Individually and collectively the faithful become the temple of God because they are the body of Christ, animated by His Spirit.

ROMANO GUARDINI

Few modern Catholic theologians are as widely known as
Romano Guardini (1885-1968). Born in Italy, he grew up in
Germany and spent his life there. Ordained a priest, he filled pro-
fessorial chairs at Berlin, Tübingen, and Munich. His book *Vom
Sinn der Kirche* (1922),[77] took note of the movement getting
underway immediately after the First World War: "A religious
process of incalculable importance has begun—the Church is
coming to life in the souls of men." There is a movement away
from individualism and subjectivism, Guardini wrote, and there
is a renewed consciousness of the religious community, the
Church, the mystical body of Christ. The Church is the spiritual
locality where the individual finds himself face to face with the
Absolute. There are three essential expressions of the Absolute in
the Church—her dogma, her moral and social system, and her
liturgy. Confronted by the Absolute, the individual recognizes
his limitations yet strives after infinity; and so he becomes human.
The man who lives in the Church is truly free because he enjoys
the advantages of the community guided by the Spirit. The
Church is the one great power which makes possible a perfect
community when members are genuine personalities.

In his book *Vom Leben des Glaubens* (1936),[78] Guardini
discussed the relationship between the Church and faith. It is God
who awakens faith in the heart of the one whom He calls; but it
is through the intermediary of the Church that God teaches and
judges the faith of the individual, according to the word: "He who
refuses to hear even the Church, let him be to you as the heathen
and the publican." By entering the community of faith, the
Church, through baptism, the individual shares in the life of
faith. At times, it is necessary for the Church to protect the life
of faith with extreme clarity and forcefulness by imposing on the
individual the rule of faith, that is, dogma. Faith is intimately
tied to the sacraments of the Church. Baptism may be represented
as the planting of a seed, the immediate effect of which is faith.
In the Eucharistic banquet, Christ unites His members into a
believing community.

Sixty years or so after he published *Vom Sinn der Kirche,* Guardini presented his second work on the Church in 1965, *Die kirche des Herrn.*[79] He had just observed his 80th birthday. In the intervening years two lines of thought had become clearer to him. First, the Church which had been shaken by all the conflicts of two thousand years and had taught a doctrine which breaks asunder all natural intelligibility ought to have disintegrated in a short time according to the laws of nature. The continued existence of the Church indicates it is supported by something more than human. Second, "there is something living in the Church which, like the energy that holds together the component parts of the atom, overcomes the tension between the structures and combines them into a whole in a way which, according to all sociological theories, is impossible on any earthly basis. It is the operation of the Holy Spirit. . ."[80] Guardini recalled the new awareness of the Church as a community immediately after the First World War. This awareness led to a consciousness of the community of mankind. The Second Vatican Council manifested a creative outburst of understanding and declaration. There was a great "opening." The Church began to speak to all without fear or harshness in order to be heard. All this was a source of great encouragement to Guardini. He expressed the hope that the difficulties encountered would not result in discouragement, that too great haste and a passion for innovation would not hinder true growth. The Church remained a "mystery" and a "rock" for Guardini—a mystery because, in her essential nature, she did not arise out of psychology or sociology or any historical necessity, but was founded by Christ and the action of the Spirit; a rock, because the Church is firm and unshakeable in her distinction between truth and error. Indifference to truth and error would mean contempt for man whose dignity consists in the very fact he exists by truth.

THE ECUMENICAL MOVEMENT

The ecumenical movement is the effort of Christians to heal the divisions among them.

The 19th century saw the rise of many international Christian organizations which drew members from disparate Protestant communities. The Y.M.C.A., for example, was founded by Sir George Williams in London in 1844, and the World's Student Christian Federation was founded by an American, Dr. John Mott, in Sweden in 1895. Protestant denominations with a common confession and organization formed international alliances. The Baptist World Alliance, for instance, was founded in London in 1905. The success of these and other international organizations coupled with a reaction against the liberalism of the 19th century and a desire to remove the scandal of divisions among Christians stimulated the modern ecumenical movement.

The modern ecumenical movement dates from the World Missionary Conference at Edinburgh, Scotland, in 1910 which met under the chairmanship of Dr. Mott (1865-1955), a Methodist layman. At this conference Anglican and Protestant missionaries deplored the effect of divisions among Christians upon their missionary efforts. An International Missionary Council was formed in 1921 as a result of this conference. In 1925 the first international conference on Life and Work met at Stockholm, Sweden, under the direction of the Lutheran archbishop of Upsala, Nathan Söderblom (1866-1931). The conference favored practical cooperation among Christian bodies while awaiting doctrinal agreement. The conference on Faith and Order was assembled at Lausanne, Switzerland, in 1927 under the leadership of Charles Henry Brent (1862-1929), a bishop of the American Episcopal Church, and Archbishop Söderblom. This conference concentrated on doctrinal matters with a view to unity in faith and order. In 1948, both conferences—Life and Work, Faith and Order—were merged at Amsterdam to form the World Council of Churches (WCC). Every major Protestant denomination is represented on the WCC as are the Orthodox and Anglicans; but large sections of individual denominations, such as the Missouri Synod of the Lutheran Church and most American Baptists, hold aloof from it. The WCC is a fellowship of Churches, not a super-Church. It provides an opportunity for discussion and joint action; but its recommendations are not binding upon any of its members. Its headquarters are at Geneva, Switzerland.

At first the official Catholic reaction to the ecumenical movement among Protestants was negative. Was the movement suggesting that the nature of Church unity desired by Christ is a matter of uncertainty and has to be discovered by discussion? After the conference in Stockholm (1925) and Lausanne (1927), Pope Pius XI issued his encyclical, *Mortalium animos* (1928), in which he declared that the unity of faith and communion desired by Christ already exists in the Catholic Church which is not merely one Church among many, but rather *the* Church of Christ. The Pope forbade Catholics to participate in any movement which questioned this position. The Orthodox delegation at Lausanne spoke of their Church in the same way.

Subsequently, the official Catholic attitude toward the ecumenical movement became more positive. Shortly after the formation of the WCC (1948), the Holy Office issued its instruction about ecumenical activity, *Ecclesia catholica*, in 1949. The unity of Christ's Church, the instruction stated, is the unity of the Catholic Church, and reunion means the acceptance of Catholicism by non-Catholic Christians; but with the permission of the proper authorities, Catholics may meet with non-Catholics in order to discuss their credal views and differences on the basis of equality and reciprocal freedom. At the same time, the instruction said: The Catholic Church takes no actual part in "ecumenical" assemblies.[8]

In the decade immediately preceding the Second Vatican Council Catholics frequently attended Protestant ecumenical gatherings as officially approved observers. Ecumenical contacts between Catholics and Protestants on a private basis increased. In 1960 Pope John XXIII established a Secretariate for the Promotion of the Unity of Christians with Cardinal Augustine Bea at its head. Non-Catholic Churches were well represented by observers at the sessions of Vatican II.

NOTES TO CHAPTER IX

1. (New York, 1909).
2. *Ibid.* 146-156.
3. *Ibid.* 171-172.
4. (Published privately).
5. DS 3403.
6. DS 3404.
7. DS 3406.
8. DS 3420-22.
9. DS 3452-53.
10. DS 3455-56.
11. DS 3458-59.
12. DS 3462.
13. DS 3475-3500.
14. Cf. U. Valeske, *Votum Ecclesiae* (München, 1962).
15. *CT* nos. 242-243.
16. *CT* 274-275.
17. *Mystici 'corporis* no. 103.
18. *CT* 67.
19. 6 ed., 1955.
20. (Zürich, 1952).
21. *AAS* 14 (1922) 673; 20 (1928) 384; 21 (1929) 664.
22. *CT* 849.
23. *CT* 843.
24. *CT* no. 520.
25. *CT* no. 519.
26. (Rome, 1937).
27. (Paderborn, 1940).
28. *Ibid.* 146-158.
29. (Paris, 1947).
30. 25 (1949) 187-195.
31. *Ibid.* 195.
32. (München, 1947).
33. *S. Th.* 3, prologue.
34. *Symbolik* 36, 6 ed. (Monaco, 1895).
35. *Die dogmatische Lehre von den heiligen Sakramenten der katholischen Kirche* (Münster, 1894) 1, 12-13.
36. *Catholicism* (London, 1950) 29.
37. (Frankfurt, 1953).
38. *CT* no. 274.
39. No. 48.
40. Trans. (Edinburgh, 1936-62).
41. *Church Dogmatics* IV/2, 195-305.
42. *Ibid.* IV/1, 643.

43. *Ibid.* IV/1, 651.
44. *Ibid.* IV/3, 2, 722.
45. *Ibid.* IV/1, 657.
46. *Ibid.* IV/1, 662-668.
47. *Ibid.* IV/1, 668.
48. *Ibid.* IV/1, 685.
49. *Ibid.* IV/1, 701.
50. *Ibid.* IV/1, 714.
51. *Ibid.* IV/2, 614-726.
52. *Ibid.* IV/3, 2, 681-901.
53. *Ibid.* IV/3, 1, 295.
54. *Theology of the New Testament* (New York, 1951) 1, 306-314; 2, 95-100. *Faith and Understanding* (New York, 1969) 1, 184-219.
55. *Systematic Theology* (Chicago, 1963) 3, 112.
56. *Ibid.* 138-139.
57. *Ibid.* 150.
58. *Ibid.* 152-155.
59. *Ibid.* 165.
60. *Ibid.* 212-215.
61. *The Protestant Era* (Chicago, 1937) 163.
62. *Ibid.* 212.
63. *Ibid.* 213.
64. *Ibid.* 194.
65. (Paris, 1937). Trans. *Divided Christendom* (London, 1939).
66. *Ibid.* ch. 1.
67. *Ibid.* chs. 2-3.
68. *Ibid.* chs. 4-6.
69. *Ibid.* ch. 7.
70. *Ibid.* ch. 8.
71. (Paris, 1950).
72. (Paris, 1953). Trans. *Lay People in the Church* (London, 1957).
73. Pt. 1.
74. Pt. 2, 1-3.
75. *Ibid.* 2, 5-7.
76. (Paris, 1958). Trans. *The Mystery of the Temple* (London, 1962).
77. Trans. *The Church and the Catholic* (New York, 1953).
78. Trans. *The Life of Faith* (Westminster, 1961).
79. Trans. *The Church of the Lord* (Chicago, 1966).
80. *Ibid.* 4-5.
81. AAS 42 (1950) 142-147.

X. THE SECOND VATICAN COUNCIL
(1962-1965)

THE BACKGROUND

The First Vatican Council had been interrupted by the outbreak of the Franco-Prussian War. Vatican I had defined the position of the Pope in the Church. It was appropriate that another council should complete its labors by defining the position of the bishops, the clergy and the laity. "The late definition," Newman wrote at the time of Vatican I, "does not so much need to be undone as to be completed." Moreover, the complexity and profundity of the changes which had overtaken the world and the Church in the first decades of the 20th century demanded the attention and consultation of all the bishops of the Catholic world. The prediction that Vatican I's definition of papal supremacy and infallibility would render further councils unnecessary was laid to rest by Pope John XXIII (1958-63). Only a few months after his election as Pope, he announced his intention in January, 1959, to convene the Second Vatican Council. He summoned the council to renew the Church and thereby further the cause of Christian unity. In the Pope's mind, renewal meant new energy for the apostolate, a new impulse to Christian living, new forms adapted to modern circumstances, the presentation of the Church's teaching in more intelligible terms, and more vigorous service to mankind. The Pope saw in the projected council a striking manifestation of the Church's unity. Pope John died before the council had completed its work; but his successor, Paul VI (1963-   ), maintained the council in existence, lending it warm support. The full council met for two or three months in the fall of each year from 1962 to 1965.

Some sessions of the council were attended by more than 2,500 bishops representing the largest part of the Catholic episcopacy. Anglican, Orthodox and Protestant observers were invited to be present and were present for all the sessions. Each of the documents published by the council—four constitutions, nine decrees, three declarations--was approved by an overwhelming majority of those voting. The documents embody the contribution of both conservative and liberal churchmen, the conservatives being intent on preserving the gains of the past while the liberals were anxious to introduce necessary changes. The objectives of both groups were by no means incompatible; and it is the task of theologians to integrate the doctrinal elements introduced by both groups. According to Pope Paul VI, in his closing speech to the council (Dec. 7, 1965), the council wished to make no extraordinary dogmatic pronouncements; rather, it wished to speak with the friendly voice of pastoral charity; and it desired to place its teaching at the service of mankind. (Of course, the theologian will realize that the teaching of the council on a particular point may be infallible on the grounds that it is taught infallibly elsewhere either by an extraordinary and solemn pronouncement of the magisterium or by the ordinary and universal magisterium of the Church.) To implement the conciliar documents, the Pope established several commissions.

The council itself described the contemporaneous situation. The world is changing rapidly. Change has brought serious difficulties in its wake. The result is an anomalous state of affairs:

> Never has the human race enjoyed such an abundance of wealth, resources and economic power, and yet a huge proportion of the world's citizens are still tormented by hunger and poverty, while countless numbers suffer from total illiteracy. Never before has man had so keen an understanding of freedom, yet at the same time new forms of social and psychological slavery make their appearance. Although the world of today has a very vivid awareness of its unity and of how one man depends on another in needful solidarity, it is most grievously torn into opposing camps by conflicting forces. For political, social, economic, racial and ideological disputes still continue bitterly, and with them the peril of war which would reduce everything to ashes. True, there is a growing exchange of ideas, but the very words by which

key concepts are expressed take on quite different meanings in diverse ideological systems. Finally, man searches for a better world without a corresponding spiritual advancement.[1]

The changes of which the council spoke are part of a revolution. Mathematics, natural science, technology, biology, psychology, and the social sciences are shaping man's point of view in an increasing measure. The human race has passed from a rather static concept of reality to a more dynamic, evolutionary one. Society is becoming industrialized, urbanized, and socialized. The media of communication are being perfected.[2]

These changes have had the effect of calling accepted values and even religion into question especially in the minds of young people. Changes have created imbalance and contradiction—among nations and classes, for example. Many people call for, and even demand, the redress of this imbalance. At the root of this demand is the desire for a full and free life worthy of a man. The council noted that external imbalance is linked with the internal conflict in the heart of man. As a weak and sinful being, he often does what he would not do and fails to do what he would.[3]

According to the council, atheism is one of the most serious problems of the age. One sector of modern atheists denies the existence of a God who is the author of all things because recognition of such a God would restrict man's freedom to be the sole artisan and creator of his own history. Another sector of modern atheists (Marxists, for example) rejects the existence of God because recognition of God diverts man's energy from striving for economic and social emancipation by the promise of a better future life.[4] Of course, other and possibly older reasons for atheism are still influential.

Three months before Vatican II published its constitution on the Church, Pope Paul VI published an encyclical on the Church, *Ecclesiam suam* (August 6, 1964). The Pope was awaiting the conciliar document on the Church; hence, he regarded his encyclical as an informal and fraternal message. The Pope had three reasons for writing the encyclical: 1) to reflect upon the mystery of the Church; 2) to find the -way to renewal of the

Church; and 3) to discuss the relationship between the Church and the world.

The Church needs to reflect upon herself, the Pope wrote. She must learn to know herself better if she wishes to be faithful to her mission. The Church has roots deep in mankind for she is part of it. The changes which mankind is undergoing at the present time make a restudy of the Church's role mandatory. Obviously, this restudy must be undertaken according to the mind of Christ as it is revealed in the New Testament and tradition.[5]

The Pope desired the Church to be as faithful as possible to the pattern set by Christ. To achieve this ideal, the Pope enumerated certain norms for the reform of the Church. Reform cannot touch either the essential concept of the Church or its basic structure. On the other hand, there is a need for new forms which are commonly regarded as acceptable and suited to the character of the times. It is the task of the council to decide specifically what new forms are to be introduced. The Pope mentioned two needs of the moment: the spirit of poverty and the spirit of charity.[6]

Turning his attention to the relationship between the Church and the world, the Pope stated the Church must recognize the existence of sin in the world. Just as a doctor tries to protect himself and others from a contagious disease and dedicates himself to its cure, so too the Church must adopt a similar attitude toward sin and the sinner. The Church ought to speak to the world about problems that concern it and in terms which the world understands. The Church speaks to men in imitation of God who has spoken to them through revelation in the course of salvation history. The dialogue which the Church wishes to initiate with the world must be characterized by clarity, meekness, trust and prudence on the part of the Church. For this dialogue, the Church must seek identification with those who are to be evangelized and try to understand their position. The Church ought to dialogue with the whole of mankind, atheists, Jews, Muslims, and separated Christians: "Let us stress what we have in common rather than what divides us." The Pope expressed the hope that dialogue between the Church and the world would be a pattern for dialogue among men and lead to peace. Finally, the Pope stated candidly that his own office is a stumbling block for many Christians; but it is a principle of unity for the Church.[7]

CONSTITUTION ON THE CHURCH

Vatican II reflected on the mystery of the Church more deeply and extensively than any other ecumenical council in the history of the Church. The council's constitution on the Church, *Lumen gentium*, promulgated by Pope Paul VI on Nov. 21, 1964, is the most basic expression of the council's mind about the Church.

The council spoke first of all about the mystery of the Church. The Church is a mystery because it is part of God's hidden plan of salvation which was revealed in Jesus Christ. At the same time, the Church is an essentially transcendent, supernatural entity. The origin and continued existence of the Church is bound up with the inner life of the Blessed Trinity. The Church received its mission from Jesus Himself. The Scriptures use various metaphors—sheepfold, piece of land, temple, holy city and others—to explain the nature of the Church. The Church is the body of Christ: as all the members of the human body, though they are many, form one body, so also are the faithful in Christ. By no weak analogy the Church may be compared to the incarnate Word: as the assumed nature inseparably united to Him serves the divine Word, so, in a similar way, does the visible social structure of the Church serve the Spirit of Christ. This Church subsists [fully] in the Roman Catholic Church although many elements of sanctification and truth are found outside its visible structure. The Church is called to follow Christ in humility and self-sacrifice.[8]

God has chosen to bring men to Himself not as isolated individuals, but as a people. He chose the race of Israel as a people to prefigure the new covenant. The new messianic people has Christ for its head and it is the Church. Christ made the new people of God a race of priests, prophets and kings. They exercise their priesthood by offering themselves as living sacrifices to God and through the sacraments. They exercise their prophetic role

by giving witness through a life of faith, charity and praise. The
entire body of the faithful cannot err in matters of belief. The
Holy Spirit also gives special graces or charisms to the faithful.
The people of God is destined to embrace all peoples; and all
men are called to belong to it. Full incorporation in the Church,
the people of God, is a matter of visible communion with the
Pope and bishops, a communion which entails charity; nevertheless, various degrees of union with the Church are possible
depending upon one's share in Christian truth and sanctification.
The Church undertakes missionary activity to bring unbelievers to
the knowledge of Christ.[9]

Having spoken of the people of God in general, the council
turned its attention to particular groups within the Church. The
council spoke first of the hierarchy. The council reaffirmed without qualification the teaching of Vatican I about the Roman
Pontiff. Then the council spoke of bishops. By divine institution
they have succeeded to the place of the apostles. The Roman
Pontiff and the bishops constitute one apostolic college which
is the subject of supreme and full authority. This college exercises its authority, for example, in an ecumenical council. Bishops
are teachers, priests, and shepherds. As a group, the whole body
of bishops is infallible when they teach the faithful with one
voice about matters of faith and morals. As individuals, bishops
are not infallible; nevertheless, they speak in the name of Christ
and the faithful are to adhere to their teaching with a religious
assent. Bishops are the high priests of the local liturgy. As vicars
and ambassadors of Christ, they govern the particular churches
entrusted to them, exercising their pastoral office after the manner of the Good Shepherd. Priests are the helpers of bishops in
their magisterial, sacerdotal and pastoral responsibilities. At a
lower level, deacons are ordained to a ministry of service.[10]

Then the council spoke of the laity. They are all the faithful except those in holy orders or a state of religious life
especially approved by the Church. The laity seek the kingdom
of God by engaging in secular professions and occupations. They
are to apply the principles of the Gospel to those situations
accessible to them alone. As a priestly people, they can offer all

their works as spiritual sacrifices to God. As a prophetic people, they can give testimony to the faith by word and deed. Christ has communicated His royal power to the laity that they might be established in royal freedom, conquer sin, and lead their brothers and sisters to that King whom to serve is to rule. The laity ought to learn the meaning and value of all creation and strive to remedy the customs and conditions of the world. The laity have the right to receive the spiritual goods of the Church from their pastors; and they should openly reveal their needs to them.[11]

The Church is indefectibly holy. Each member of the Church is called to holiness—the love of God and neighbor. Each one can cultivate holiness in the state to which he is called, the ministers of the Church by fidelity to their ministry, the laity by their secular occupations and responsibilities. Holiness is fostered by reception of the sacraments, liturgical worship, prayer, self-denial, and the observance of the evangelical counsels.[12] The evangelical counsels—poverty, chastity and obedience—are based on the words and example of Our Lord. Religious practice the evangelical counsels in a state especially approved by the Church. The religious state manifests clearly that the kingdom of God surpasses all earthly considerations.[13]

The Church will attain its full perfection only in the glory of heaven. The promised restoration which we are all awaiting has already begun in Christ who is sitting at the right hand of the Father. Joined with Christ in the Church we are sons of God but we have not yet appeared with Christ in glory. There is a union of charity and a communion of spiritual goods between the saints in heaven, the dead who are being purified and those who are exiled on earth.[14]

The virgin Mary is the mother of God. She is the mother of men in the order of grace. She cooperated with her divine Son in the work of saving men and she continues to intercede for them in heaven. Mary is a type of the Church inasmuch as she is a mother and a virgin. Because she is the mother of God, she is justly venerated by the Church. Veneration of Mary is simply the recognition and approbation of God's work in her and through her.[15]

CONSTITUTION ON THE SACRED LITURGY

The constitution on the sacred liturgy, *Sacrosanctum con-, cilium,* promulgated by Pope Paul VI on Dec. 4, 1963, reaffirmed the teaching of Pius XII's *Mediator Dei.* Christ is always present in His Church, especially in her liturgical celebrations. "In the liturgy the whole public worship is performed by the mystical body of Jesus Christ, that is, by the head and His members." It follows that every liturgical celebration is a sacred action surpassing all others.[16] The sacred liturgy does not exhaust the entire activity of the Church. Before men can come to the liturgy they must be called to faith and conversion.[17] "Nevertheless the liturgy is the summit toward which the activity of the Church is directed. . . The aim and object of apostolic works is that all who are made sons of God by faith and baptism should come together to praise God in the midst of His Church, to take part in the sacrifice, and to eat the Lord's supper."[18] The Church earnestly desires that all the faithful should be led to full, conscious and active participation in liturgical celebrations.[19]

Some elements of the liturgy are divine in origin; they are immutable. Other elements of the liturgy are human in origin; they are subject to change.[20] When liturgical changes are made, however, certain norms must be observed. As a general norm, regulation of the sacred liturgy depends solely on the authority of the Church, that is, on the Holy See and the bishop.[21] The unstated justification for this norm is the doctrinal, liturgical and pastoral responsibility of the hierarchy described in chapter 3 of the constitution on the Church. A second norm of liturgical revision is based upon the variety of offices which exists within the Church as a worshiping community. Liturgical services should involve the whole local community, each member actively participating according to his specific role.[22] A third norm has to do with the didactic and pastoral purposes of the liturgy. The rites of the Church should be simple, short, clear, and without repetition so that the faithful may be instructed and edified.[23] Finally, liturgical rites should make provision for cultural adaptations in accordance with the needs of different national and racial groups.[24]

The remaining paragraphs of the constitution are devoted to the practical application of these principles to the Holy Eucharist, the other sacraments and sacramentals, the divine office, the liturgical year, sacred music, art and furnishings.

CONSTITUTION ON DIVINE REVELATION

This constitution, *Dei verbum*, was published Nov. 18, 1965. It teaches that God has chosen to reveal Himself by deeds and words in the history of salvation. "God, who at sundry times and in divers manners spoke in times past to the fathers by the prophets, last of all in these days has spoken to us by His Son" (Heb 1:1-2). The obedience of faith is the appropriate response to God who has revealed Himself.[25]

What the apostles learned from Christ they handed on by preaching, example, and writing. The apostolic preaching is expressed in a special way in the inspired books of the New Testament. The tradition which comes from the apostles develops in the Church with the help of the Holy Spirit through a growth in understanding.

> The task of authentically interpreting the word of God, whether written or handed on, has been entrusted exclusively to the living teaching office of the Church. This teaching office is not above the word of God, but serves it, teaching only what has been handed on, listening to it devoutly, guarding it scrupulously and explaining it faithfully in accord with a divine commission and with the help of the Holy Spirit... It is clear, therefore, that sacred tradition, Sacred Scripture and the teaching authority of the Church, in accord with God's most wise design, are so linked together that one cannot stand without the others, and that all together and each in its own way under the action of the one Holy Spirit contribute effectively to the salvation of souls.[26]

The books of both the Old and New Testament were written under the inspiration of the Holy Spirit. They have God as their author who employed men in writing them. The Scriptures teach without error that truth that God wished to communicate for the salvation of men. The interpreter must discover the meaning the sacred writers really intended. The interpretation of the Scriptures is subject finally to the judgment of the Church to whom they have been entrusted.[27]

God's revelation of Himself to the nation of Israel is found in the books of the Old Testament. This revelation was given primarily to prepare for the coming of Christ.[28] The revelation of God to men through Jesus Christ is set forth in the books of the New Testament, especially the gospels. The gospels faithfully hand on what Jesus Christ, while living among men, really did and taught for their eternal salvation. Besides the four gospels, the canon of the New Testament also contains the epistles of Paul and other apostolic writings.[29] The Church must be nourished and guided by Sacred Scripture which is employed so widely in the liturgy. Easy access to the Scriptures should be provided to all the faithful. The study of the sacred page must be, as it were, the soul of theology. "Ignorance of the Scriptures is ignorance of Christ."[30]

CONSTITUTION ON THE CHURCH IN THE MODERN WORLD

This constitution, *Gaudium et spes,* was published Dec. 7, 1965. Having described in some detail the effects of change upon the world, the constitution reaffirmed at the outset the dignity of the human person. The human person was created in the image of God. He is capable of knowing and loving his creator. He is the master of all earthly creatures. Though made of body and soul, he is one. In his heart he has a law written by God. He is free and only in freedom can he direct himself toward goodness. He is called to communion with God. It is the incarnate Son of God who fully reveals man to himself.[31]

From this conception of human dignity, the Second Vatican Council drew the appropriate conclusions: "There must be made available to all men everything necessary for leading a life truly human, such as food, clothing, and shelter; the right to choose a state of life freely and to found a family, the right to education, to employment, to a good reputation, to respect, to appropriate information, to activity in accord with the upright norm of one's own conscience, to protection of privacy and to rightful freedom, even in matters religious."[32]

Since all men have been created after the image of God, since they have the same nature and origin, since they have been redeemed by Christ and share the same opportunity for a blessed immortality, all men are basically equal. It would be unrealistic, of course, to overlook the great physical, intellectual and moral differences that distinguish individuals. "Nevertheless, with respect to the fundamental rights of the person, every type of discrimination whether social or cultural, whether based on sex, race, color, social condition, language or religion, is to be overcome and eradicated as contrary to God's intent. . . Therefore, although rightful differences exist among men, the equal dignity of persons demands that a more humane and just condition of life be brought about."[33] Excessive economic and social differences among men violate the dignity of the human person.[34]

Then the council reflected upon the dignity of human activity. According to the council, mankind has received a mandate from the creator to subject the earth and all it contains to himself (man). By his labor he implements the plan of his creator. The Church does not regard the marvelous achievements of human activity as opposed to the works of God. These achievements are the fulfillment of God's design. To the extent that human activity contributes to the genuine good of the human race and enables men, as individuals and as members of society, to attain their purpose in life, to that extent it is good and praiseworthy.

In a sense, human activity which is concerned with the things of this world is autonomous. The things of this world are regulated by their own principles which man must discover and utilize. The Church has no fear that the discovery of these principles will be harmful to religion, for both the world and religion are derived from the same God. On the other hand, no human activity is totally autonomous in the sense that it may proceed without any reference whatsoever to the creator. The creature may never be totally divorced from the creator.[35]

These remarks about the dignity of the human person and his activity clarify the relationship between the Church and the world. The purpose of the Church can be realized fully only in the future world; but the Church serves as a leaven in this world by sustaining human dignity and revealing the total dimensions of human activity. By virtue of the gospel committed to her, the Church proclaims the rights of man without prejudice to the divine law. By her universality the Church is a bond and example of human solidarity. The Church encourages its members to meet their responsibilities in this world, for the Christian who neglects his temporal duties neglects his duties to his neighbor and his God. The Church is acutely conscious of the distance between the gospel and the failings of Christians. While the Church aids human society, the Church is simultaneously its beneficiary. The experience of the past, scientific progress and cultural treasures benefit the Church too.[36]

In its discussion of the place of the Church in the modern world, the Second Vatican Council singled out a number of subjects for particular consideration. These subjects were marriage and the family, human culture, the social, economic and political dimensions of modern life, the relationship between nations and peace. The council examined each of these subjects in the light of the gospel and human experience with the dignity of the human person and his activity as an important presupposition. Some of the ideas expressed by the council are recalled in the paragraphs that follow.

First of all, with respect to marriage and the family: marriage has been established by the creator; it is qualified by His laws; it is contracted by the irrevocable consent of the parties involved. Marriage is a union which exists for the procreation and education of children. It enables husband and wife to render love and service to each other. The natural institution of marriage has been elevated to the dignity of a sacrament. It is profaned by adultery and divorce.

Bringing children into the world is a serious responsibility which must be weighed carefully. The Second Vatican Council said: "Let parents thoughtfully take into account both their own welfare and that of their children, those already born and those whom the future may bring. For this accounting they need to reckon with both the material and spiritual conditions of the times as well as of their state in life. Finally, they should consult the interests of the family group, of temporal society, and of the Church itself. The parents themselves and no one else should ultimately make this judgment in the sight of God. But in their manner of acting, spouses should be aware that they cannot proceed arbitrarily, but must always be governed according to a conscience dutifully conformed to the divine law itself, and should be submissive toward the Church's teaching office, which authentically interprets that law in the light of the gospel."[37]

The education of children requires that they be prepared to choose and to follow their vocation in life and, if they decide to marry, to establish their families in favorable moral, social, and economic conditions. The position of parents obliges them to guide their children in these matters, and children have the corresponding duty to listen to them. Still, parents may exercise no pressure upon their children either to marry or to choose a specific partner. Children owe their parents gratitude, love and trust; and they ought to stand by their parents in hardships and the loneliness of old age.[38]

Secondly, the Second Vatican Council turned its attention to the subject of human culture. Culture signifies a particular stage of advancement in civilization. It comprehends the values, manner of life, social institutions, customs, religion, science, literature and arts of a particular people. Mention has already been made of the recent and profound changes in human culture. Modern culture is assuming an aspect that is scientific and technological, industrialized, urbanized and planned, and increased contact among nations is producing a more uniform culture. At the same time, the appearance of the new culture threatens (though not necessarily) the survival of certain traditional values.

The technological and scientific progress of the human race is fully in accord with the design of God; but it can foster an exclusive reliance on observable data and·an agnosticism about everything else. While this unfortunate result is possible, one must not overlook the positive values of modern culture. "Among these values are included scientific study and fidelity toward truth in scientific inquiries, the necessity of working together in technical groups, a sense of international solidarity, a clearer awareness of the responsibility of experts to aid and even to protect men, the desire to make the conditions of life more favorable for all, especially for those who are poor in culture or who are deprived of the opportunity to exercise responsibility."[39]

There are many ties between the message of salvation and human culture. When God spoke to mankind, he did so in the context of the prevailing culture. The Church too has employed different cultures to convey her message. Yet the message of the Church is not bound up with any particular culture, past or present. Moreover, it is the function of the Church to encourage the praiseworthy elements of a particular culture and to combat its pernicious ones.

At the present time it is possible to raise the general level of cultural achievement by employing the means that have become available: the new possibilities for national and international cooperation, the increased circulation of books, the use of radio and television, the utilization of the longer periods of leisure for study, and travel. The Church welcomes the expansion of cultural possibilities; nevertheless, it reminds the world "that culture is to be subordinated to the integral perfection of the human person, to the good of the community and of the whole society. Therefore it is necessary to develop the human faculties in such a way that there results a growth of the faculty of admiration, of intuition, of contemplation, of making personal judgment, of developing a religious, moral and social sense."[40]

In the third place, the Second Vatican Council turned its attention to the economic and social dimensions of modern life. The recent progress in the methods of production and the exchange of goods and services has been remarkable; but this progress has not benefited a large part of the human race. As a result, grave inequalities exist. The Church encourages the production of goods and services; however, the council pointed out: "The fundamental finality of this production is not the mere increase of products nor profit or control but rather the service of man, and indeed of the whole man with regard for the full range of his material needs and the demands of his intellectual, moral, spiritual, and religious life; this applies to every man whatsoever and to every group of men, of every race and of every part of the world."[41]

Furthermore, the control of economic matters ought not to be in the hands of a few individuals or even of a few nations. On the contrary, it is desirable that at every level the largest number of people and nations have an active share in that control.

The human labor which is expended in the production of goods and services is superior to the other elements of production which are mere tools. Human labor is the activity of a person. By it a man associates himself with Jesus who labored with His own hands at Nazareth. Society has the duty to help citizens find employment, and the remuneration for employment ought to be such that a man can provide for himself and his family.

The Second Vatican Council also took this position: "In economic enterprises it is persons who are joined together, that is, free and independent human beings created to the image of God. Therefore, with attention to the functions of each—owners or employers, management or labor—and without harm to the necessary unity of management, the active sharing of all in the administration and profits of these enterprises in ways to be properly determined is to be promoted."[42]

Private property confers an autonomy on the person and the family which is consonant with human freedom. It is an incentive to meet one's responsibilities. However, public authority must intervene in situations where property is abused to the detriment of the common good.[43]

In the fourth place, the Second Vatican Council turned its attention to political institutions. Political institutions exist for, and are demanded by, the common good. The common good is the sum of those conditions which enable the individual, the family and larger groups to fulfill their proper functions. If a community is to secure the common good, if it is to avoid chaos, there must be an authority to achieve the necessary order. Hence, political institutions and authority are related to human nature itself and to the plan of God, even though the choice of a political system and the appointment of officials are left to the citizens.

At present, a growing number of persons wish to play a more

active role in the political life of the community. Such a wish is fully in accord with the dignity of the human person as a free and responsible agent. Nevertheless, responsible participation in affairs of government supposes a certain measure of political education. Political education is necessary for young people especially, but also for the people as a whole. Political education includes the recognition that individuals and groups can have legitimate differences about solutions to political problems.

The complex circumstances of our day make it necessary for public authority to intervene more often in social, economic and cultural matters in order to further the common good.

The Second Vatican Council expressed this caution too: "It is very important, especially where a pluralistic society prevails, that there be a correct notion of the relationship between the political community and the Church, and a clear distinction between the tasks which Christians undertake, individually or as a group, on their own responsibility as citizens guided by the dictates of a Christian conscience, and the activities which, in union with their pastors, they carry out in the name of the Church."[44]

Finally, the council discussed the subject of peace and the community of nations. According to the council, "peace is not merely the absence of war; nor can it be reduced solely to the maintenance of a balance of power between enemies; nor is it brought about by dictatorship. Instead, it is rightly called an enterprise of justice. Peace results from the order structured into human society by its divine founder and actualized by men... This peace on earth cannot be obtained unless personal well-being is safeguarded and men freely and trustingly share with one another the riches of their inner spirits and their talents. A firm determination to respect other men and people and their dignity, as well as the studied practice of brotherhood, is absolutely necessary for the establishment of peace. Hence, peace is likewise the fruit of love, which goes beyond what justice can provide."[45]

The council recognized the right of government to legitimate defense; but it took this stand: "Any act of war aimed indiscriminately at the destruction of entire cities or extensive areas along with their population is a crime against God and man himself. It merits unequivocal and unhesitating condemnation."[46] The council stated that the arms race is a treacherous trap and appealed for an end to it. The council also encouraged international meetings as the first step to true peace.

The creation of international bodies to work for peace and to meet the needs of the nations of the earth is imperative. The organizations that already exist for this purpose deserve commendation and support.[47]

Undoubtedly, the proposals of the Church in this constitution are general in scope, but they were made deliberately so in view of the immense variety of conditions and forms of human culture.

Several of the decrees published by the Second Vatican Council, especially those dealing with the office of bishops, the ministry of priests and religious, and the apostolate of the laity, elaborate principles stated summarily in the constitution on the Church, *Lumen gentium;* hence, these decrees are not reviewed here. The two decrees chosen for review have to do with ecumenism and the missionary activity of the Church.

DECREE ON ECUMENISM

The decree on ecumenism, *Unitatis redintegratio,* was published Nov. 21, 1964. The restoration of unity among Christians was one of the principal objectives of Vatican II. The council noted that the divisions among Christians are opposed to the will of Christ and scandalize the world. The ecumenical movement aims at healing these divisions.

It is only through Christ's Catholic Church, committed to Peter, the apostolic college and their successors that one can benefit fully from the means of salvation. All should be fully incorporated in this Church; nevertheless, those who are members of separated Churches but believe in Christ and have been truly baptized are in communion with the Catholic Church even though this communion is imperfect. An important means for promoting the ecumenical movement is dialogue. The purpose of dialogue is to give experts from different Churches the opportunity to explain the teaching of their communion in greater depth.[48]

The Church can foster Christian unity by renewing herself. Christ summons the Church to constant renewal. There can be no ecumenism worthy of the name without a change of heart. Change of heart along with public and private prayer is the soul of the ecumenical movement. When Catholics and non-Catholics worship together, they invoke God's blessing upon their efforts at reconciliation. There is a danger, however: they may belie their disunity. When Catholics engage in dialogue with non-Catholics, they should present the Catholic faith without equivocation, remembering though that there is a hierarchy of truths. Cooperation in a social apostolate can bring Catholics and non-Catholics together.[49]

The ecumenical activity which the Second Vatican Council recommended must take into consideration two major divisions that now rend Christendom—the division between the Catholic Church and the Eastern Churches and the division between the Catholic Church and the Christian Churches and communities of the West. These divisions, of course, did not arise at the same time or for the same reasons.

The Catholic Church gladly acknowledges the existence of many ties between it and the Christian Churches of the East—true sacraments, apostolic succession, veneration of Mary and the saints, and a monastic tradition. The unity of the Church demands only that there be "one Lord, one faith, one baptism, one God and Father of all" (Ep 4:5-6). It does not demand that the Christian Churches of the East abandon their ancient laws and customs or their theological expression of Christian doctrine. There are many ties too between the Roman Catholic Church and the Christian Churches and communities of the West including confession of Jesus Christ as the mediator between God and men, reverence for the Bible, the celebration of baptism and the Lord's Supper, and other forms of public and private prayer. The council praised non-Catholic Christians of the West: "Their faith in Christ bears fruit in praise and thanksgiving for the blessings received from the hand of God. Among them too is a strong sense of justice and true charity toward their neighbor. This active faith has been responsible for many organizations for the relief of spiritual and material distress, the furtherance of the education of youth, the improvement of the social conditions of life, and the promotion of peace throughout the world."[50]

The dialogue between the Catholic Church and the Christian Churches of the East and West is subject to certain dangers. One of these dangers is a superficiality that fails to disclose accurately the positions of the parties involved. Another is the possibility of raising needless obstacles by preconceived judgments. Despite these dangers, however, and notwithstanding the very serious differences that now divide Christians, they will not be dismayed in their quest for unity. They will be encouraged by the prayer of Jesus "that all may be one."[51]

DECREE ON MISSION ACTIVITY

This decree, *Ad gentes,* was published Dec. 7, 1965. The pilgrim Church is missionary by her very nature. What the Lord preached or what was accomplished in Him for the salvation of the human race must be spread abroad and published to the ends of the earth. The Church has received an express command from its founder to this effect.

The missionary activity of the Church is to be distinguished from its pastoral and ecumenical activity. The pastoral activity of the Church is concerned with the faithful themselves; the ecumenical activity of the Church is directed toward the restoration of Christian unity; but the missionary activity of the Church seeks to establish the Church where it does not exist already. The Second Vatican Council explained the nature of missionary activity and the related term, missions, in this way: "Missions is the term usually given to those particular undertakings by which the heralds of the Gospel, sent out by the Church and going forth into the whole world, carry out the task of preaching the Gospel and planting the Church among peoples or groups who do not yet believe in Christ. These undertakings are brought to completion by missionary activity and are mostly exercised in certain territories recognized by the Holy See. The proper purpose of this missionary activity is evangelization and the planting of the Church among those peoples and groups where it has not yet taken root."[52]

"By means of this activity, the mystical body of Christ unceasingly gathers and directs its forces toward its own growth. The members of the Church are impelled to carry on such missionary activity by reason of the love with which they love God and by which they desire to share with all men the spiritual goods of both this life and the life to come."[53]

The missionary activity of the Church is committed to an enormous task, for two billion human beings have not yet heard the Christian message. To bring the Christian message to this vast number of people, the Church must rely heavily upon those Catholics who live among them or who have been sent to them. These Catholics can bear testimony to the truth by living according to the maxims of the gospel, by associating themselves with the common struggle against poverty, disease and ignorance, by identification with the people among whom they live.

Those who have expressed the intention of becoming Catholics are admitted to the catechumenate. The catechumenate is a period devoted to instruction in the doctrines of the Catholic faith and to practice of the Christian way of life. The catechumenate is climaxed by the reception of baptism and the Holy Eucharist and by formal admission to the Church. The work of planting the Church in a community reaches an intermediate stage of development when it achieves a certain stability. This stability is marked by the integration of the faithful into the life of the community, by the presence of native ministers and laymen, and by the existence of those institutions and activities that are necessary for the growth of the Church. The immediate concern of the young Church is the evangelization of its own country. For this reason, it is important that newly-founded Churches employ every means to establish a mature Christian laity who can make the Church present in those situations accessible to them alone. Young Churches ought to assimilate the customs and traditions of their people, their wisdom and learning, their arts and disciplines, that is, whatever can contribute to the

glory of God, the enrichment of Christian life and the spread
of the Church.[54]

Missionaries are the vanguard of the Church's missionary
activity. The Holy Spirit calls certain religious congregations
and individuals to undertake missionary activity. Fruitful missionary activity requires that missionaries be trained properly.
Proper training of the missionary includes a competent knowledge
of the Catholic faith, a grasp of the universality of the Church
and the diversity of peoples, an insight into the character of the
people to whom he is sent, fluency in their language and skill
in the art of communication. The missionary should be characterized by initiative, perseverance, an open mind and heart,
flexibility and a spirit of cooperation.[55]

The missionaries in the field need and, indeed, are entitled
to the support of the entire Church; for evangelization is the duty
of every member of the Church according to his position and
capacity. Individual bishops, insofar as their own discharge of
their duty permits, are obliged to enter into a community of
work among themselves and with the successor of Peter, upon
whom was imposed in a special way the great duty of spreading
the Christian faith. With all their energy, therefore, they must
supply to the missions both workers for the harvest and also
spiritual and material aid, both directly and on their own account,
as well as by arousing the ardent cooperation of the faithful.
Finally, the bishops, in a universal fellowship of charity, should
gladly extend their fraternal aid to other churches, especially to
neighboring and more needy dioceses.

Priests are collaborators of the bishops; hence, they too have
a responsibility toward the missions. Vatican II described the
contribution priests can make to missions: "Priests should stir up
and preserve amid the faithful a zeal for the evangelization of
the world, by instructing them in sermons and Christian doctrine
courses about the Church's task of announcing Christ to all
nations; by enlightening Christian families about the necessity
and honor of fostering missionary vocations among their own
sons and daughters, by promoting missionary fervor in young
people so that among them there may arise future heralds of the

gospel. Let priests teach the faithful to pray for the missions, and let them not be ashamed to ask alms of them for this purpose.[56]

Evangelization cannot go forward without. the cooperation of laymen in all these matters. The mobilization of every resource within the Church is necessary to cope with the immense challenge of the missions.[57]

Of the three declarations issued by Vatican II—on religious freedom, Christian education, and the Catholic Churches of the East, the one on religious freedom seems to represent the greatest doctrinal development. It is this declaration which is chosen for review here.

DECLARATION ON RELIGIOUS FREEDOM

This declaration was published Dec. 7, 1965. Religious freedom has to do with immunity from coercion in civil society. It has nothing to do with the moral duty of men to embrace the truth and the Church of Christ. Vatican II declared "that the human person has a right to religious freedom. This freedom means that all men are to be immune from coercion on the part of individuals or of social groups and of any human power, in such wise that no one is to be forced to act in a manner contrary to his own beliefs, whether publicly or privately, whether alone or in association with others, within due limits."[58] The right to religious freedom is based on the dignity of the human person. Because human persons are endowed with reason and free will and are therefore responsible moral agents, they have the obligation to seek and embrace truth, especially religious truth. However, they cannot discharge this obligation as free and responsible agents unless they are immune from all external coercion. A man is bound to follow his conscience; and he is not to be forced to act in opposition to his conscience.

From these principles the council drew the appropriate conclusions. Individuals also have a right to religious freedom when they act in concert. It is natural for persons to band together to give expression to their religious convictions. Hence, religious communities rightfully claim freedom to worship the Supreme

Being publicly, to select and train their own ministers, to erect buildings for religious purposes, to give public witness to their beliefs, and to establish educational, cultural, charitable and social organizations.

Parents have the right to determine the form of religious education which their children receive. The State, therefore, should not penalize parents directly or indirectly when they choose a particular school or means of education for their children.

Religious freedom, however, is not unlimited. The council made this point: "The right to religious freedom is exercised in human society; hence, its exercise is subject to certain regulatory norms. In the use of all freedoms the moral principle of personal and social responsibility is to be observed. In the exercise of their rights, individuals and groups are bound by the moral law to have respect both for the rights of others and for the common welfare of all. Men are to deal with their fellows in justice and civility."[59] Of course, society has the right to defend itself against possible abuses committed on the pretext of freedom of religion; but the freedom of man is not to be curtailed except when and insofar as necessary.

The council noted that Jesus did not employ force to gain acceptance for His message. He left each man free to hear the truth and be guided by his own conscience. Inspired by the example of Christ, the apostles acted in a similar manner. Without doubt, they sought to convert men to Christianity, but they eschewed coercion. They preached the word of God with confidence that the word itself was capable of winning men's hearts. If the Church is to be faithful to the example of Christ and the apostles, the Church may not force anyone to accept the Catholic religion.

In turn, the Church claims freedom for itself. The freedom of the Church is the fundamental principle regulating its relationship to the State. The Church claims freedom for herself as a spiritual society charged with the mandate of preaching the gospel to every creature. The Church also claims freedom for herself as a society of men who have the right to live in society in accordance with the precepts of the Christian faith.

10

The Church applauds those modern States which have recognized the right to religious freedom; but the Church deplores the fact that certain governments repress religion even though the right to religious freedom is recognized in their constitutions.

NOTES TO CHAPTER X

1. Constitution on the Church in the Modern World (*Gaudium et spes*) no. 4.
2. *Ibid*. nos. 5-6.
3. *Ibid*. nos. 7-10.
4. *Ibid*. nos. 19-20.
5. *Ecclesiam suam* pt. 1.
6. *Ibid*. pt. 2.
7. *Ibid*. pt. 3.
8. Constitution on the Church (*Lumen gentium*) c. 1.
9. *Ibid*. c. 2.
10. *Ibid*. c. 3.
11. *Ibid*. c. 4.
12. *Ibid*. c. 5.
13. *Ibid*. c. 6.
14. *Ibid*. c. 7.
15. *Ibid*. c. 8.
16. Constitution on the Sacred Liturgy (*Sacrosanctum concilium*) no. 7.
17. *Ibid*. no. 9.
18. *Ibid*. no. 10.
19. *Ibid*. no. 14.
20. *Ibid*. no. 21.
21. *Ibid*. no. 22.
22. *Ibid*. no. 26.
23. *Ibid*. nos. 33-34.
24. *Ibid*. nos. 37-38.
25. Constitution on Divine Revelation (*Dei verbum*) c. 1.
26. *Ibid*. no. 10.
27. *Ibid*. c. 3.
28. *Ibid*. c. 4.
29. *Ibid*. c. 5.
30. *Ibid*. c. 6.
31. Constitution on the Church in the Modern World (*Gaudium et spes*) pt. 1, c. 1.
32. *Ibid*. no. 26.
33. *Ibid*. no. 29.
34. *Ibid*. pt. 1, c. 2.
35. *Ibid*. pt. 1, c. 3.

36. *Ibid.* pt. 1, c. 4.
37. *Ibid.* pt. 2, c. 1, no. 50.
38. *Ibid.* pt. 2, c. 1.
39. *Ibid.* pt. 2, c. 2, no. 57.
40. *Ibid.* pt. 2, c. 2, no. 59.
41. *Ibid.* pt. 2, c. 3, no. 64.
42. *Ibid.* pt. 2, c. 3, no. 68.
43. *Ibid.* pt. 2, c. 3.
44. *Ibid.* pt. 2, c. 4, no. 76.
45. *Ibid.* pt. 2, c. 5, no. 78.
46. *Ibid.* pt. 2, c. 5, no. 80.
47. *Ibid.* pt. 2, c. 5.
48. Decree on Ecumenism (*Unitatis redintegratio*) c. 1.
49. *Ibid.* c. 2.
50. *Ibid.* no. 23.
51. *Ibid.* c. 3.
52. Decree on Mission Activity (*Ad gentes*) no. 6.
53. *Ibid.* no. 7.
54. *Ibid.* cc. 2-3.
55. *Ibid.* c. 4.
56. *Ibid.* no. 39.
57. *Ibid.* cc. 5-6.
58. Declaration on Religious Freedom (*Dignitatis humanae*) no. 2.
59. *Ibid.* no. 7.

XI. AFTER THE SECOND VATICAN COUNCIL

Vatican II was both an end and a beginning. It was an end in the sense that the council ratified, as it were, and implemented the objectives of several important pre-conciliar movements. The council fostered a more active and intelligent participation in the liturgy on the part of the laity. The council advocated a wider appreciation and use of the Bible among Catholics. It adopted certain themes such as the people of God and the universal sacrament of salvation to describe the mystery of the Church.

Yet, as Pope Paul VI remarked in a letter to the International Theological Congress of Rome, Sept. 21, 1966, the conciliar decrees were not so much a destination as a point of departure toward new goals. The seeds of life planted by the council, he said, must grow and achieve full maturity. In an address to a general audience, Nov. 16, 1966, the Pope reflected upon the words of Christ, "I will build my Church." The Church is a building under construction. The Church must be built according to the plan drawn up by Christ Himself. It is an unceasing task. Everyone knows, the Pope said, that the council has set the Church in motion in every field of its activity, that it has given Catholics a sense of renewal. The process of renewal has filled the heart of the Pope with fervor and hope and, he admitted, with a bit of anxiety over the proper direction and success of this renewal.

The Second Vatican Council gave vigorous support to the ecumenical movement. Pope John summoned the council to renew the Church and thereby further the cause of Christian unity. The teaching and exhortation of the council with respect to the liturgy, the Bible, the responsibility of the layman, collegiality, the relationship between the Church and the world, religious men and women, bishops and priests, and missionary activity will contribute to the renewal of the Church which "is essentially grounded in an increase of fidelity to her own calling. Undoubtedly, this is the basis of the movement toward unity."[1] Moreover, the council adopted a positive attitude toward non-Catholics by describing in considerable detail what they have in common with Catholics. Finally, the council recommended various means of fostering ecumenism—dialogue, common involvement in social concerns, prayer, and a change of heart. The result has been to sustain the growing spirit of friendship and trust among Christians.

The Second Vatican Council engendered in Catholics a new openness to the world—a willingness to hear and consider what the world has to say and give, a new appreciation of the intrinsic goodness of the world as the effect of God's creative activity. Often the world is viewed in the New Testament as mankind in its fallen state, as alienated from God, and hostile to God and Jesus Christ. Christians are not to identify themselves with the world in this sense. On the other hand, the world as it has come from the hand of God is good; it includes the whole human family and the realities among which it lives; it is this world which has been emancipated by Christ and must now be fashioned anew according to God's design. From this point of view the council encouraged Catholics to involve themselves in the problems of the world. Problems of special urgency, according to the constitution on the Church in the modern world, have to do with marriage and the family, the development of culture, the political community, economic and social life, and the preservation of peace. Concern for a solution to the problems of the world is a practical consequence of the commandment of Christ, "You shall love your neighbor as yourself."

In his book, *Coresponsibility in the Church*,[2] Leon-Joseph

Cardinal Suenens of Belgium expressed his personal view that the most fruitful effect of Vatican II was the rediscovery of the people of God as a whole and then, by way of consequence, the recognition of the coresponsibility of every member of the Church. By baptism a human being is incorporated into the Christian community, the people of God. Membership in the Christian community entails certain responsibilities. Within the Christian community, however, it is possible to differentiate individuals and groups on the basis of divinely conferred functions and charisms. The Pope is the vicar of Christ and the head of the episcopal college. Bishops are teachers, high priests of the liturgy, and pastors. Priests and deacons are collaborators with the bishops. The laity seek the kingdom of God by engaging in secular professions and occupations. "The distinction, however, which the Lord made between the sacred ministers and the rest of the people of God entails a unifying purpose, since pastors and the other faithful are bound to each other by mutual need."[3] In other words, each member of the people of God has a specific function. The welfare of the whole depends upon the responsible performance of that function. Vatican II defined the diversity of functions within the Church, emphasizing the importance and need of all of them.

Vatican II explained and implemented the idea of collegiality which is related to that of coresponsibility. The council's teaching on collegiality is developed most explicitly in its constitution on the Church, *Lumen gentium*, where it is concerned with the episcopal college. The term, college, is not taken in its technical sense to designate a group of equals, but in the more general sense of a unified group. The further determination of the constitution of this college depends on the doctrine of episcopal collegiality as a whole. The college of bishops, the constitution states,[4] is "the subject of supreme and full power over the universal Church, provided we understand this body together with its head, the Roman Pontiff." Episcopal collegiality can be exercised in a solemn way in an ecumenical council; or it can be exercised by all the bishops scattered throughout the world provided that the head of the college, the Pope, calls them to a collegiate action. As a consequence of the council's teaching on episcopal collegiality, one may expect a more frequent and explicit exercise of it in the future.

In many ways Vatican II encouraged consultation and a free exchange of views among the members of the Church. "Among the collaborators of the bishop in the government of the diocese are numbered those priests who constitute his senate or council. . . It is greatly desired that in each diocese a pastoral commission may be established over which the diocesan bishop himself will preside and in which specially chosen religious and lay people will participate. The duty of the commission will be to investigate and weigh pastoral undertakings and to formulate practical conclusions regarding them."[5] "The laity should openly reveal their needs and desires to their pastors with that freedom and confidence which is fitting for children of God and brothers in Christ. They are, by reason of the knowledge, competence or outstanding ability which they may enjoy, permitted and sometimes even obliged to express their opinion on those things which concern the good of the Church."[6]

The Second Vatican Council did not encourage religious indifferentism. Surely the council adopted a positive attitude toward the religious values of non-Catholic Churches and religions. Moreover, the council was acutely conscious of the pilgrim status of the Catholic Church. The council stated quite clearly, however, the obligatory character of Roman Catholicism: "Whosoever knowing that the Catholic Church was made necessary by Christ, would refuse to enter it, could not be saved."[7] "Our separated brethren, whether considered as individuals or communities and Churches, are not blessed with that unity which Jesus Christ wished to bestow. . . . It is only through Christ's Catholic Church which is the all-embracing means of salvation that they can benefit fully from the means of salvation."[8] In the documents of the council there are many references to the fact that Christ placed His Church under the leadership of Peter and his successors, the Popes; so that where Peter and his successors are, there is the Church of Christ.

One of the by-products of the Second Vatican Council was confusion on the part of many Catholics. In response to the profound changes which the modern world has experienced, Vatican

II introduced many changes into the Catholic Church. Many of the faithful were confused by certain breaks with the past. It was difficult for them to distinguish the unchangeable tradition of the Church from human and sociological traditions which, even though they were ancient, were distinct and separable from the core of the faith. The dismantling of human structures by Vatican II seemed to be the destruction of vital portions of the Church. Other Catholics, caught up too enthusiastically in the changes introduced by Vatican II, unknowingly wished to discard even that which may not be discarded because it is derived from Christ; for example, the papal office. Unwittingly they wished to throw out the baby with the bath water. Still other Catholics were dismayed by the slow pace of change even when that change had been sanctioned by Vatican II. They did not realize that social and institutional change is often difficult to achieve in view of the natural resistance to change especially where large groups are concerned.

HANS KUNG

The storm petrel of post-conciliar ecclesiology within the Catholic Church has been Hans Küng (1928-   ), dean of the Catholic theological faculty of the university of Tübingen, Germany. His book, *Konzil und Wiedervereinigung*,[9] was possibly the most widely read of all the publications occasioned by Pope John's announcement of his intention to summon an ecumenical council. The main thesis of the book is that the key to Christian unity lies in the reform and renewal of the Church, in her fidelity to the gospel. (This idea was underscored subsequently by Vatican II's decree on ecumenism.) The renewal of the Church is always necessary because it is composed of sinful human beings. Reform without schism demands that we give priority to charity and pastoral considerations, that we remain a part of the whole community, that we be patient while avoiding delays, that we return to the sources of things. In his book, Küng wrote that the chief difficulty in the way of reunion lies in the two different concepts of the Church, and especially of the concrete organizational structure of the Church. Many of Küng's concrete proposals for reform, such as the strengthening of national episcopal conferences and the decentralization of administration within the Church, were voiced by others too.

Küng's book, *Strukturen der Kirche*,[10] was also written before, and in anticipation of, Vatican II. Küng distinguished between an ecumenical council called into existence by God (the Church) and an ecumenical council called into existence by man —Vatican II, for example. A council taken in the latter sense is a human, though a true and real, representation of the Church. A council should reflect the notes of the Church: the unity of the Church by a real union of hearts and minds among the conciliar fathers; the catholicity of the Church by a recognition of diversity within the Church; and the holiness of the Church by fidelity to the gospel and abstraction from demonstrations of spiritual power. Just as the Church in the New Testament was a structured community, so the council must be a structured assembly if it is to reflect the nature of the Church. Both pastors and laity must be represented. A structure of crucial importance for an ecumenical council is the Petrine office. The primatial authority of the Pope is limited by the office of bishops and the principle of subsidiarity. The purpose of the papal office is service. By *divine* law the Pope does not have the exclusive right to summon an ecumenical council. Papal infallibility does not exist to manifest a new teaching, but to preserve reverently and expound faithfully the deposit of faith. That a papal definition may 'be infallible "the necessity of a simultaneous or subsequent consensus of the episcopate is to be excluded, yet it is not to be maintained that the pope can define a truth without as a basis, the prior existence of a consensus of the Church."[11]

After the conclusion of the Second Vatican Council, Küng published a lengthy volume, *Die Kirche*,[12] which is dedicated to Dr. Michael Ramsäy, Archbishop of Canterbury. The book is divided into five parts. The first part is concerned with the nature of the Church as an historical reality. The essential reality of the Church is embodied in historical forms which change with the passing of time. This idea applies even to the Church in the New Testament; nevertheless, the Church must ever preserve its link with God's saving act in Jesus Christ. The testimony of the apostolic Church which has been enshrined in the New Testament remains normative for the Church in all ages. The second part discusses the connection between Jesus and the beginning of the Church. Jesus did not found a Church during his earthly life, although He did lay the foundation of the Church by His preaching and ministry. The Church emerged only with the rise of faith in the risen Lord. The Church is distinct from the kingdom of God which it must serve. The third part is an analysis of three important Biblical images of the Church—as the new people of God, the creation of the Holy Spirit, and the body of Christ.

The fourth part of Küng's book, *The Church*, is concerned with the four "dimensions" of the Church mentioned in the Nicene Creed. The Church is essentially one—one people of God, one body of Christ, one spiritual creation. Today, in opposition to the will of Christ, the Church is divided. Visible unity must be reestablished. The standard of unity must be the gospel taken as a whole. The catholicity of the Church consists in a notion of entirety based on the identity of the Church with its Biblical norm and resulting in universality. The Church is holy because God makes it holy by sanctifying the sinner and thereby founding the communion of saints. "Infallibility means a fundamental remaining in the truth which is not disturbed by individual errors."[13] The Church is apostolic because it was founded on the apostles. The whole people of God shares in the apostolic mission.

The fifth part deals with offices in the Church. All believers are priests and clergy. The Church is a fellowship of different ministries. Authority in the Church comes from Christ and not from the community; but all should have a voice in its exercise. The papal office is the chief obstacle to Christian unity; but it has an important contribution to make to the life of the Church. It is a primacy of service, a pastoral primacy.

Subsequently, in his book, *Unfehlbar? Eine Anfrage*,[14] Küng questioned the infallibility of the Church. He concluded that Church pronouncements are not guaranteed as infallible a priori. Church pronouncements are true when they correspond to the original Christian message; but neither the New Testament nor ancient Christian tradition guarantees them protection from error by the Holy Spirit. Küng prefers to speak of the indefectibility of the Church rather than infallibility; that is, the truth of the gospel ultimately prevails in the Church despite the errors of members of the Church including Popes and bishops.

HUMANAE VITAE

Pope Paul VI published his encyclical, *Humanae vitae*, dealing with the regulation of birth, in 1968. The encyclical stimulated a lively reaction. The Pope asserted that the teaching authority of the Church has been constituted the "guardian and authentic interpreter of all the moral law, not only, that is, of the law of the gospel, but also of the natural law, which is also an expression of the will of God, the faithful fulfillment of which is equally necessary for salvation."[35] In his capacity as an authentic teacher within the Church, the Pope rejected as immoral abortion, direct sterilization, and any act which proposes, whether as an end or a means, to render procreation impossible.[16]

The reaction to *Humanae vitae* was varied. Many Catholics accepted its teaching without hesitation. They viewed it as an expression of the Church's magisterium. They recalled the words of the Second Vatican Council: "In their manner of acting, spouses should be aware that they cannot proceed arbitrarily, but must always be governed according to a conscience dutifully conformed to the divine law itself, and should be submissive toward the Church's teaching office, which authentically interprets that law in the light of the gospel."[17]

The reaction of Hans Küng to *Humanae vitae* was unique in a certain sense. In his book, *Infallibility? An Inquiry*, he rejected the papal condemnation of artificial contraception as erroneous. Nonetheless, he held that the condemnation of contraception by the ordinary and universal magisterium of the Church, even prior to *Humanae vitae*, met all the requirements for an infallible teaching as they were enumerated by theologians. Instead of rejecting artificial contraception, however, he rejected infallibility.

Many other Catholics too disagreed with the papal condemnation of artificial contraception. The condemnation, they felt, was based upon an overly rigorous notion of the natural law.

Humanae vitae they said, viewed the individual act of contraception in an exclusively physical way without considering it in a larger context. Since the papal encyclical, according to these Catholics, was not an infallible pronouncement, it was subject to error; and, as a matter of fact, the Pope did err. The alleged papal error could have been avoided, they maintained, if there had been greater dialogue between the Pope and the laity.

MYSTERIUM ECCLESIAE

In reply to Hans Küng's book, *Infallibility?* (but without mentioning him or it by name), the Sacred Congregation for Teaching the Faith published *Mysterium Ecclesiae*[18] (*The Mystery of the Church*) June 24, 1973. Citing Vatican II, the congregation reaffirmed the identity of the Catholic Church as the Church which Christ founded.

Then turning its attention to the subject of infallibility, the congregation stated that the body of the faithful as a whole cannot err in matters of belief. The pastors of the Church teach the faithful with the authority of Christ. The pastors of the Church can anticipate or demand the assent of the faithful in matters of faith and morals. Through the assistance of the Holy Spirit, they can teach infallibly in the circumstances defined by Vatican I and repeated by Vatican II. The infallibility of the magisterium extends not only to the deposit of faith, but also to those matters without which that deposit cannot be rightly preserved and expounded. The dogmas of the Church are the unalterable norm both for faith and for theological science. It follows that the faithful are in no way permitted to see in the Church merely a fundamental permanence in truth which, as some assert, could be reconciled with errors contained here and there in the propositions that the Church's magisterium teaches. Unquestionably, though, the dogmatic formulas of the Church must be understood in their historical context. These formulas express incompletely (but not falsely) the permanent reality.

The congregation concluded its statement by a reflection upon the priesthood of the laity and the hierarchical priesthood. These differ from each other not only in degree but also in essence; yet they are mutually complementary within the communion of the Church.

NOTES TO CHAPTER XI

1. Decree on Ecumenism, no. 6.
2. (New York, 1968).
3. Constitution on the Church in the Modern World, no. 32.
4. Constitution on the Church, no. 22.
5. Decree on the Pastoral Office of Bishops, no. 27.
6. Constitution on the Church, no. 37.
7. Constitution on the Church, no. 14.
8. Decree on Ecumenism, no. 3.
9. Trans., *The Council, Reform and Reunion* (New York, 1961).
10. Trans., *Structures of the Church* (New York, 1964).
11. *Ibid.* 371.
12. Engl. transl., *The Church* (New York, 1967).
13. *Ibid.* 342.
14. Trans., *Infallibility? An Inquiry* (New York, 1971).
15. *Humanae vitae,* no. 4.
16. *Ibid.* no. 14.
17. Constitution on the Church in the Modern World, no. 50.
18. *AAS* 65 (1973) 396-408.

BIBLIOGRAPHY

Readers are referred, first of all, to the primary works cited in the text and the standard works listed at the beginning of this book. The following list includes useful secondary works among which Y. Congar's *L'Église de saint Augustin à l'époque moderne* (Paris, 1970) is particularly helpful.

I. The New Testament

J. Bauer, *Sacramentum Verbi* (New York, 1970).

R. Brown, J. Fitzmyer, R. Murphy (ed.), *The Jerome Biblical Commentary* (Englewood Cliffs, 1968).

R. Brown *et. al.* (ed.), *Peter in the New Testament* (Minneapolis, 1973).

P. Burns (ed.), *Mission and Witness* (Westminster, 1965).

L. Cerfaux, *The Church in the Theology of St. Paul* (New York, 1959).

Y. Congar, *Jesus Christ* (New York, 1966).

H. Fries (ed.), *Handbuch theologischer Grundbegriffe* (München, (1962)

J. Gilbert *et. al. The Birth of the Church* (Staten Island, 1968).

O. Karrer, *Peter and the Church* (New York, 1963).

H. Küng, *The Church* (New York, 1967).

X. Leon-Dufour, *The Gospels and the Jesus of History* (New York, 1968).

J. McKenzie, *Dictionary of the Bible* (Milwaukee, 1965).
The Power and the Wisdom (Milwaukee, 1965).

J. Schmid, *Das Evangelium nach Matthäus* (Regensburg, 1959).
Das Evangelium nach Markus (Regensburg, 1963).
Das Evangelium nach Lukas (Regensburg, 1960).

R. Schnackenburg, *The Church in the New Testament* (New York, 1965).
God's Rule and Kingdom (New York, 1963).
D. Stanley, *The Apostolic Church in the New Testament* (Westminster, 1965).
B. Vawter, *The Four Gospels* (New York, 1967).

II. The Fathers

B. Altaner, *Patrology* (New York, 1960).
G. Bardenhewer, *Patrology* (St. Louis, 1908).
B. Butler, *The Idea of the Church* (Baltimore, 1962).
T. Carroll, *The Venerable Bede* (Washington, 1946).
H. von Campenhausen, *Ecclesiastical Authority and Spiritual Power* (Stanford, 1969).
F. Cayré, *Manual of Patrology* (Paris, 1940).
J. Colson, *L'Évêque dans les Communautés Primitives* (Paris, 1951).
Les Fonctions Ecclésiales (Paris, 1956).
R. Evans, *One and Holy: The Church in Latin Patristic Thought* (London, 1939).
S. Grabowski, *The Church. An Introduction to the Theology of St. Augustine* (St. Louis, 1957).
J. Kelly, *Early Christian Doctrines* (New York, 1959).
T. Jalland, *The Life and Times of St. Leo the Great* (London, 1941).
A. McGiffert, *A History of Christian Thought* (New York, 1932).
J. Plumpe, *Mater Ecclesia* (Washington, 1943).
E. Portalie, *A Guide to the Thought of St. Augustine* (Chicago, 1960).
J. Quasten, *Patrology* (Westminster, 1950).
H. Rahner, *Symbole der Kirche* (Salzburg, 1964).
N. Sharkey, *Saint Gregory the Great's Concept of Papal Power* (Washington, 1950).
W. Simonis, *Ecclesia Visibilis et Invisibilis* (Frankfurt, 1970).
J. Tixeront, *A Handbook of Patrology* (St. Louis, 1934).
J. Willis, *The Teachings of the Fathers of the Church* (New York, 1966).

III. The Carolingian Era and the Gregorian Reform

O. Blum, *St. Peter Damian* (Washington, 1947).
Y. Congar, *L'Ecclésiologie du haut Moyen-Age* (Paris, 1968).
F. Dvornik, *Byzance et la Primauté romaine* (Paris, 1964).
   The Photian Schism (Cambridge, 1948).
H. de Lubac, *Corpus Mysticum* (Paris, 1949).
J. Meyendorff, *The Orthodox Church* (New York, 1962).
K. Morrison, *The Two Kingdoms. Ecclesiology in Carolingian Political Thought* (Princeton, 1964).
S. Runciman, *The Eastern Schism* (Oxford, 1955).
H. Symonds, *The Church Universal and the See of Rome* (London, 1939).
W. Ullmann, *The Growth of Papal Government in the Middle Ages* (London, 1955).
   Principles of Government and Politics in the Middle Ages (London, 1955).

IV. The Golden Age of Scholasticism

P.W. and A.J. Carlyle, *A History of Medieval Political Theory in the West* (Edinburgh-London, 1950).
S. Chodorow, *Christian Political Theory and Church Politics in the Mid-Twelfth Century* (Berkeley, 1972).
A. Cicognani, *Canon Law* (Westminster, 1949).
D. Culhane, *De corpore mystico doctrina Seraphici* (Mundelein, 1934).
C. Dawson, *The Formation of Christendom* (New York, 1967).
   Medieval Essays (New York, 1954).
W. Farrell, *A Companion to the Summa* (New York, 1941).
J. de Ghellinck, *Le mouvement theologique du xiie siècle* (Bruxelles-Paris, 1948).
M. Grabmann, *Die Lehre des hl. Thomas von Aquin v.d. Kirche als Gotteswerk* (Regensburg, 1903).
F. Holböck, *Der eucharistische und der mystische Leib Christi* (Rome, 1941).
E. Kantorowicz, *The King's Two Bodies* (Princeton, 1957).
E. Lewis, *Medieval Political Ideas* (New York, 1954).

E. Mersch, *The Whole Christ* (London, 1938).
B. Tierney, *Foundations of the Conciliar Theory* (Cambridge, 1955).
  The Crisis of Church and State 1050-1300 (Englewood Cliffs, 1964).
  Origins of Papal Infallibility (Leiden, 1972).
S. Tromp, *Corpus Christi quod est Ecclesia* (Rome, 1946).
W. Ullmann, *Medieval Papalism* (London, 1949).
W. Williams, *St. Bernard, The Man and His Message* (Manchester, n.d.).

V. The 14th and 15th Centuries

G. Alberigo, *Cardinalato e Collegialità* (Firenze, 1969).
F. Copleston, *A History of Philosophy* (Westminster, 1953) 3.
A. Fliche, V. Martin, *Histoire de l'Église* (Paris, 1962, 1951) 14-15.
E. Gewirth, *Marsilius and the Medieval Political Philosophy* (New York, 1951).
E. Jacob, *Essays in the Conciliar Epoch* (Notre Dame, 1963).
J. McGowan, *Peter d'Ailly and the Council of Constance* (Washington, 1936).
W. Maguire, *John of Torquemada. The Antiquity of the Church* (Washington, 1957).
F. Oakley, *The Political Thought of Pierre d'Aily* (New Haven, 1964).
H. Oberman,, *The Harvest of Medieval Theology* (Cambridge, 1963).
M. Spinka, *John Hus' Concept of the Church* (Princeton, 1966).
B. Tierncy, *Foundations of the Conciliar Theory* (Cambridge, 1955).
W. Ullmann, *The Origins of the Great Schism* (London, 1948).
M. Wilks, *The Problem of Sovereignty in the Later Middle Ages* (Cambridge, 1964).

VI. The Reformation and Counter-Reformation

L. Bouyer, *The Spirit and Forms of Protestantism* (Westminster, 1956).

Y. Congar, *Vraie et fausse réforme dans l'Église* (Paris, 1950).

C. Dawson, *The Dividing of Christendom* (New York, 1965).

T. Foley, *The Doctrine of the Catholic Church in the Theology of John Driedo of Louvain* (Washington, 1946).

J. Hardon, *Robert Bellarmine's Concept of the Church* in Studies in Medieval Culture, ed. by J. Sommerfeldt (Western Mich. Univ.) II (1966) 120-127.

P. Hughes, *A Popular History of the Reformation* (Garden City, 1957).

H. Jedin, *A History of the Council of Trent* (St. Louis, 1957).

J. McNeill, *The History and Character of Calvinism* (New York, 1967).

B. Milner, *Calvin's Doctrine of the Church* (Leiden, 1970).

F. Murray, *St. Robert Bellarmine on the Indirect Power* in Theological Studies 9 (1948) 491-535.

M. O'Connell, *Thomas Stapleton and the Counter Reformation* (New Haven, 1964).

W. van de Pol, *World Protestantism* (New York, 1964).

R. Pole, *The Unity of the Church*. Transl. by J. Dwyer (Westminster, 1965).

H. Preus, *The Communion of Saints. A Study of the Origin and Development of Luther's Doctrine of the Church* (Minneapolis, 1948).

G. de Santillana, *The Crime of Galileo* (Chicago, 1955).

G. Tavard, *The Quest for Catholicity* (New York, 1964).

H. Woodhouse, *The Doctrine of the Church in Anglican Theology 1547-1603* (London, 1954).

VII. The 17th and 18th Centuries

Y. Congar, *L'Église de saint Augustin à l'époque moderne* (Paris, 1970).

H. Daniel-Rops, *The Church in the Seventeenth Century* (London-New York, 1963).

The Church in the Eighteenth Century (London-New York, 1964).

M. Goodwin, *The Papal Conflict with Josephinism* (New York, 1938).

R. Graham, *Vatican Diplomacy* (Princeton, 1959).
V. Martin, *Les origines du Gallicanisme* (Paris, 1939).
J. Mayr, *Die Ekklesiologie H. Tournélys* (Essen, 1964).
A. Robertson, *Fra Paolo Sarpi, The Greatest of the Venetians* (London, 1911).
D. Sharrock, *The Theological Defense of Papal Power by St. A. de L.* (Washington, 1961).
J. Steinmann, *Pascal* (London, 1966).
J. Todd, *John Wesley and the Catholic Church* (London, 1958).
D. Trueblood, *Robert Barclay* (New York, 1968).

VIII. The 19th Century

R. Aubert, *Vatican I* (Paris, 1964).
K. Buchheim, *Ultramontanismus und Democratie* (München, 1963).
C. Butler, *The Vatican Council* (London, 1930).
R. Corrigan, *The Church and the Nineteenth Century* (Milwaukee, 1938).
E. Fairweather (ed.), *The Oxford Movement* (New York, 1964).
E. Hales, *The Catholic Church in the Modern World* (Garden City, 1958).
Pio Nono (New York, 1954).
M. Jugie, *Theologia Dogmatica Christianorum Orientalium* (Paris, 1931).
K. Latourette, *The Nineteenth Century in Europe* (New York, 1959).
S. Leslie, *Cardinal Manning* (New York, 1954).
D. Mathew, *Lord Acton and His Times* (Alabama, 1968).
M. Nédoncelle *et. al.*, *L'Ecclésiologie au xixe siècle* (Paris, 1960).
J. Quinn, *The Recognition of the True Church according to J.H. Newman* (Washington, 1954).
B. Reardon, *Religious Thought in the Nineteenth Century* (Cambridge, 1966).
P. Santi, *La Chiesa cattolica* (Torino, 1960).
H. Savon, *Johann Adam Möhler* (Glen Rock, 1966).
T. Ware, *The Orthodox Church* (Baltimore, 1963).
N. Zernov, *Eastern Christendom* (London, 1963).

IX. The 20th Century: The Age of the Church

C. Armbruster, *The Vision of Paul Tillich* (New York, 1967).
H. Fries, *Bultmann, Barth and Catholic Theology* (Pittsburgh, 1967).
J. Hamer, *Karl Barth* (Westminster, 1962).
K. McNamara, *The Idea of the Church* in *The Irish Theol. Quarterly* 33 (1966) 99-113.
E. Menard, *L'Ecclesiologie hier et aujourd'hui* (Paris, 1966).
C. O'Grady, *The Church in the Theology of Karl Barth* (Washington, 1968).
The Church in Catholic Theology (Washington, 1969).
W. van de Pol, *World Protestantism* (New York, 1964).
J. Rea, *The Common Priesthood of the Members of the Mystical Body* (Westminster, 1947).
O. Rousseau, *The Progress of the Liturgy* (Westminster, 1951).
M. Schmaus, *Katholische Dogmatik* (München, 1958) 3/1.
G. Thils, *Histoire doctrinale du Mouvement oecuménique* (Louvain, 1963).
U. Valeske, *Votum Ecclesiae* (München, 1962).
A. Vidler, *A Variety of Catholic Modernists* (Cambridge, 1970).

X. The Second Vatican Council

W. Abbott (ed.), *The Documents of Vatican II* (New York, 1966).
G. Baraúna (ed.), *La Chiesa del Vaticano II* (Firenze, 1965).
L. Bouyer, *The Liturgy Revived* (Notre Dame, 1964).
J. Deretz, A. Nocent (ed.), *Dictionary of the Council* (London, 1968).
C. Hollis, *The Achievements of Vatican II* (New York, 1966).
B. Leeming, *The Vatican Council and Christian Unity* (New York, 1966).
F. McManus, *Sacramental Liturgy* (New York, 1967).
K. McNamara (ed.), *The Constitution on the Church* (Chicago, 1968).
C. O'Donnell (ed.), *The Church in the World* (Milwaukee, 1967).

H.Vorgrimler (ed.), *Commentary on the Documents of Vatican II* (New York, 1966).

XI. After the Second Vatican Council

A. Dulles, *The Dimensions of the Church* (Westminster, 1967).
    The Survival of Dogma (Garden City, 1971).
    Models of the Church (Garden City, 1974).
E. Gratsch, *The Basis of Roman Catholicism* (New York, 1967).
H. Küng, *The Church* (New York, 1967).
A. Lang, *Fundamentaltheologie* (München, 1968).
J. McKenzie, *Authority in the Church* (New York, 1966).
A New Catechhism (New York, 1969).
Paul VI, *The Pope Speaks* (Washington, 1963-   ).
J. Powell, *The Mystery of the Church* (Milwaukee, 1967).
K. Rahner, *The Christian of the Future* (New York, 1967).
L. Suenens, *Coresponsibility in the Church* (New York, 1968).

INDEX

An Interesting Thought

The publication you have just finished reading is part of the apostolic efforts of the Society of St. Paul of the American Province. A small, unique group of priests and brothers, the members of the Society of St. Paul propose to bring the message of Christ to men through the communications media while living the religious life.

If you know of a young man who might be interested in learning more about our life and mission, ask him to contact the Vocation Office in care of ALBA HOUSE, at 2187 Victory Blvd., Staten Island, New York 10314. Full information will be sent without cost or obligation. You may be instrumental in helping a young man to find his vocation in life. *An interesting thought.*

T 51253